the good website guide 2003

SIMON EDWARDS

the good website guide 2003

MITCHELL BEAZLEY

The Good Website Guide 2003
by Simon Edwards
Revised and updated by Julian Mosedale

Published in Great Britain in 2003 by Mitchell Beazley,
an imprint of Octopus Publishing Group Ltd,
2–4 Heron Quays, Docklands, London, E14 4JP

Copyright © Octopus Publishing Group Ltd 2003

All rights reserved. No part of this work may be reproduced or utilised in any form or by any means, electronic or mechanical, including photocopying, recording or by any information storage and retrieval system, without the prior written permission of the publishers.

ISBN 1 84000 725 7

A CIP catalogue record for this book is available from the British Library

The author and publishers would be grateful for any information that will assist them in keeping future editions up to date. Although all reasonable care has been taken in the preparation of this book, neither the publishers nor the author can accept liability for any consequences arising from the use thereof, or from the information contained therein.

Commissioning Editor	Vivien Antwi
Project Editor	Peter Taylor
Editor	Siobhán O'Connor
Design	Alexa Brommer
Production	Alexis Coogan
Checker	Siobhán O'Connor

Typeset in Clearface Gothic, Franklin Gothic, and Helvetica Neue

Printed and bound by Mackays of Chatham

CONTENTS

6	Introduction
10	Surfing the Net
18	Shopping on the Internet
26	**Art, Design, and Architecture**
	Architecture • Art and artists • Fashion • Photography
36	**Books**
	Author sites • Browsers • For book lovers • For writers • News and reviews • Online shops • Online texts to download • Publishers' sites • Writers' prizes and libraries
50	**Computers**
	Computer reference sites • Hardware • Literature/articles • Major manufacturers • Search sites • Software and downloads • Stores • Web page construction help
67	**Education**
	Alternative teaching sites • For graduates • For students • For teachers and parents • Intelligence sites • Language sites • Learning • Mathematics sites • School revision • Science sites • Social sciences sites
86	**Entertainment**
	Cartoons and comics • Electronic equipment • Events • Films • Jokes • Magic sites • Movies and television • Music, sound, and video • Sci-fi sites • Theatre • Theme parks • Treading the boards • Television, radio, and ads
108	**Food and Drink**
	Drink • Luxury food • Recipes • Reviews • Safety and other issues • Supermarkets • World foods and restaurants
119	**Games**
	Computer games • News and software • Old favourites • Online games and puzzles • Role-playing games • Rules and information • Toy histories and collectibles
132	**Health**
	Alternative therapies • Beauty sites • Dental health • Disorders and illnesses • Family health • Fitness • Information and advice • Interactive sites • Nutrition • Pharmaceuticals • Psychology • Sexual matters
150	**Hobbies**
	Animals • Collections • Crafts • Electronic parts and kits • Genealogy • Motoring • Pot luck • Space
164	**Home and Lifestyle**
	Clothes and jewellery • Discounts, ads, and auctions • Furnishings • Home improvement • Lifestyle • Upkeep • Utilities
180	**Money**
	Internet banks • Jobs • Money management • Property and mortgages • Stocks and shares • Your money
197	**Music**
	Concert information • For musicians • Magazines • MP3 • Musicals and classical music • Popular music • Radio
211	**The Natural World**
	Conservation groups • Geography and environment • Learn about nature • Museums, zoos, and parks
226	**News**
	Financial and business news • Have we got news for you • News on demand • Papers and magazines • Radio • Technology news • TV • Weather
242	**Reference**
	Any questions? • Bits and pieces • Dictionaries/encyclopedias • Legal issues • Museums • Myths and conspiracies
256	**Society, Politics, and Religion**
	Charities • National culture • Political parties and issues • Religious sites • Social issues
268	**Sport**
	Athletics • Ball sports • Big sporting events • Contact sports • Equestrian sports • Extreme sports • Martial arts • Motor sports • Sports news and information • Target sports • Water sports
284	**Travel**
	Cruises and flights • For the adventurous • Holiday bargains • Holidays in Europe • Holidays in North America • Information and advice • Transport and maps • Travel guides
302	Netiquette and Security
307	Glossary and Index

INTRODUCTION

This handbook will help to guide you through your explorations of the exciting world wide web. Many people have already discovered the huge amounts of useful services, shops, and information that are available. Don't worry if you are not actually one of these people. If you have a computer, an Internet connection, and this book, then you will soon be zooming around the web, visiting the places that you need, and learning how to avoid the ones that you don't.

— Getting connected —

Essential terms

There are a few technical terms that you will need to know. Don't worry, though. You don't have to understand how the Internet works to use it, but knowing a few buzzwords will help to make your journey much easier. The Internet can be divided into different areas. The bit people are talking about, where you "surf" for information, look at lush pictures, and generally "get connected", is called the web. Other places include newsgroups, chat, and FTP sites. We will concentrate on the web here, as it will be the most useful for you.

Sites and addresses

The web itself is made up of many different areas, called sites. Each one has a unique name, or address. Web addresses frequently appear in advertisements or at the end of television programmes. The proper name for a web address is an URL (often pronounced "earl"), which means uniform resource locator. Most of the time you won't need to know this, but the writers of some websites assume their readers have lots of technical knowledge and will refer to URLs. If you are having trouble with the concept of the web, imagine that it is similar to the teletext service available with most televisions. But instead of typing in a three-figure number to find the news headlines, television programme showing times, or sports results, you enter words. And you'll find that the web can be much more powerful, too, with photographic-quality pictures and interesting articles.

Browsers and plug-ins

To access a website, your computer needs to be connected to the Internet and be able to run a program called a web browser – the two most commonly used are Microsoft Internet Explorer and Netscape Navigator. It is almost certain that Internet Explorer will already be installed on your PC. The browser acts as your window on to the web. It will show you pictures and text, and will sometimes play sounds. Modern browsers also support moving video images and other technologies that provide animations and interactive buttons. Sometimes a website might expect your browser to be equipped with a piece of software to display multimedia – Flash is the most common – but don't worry if you don't have it as most of the time you'll be offered the opportunity to download the appropriate program. This program is called a "plug-in".

An example site

Here's an example of a website. *The Times* newspaper has a website that contains much of the same information that you would find in the physical paper version. Its address is www.timesonline.co.uk. You would visit this site by connecting to the Internet, loading your web browser program, and typing the web address (URL) into the address box, or bar.

Once you have connected, you will be given the option to look at the various areas covered by the site, such as world news, sport, or business. The site is updated daily, so you can refer to it in much the same way as you would a newspaper. The added benefit, however, is that new stories can be included as soon as they happen, so readers – like you – don't have to wait until the next day for articles to be published.

Navigating sites using links

Once you have found an interesting website (this book contains the addresses to more than 1500 of these), you'll obviously want to read its contents. The beauty of the web is that you can choose which bits to look at without having to plough through the whole thing. Websites are not like books, which you should read from beginning to end. Web pages allow you to link a word or phrase to another page so that, when you click on it with your mouse, your browser goes straight to another article without you having to type in a further address. By clicking on the link, you will be sent immediately to the related site that usually offers further information. The linked text is usually written in a different colour and is often underlined, although different sites have different styles. Some links merely change colour when your mouse moves over them – the cursor also changes to a hand when you hover over a link. Most websites have simple menus that make browsing easier. It's usually obvious.

For example, if this book were a website, you might expect to click on the underlined text to find out what the term "website" actually means. These links are called hyperlinks and are not just restricted to the text. Pictures can also be used as hyperlinks. Alternatively, when visiting an art gallery's site, you can expect to click on any of their small pictures, called thumbnails, to view a larger version.

When you position your cursor over words providing links to other websites, your cursor will change from an arrow shape to a pointing hand.

Making a list

Armed with this knowledge, you are ready to take your first tentative steps on to the web. Once you've found a site you like, it is often a good idea to make a note of its address so that you can return to it easily. Your web browser program will be able to do this for you, by using its Bookmark (Netscape Navigator) or Favourites (Internet Explorer) list.

Once you have found a set of sites you really like, you'll probably want to keep returning to them, particularly those that provide regular news stories. It's worth spending a bit of time whittling down the numbers. If you try to visit too many, you'll end up not bothering at all in the long run, which would be a shame because the Internet is more up to date than any newspaper or magazine can ever be. Create a short list, and get into the habit of checking the sites on it regularly. Alternatively, many sites have newsletters that they send to you by e-mail on a daily basis.

A brief history of the web

The Internet has been around for ages, although the web has only really caught on since the mid-1990s. Until 1991, the web was dominated by the experts that developed it. The first proper web browser, which could show pictures and run on the common PC, was introduced in 1993. It was called Mosaic and was the forerunner to modern browsers such as Internet Explorer and Navigator. It was so easy to use that the use of the web grew by 341,634 per cent within the browser's first year. Since then, web browsers have had more features added to them, including the ability to make secure financial transactions.

The most important thing to happen to increase the web's popularity has been the introduction of free access. Generally, those in the United States have to pay subscription fees to Internet service providers (ISPs), but don't pay for the phone calls made to establish connections. In the United Kingdom, Internet users used to pay for phone calls and subscription fees. They signed up in droves when ISPs offered subscription-free accounts. Over the past year and a half, interesting new deals have appeared for Internet users. You can now pay a monthly subscription fee of around £15 that includes free Internet phone calls, thus eliminating the worry of astronomically large phone bills.

You will be probably be accessing the web by computer, either at home or at work. It may be a Mac, but is more likely to be a PC. However, games consoles with Internet features and Internet-equipped digital television services mean that you don't have to be deskbound when going online. For a while it looked like mobile phones would allow us to use the Internet while on the move, but WAP (Wireless Application Protocol) phones turned out to be too slow and unreliable. We've been expecting to see the launch of new, faster and more powerful phones that use GPRS and 3G technologies – but these have been slow to catch on.

How to use this book

This guide brings you more than 1500 of the best websites available on the Internet. Whether you are a keen traveller, a bookworm, or a sports fanatic, you will find something here for you. If you can't find what you are looking for in the main area, then look to the "see also" section at the back of each chapter, where a number of other sites are concisely described. They may well take you to the ideal site.

Each entry is given in alphabetical order, either according to its official company name or a brief summary of the site's contents. The website address, or URL, is then given. While all addresses have "http://" in front of them, it is not necessary to type this into the address bar, as your computer should do this automatically. Please note, however, that not all websites begin with "www", and in this book this prefix has only been given when it is actually part of the address.

Unfortunately, the nature of the Internet and e-commerce means that websites are prone to change, both in design and location. Although we can warrant that the sites included in this book were correct at the time of going to press, we, the author and the publishers, do not accept responsibility for any errors that may occur as a result of these changes, but apologize for any inconvenience this may cause you.

SURFING THE NET

The Internet is packed with information about absolutely everything. Most of it is free, much of it is accurate, but actually finding the bits you need is not always as straightforward as you might hope. Don't panic, though. Once you've read this crash course in Internet navigation, the tangled mess that is the web will be under your control. You'll learn about web directories, search engines, and even how to guess a site's address, sometimes with astonishing accuracy. Remember, too, that many sites provide links to other, similar pages. A directory or search engine might not give you exactly the information you want, but the pages they do yield can take you closer to your ultimate goal.

Web directories

There is more than one way to find useful information on the web. The simplest method is to use a website directory. This is a site that stores lists and lists of Internet sites, a bit like the "A–Z guide" in this book. The best web directories have clearly defined categories that will make it easy for you to find your particular area of interest. If you want to find out about health-related issues, perhaps to learn more about asthma, then browse through the available categories until you find one called "Health". This would contain subcategories for you to burrow down into – and eventually you should find a shortlist of websites referring to asthma. Some website directories have an often quite basic search feature, which you can use to help you to find the best categories to attack.

Searching with a web directory

Yahoo! (**www.yahoo.com** or **uk.yahoo.com**) is the world's most popular web directory, and we are using it here to show you what a search is actually like. In this instance, we are searching for information on the hit film *The Matrix*. Initially you might enter something such as "the matrix" into the search box, and then press the Search button to start things moving (see step 1, opposite). The

Surfing the Net 11

Add some key words and press "Search"

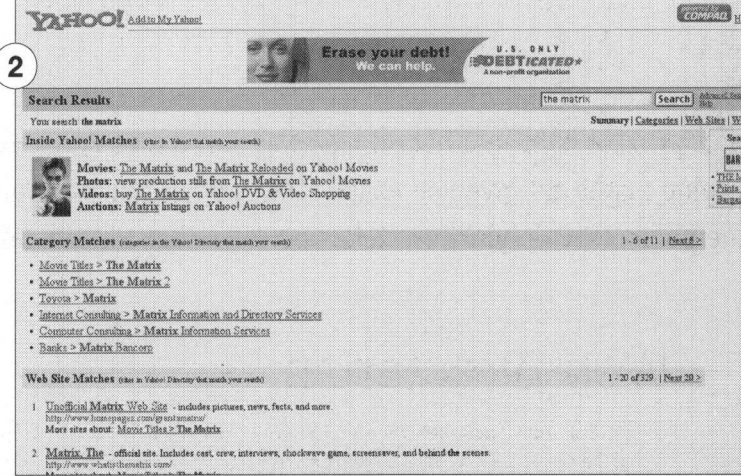

This is just a small number of the sites Yahoo! has listed

"Entertainment > Movies and Film" section looks like a safe bet, so click on it to see a list of sites, and other subcategories (see step 2, above). A website's title and address can often give you a clue as to how useful it's going to be. It is worth remembering that the official websites are not necessarily the best. Once you get a feel for a directory, you'll be able to head straight for the right categories. For example, it makes sense to start at "Recreation and Sport" when searching for your favourite soccer team's home page.

— Local information

If you are looking for information on local businesses, then the easiest method is to use the electronic equivalent of the local telephone directory. Many will go further than just providing telephone numbers and addresses. Some, such as Scoot (**www.scoot.co.uk**), will give you information about what films your local cinema is showing. It will also provide access to a full timetable, as well as giving you the option to book tickets online. Links to the companies' websites, if they exist, are also available.

Guestimate

If you know the company's name, then there is a very simple and very fast way to find its website – guess! Imagine that there is a hardware store that sells nails, screws, and other bits and pieces. It's called "Mr Grommet". There is a fair chance that, if the company has a website, its address would be **www.mrgrommet.com**. You can type the address right into your web browser and see what comes up. The worst thing that can happen is an error message saying that the page doesn't exist. If so, try **www.mrgrommet.co.uk**, **www.mrgrommet.uk.com**, and possibly **www.mrgrommet.net**. What about **www.mr-grommet.com**? Try generic names when starting out with such searches. Do you want to know about hamsters? Then try **www.hamsters.com**.

How web addresses work

Most website addresses are in three parts – beginning with "www", which stands for world wide web. The words that follow can be almost anything, but usually make up the name of the company in question. The last bit, the ".com", ".co.uk", or ".net" indicates where or what the site is. You can deduce the basic nature of a site from its address. See the list opposite for descriptions of common endings.

Check a website's ending to see if it belongs to a government department or an educational facility, or if it is located on the other side of the world. The latter sites can often load much more slowly than sites that are closer to home. This is because it takes time for digital information to flow through the many computers that make up the Internet – and the further away a site is, the greater the number of computers that will become involved. Some of these computers may well be too busy to help straight away.

Some popular sites exist in more than one place. For example, the main Microsoft website may be in the United States, but there are copies of it hosted all over the world. Americans will find that the **www.microsoft.com** address will work just fine for them. However, British users would be much better off going to **www.microsoft.co.uk**, or **www.microsoft.com/uk**. If you are given a choice, it is always best to choose a site that is either in or near your own country. Links to international "mirror" sites are almost always provided on the main site's first page, so they are easy to find.

Surfing the Net 13

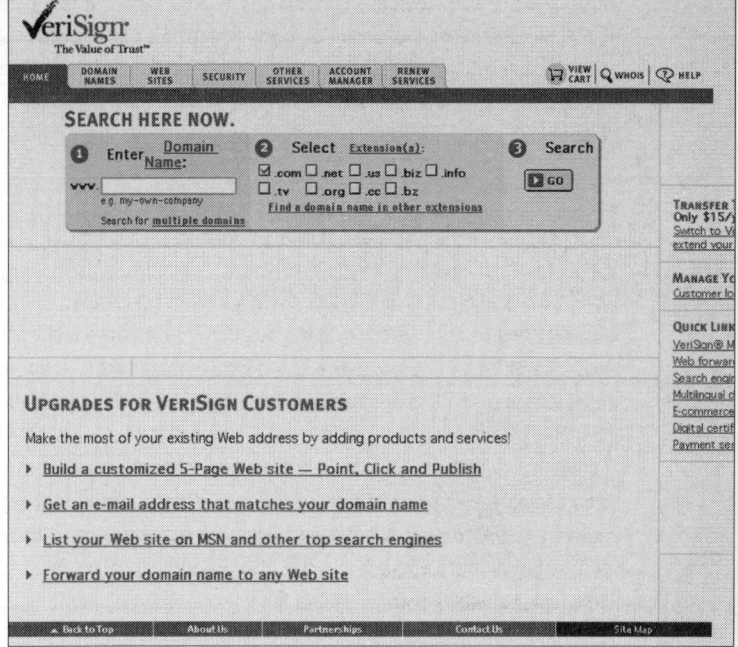

Register your domain name with a registration service such as www.networksolutions.com

Common web address suffixes

Here are some common web address suffixes, called top level domains (TLDs):

.com	A company, often based in the United States – but not always
.org	A non-commercial organization, sometimes charitable
.net	Usually reserved for networks, such as your Internet service provider
.co.uk	A British company
.org.uk	A British organization
.gov	These sites are run by US governmental departments
.gov.uk	Add a country's suffix for other nations' governments
.mil	The military
.ac.uk	British academic sites, run by universities and colleges
.edu	US educational facilities
.au	Australian site
.fr	French site
.de	German site
.it	Italian site
.jp	Japanese site
.ru	Russian site

Judge a site by its cover. A site address such as **www.nhsdirect.nhs.uk** (NHS Direct) or **www.fda.gov** (Food and Drug Administration) is much more likely to contain trustworthy information than an amateur one. And remember that there is no guarantee that a site has been designed for English readers. If the address ends with a Japanese or German code, you're likely to need a phrase book. You can find more information on TLDs at the Internic website (**www.internic.net**).

Search engines

A search engine is a website that has access to an incredibly large index of websites right across the network. You tell it what you want to find by using key words and phrases, and it consults the index, throwing up links to possibly useful sites. Because there is no single official index that these sites can use, search engines have to create their own. Some share, but the main ones use different technologies to gather and sort information. The result is that not all search engines are of equal quality. But even the best search engines cannot search the whole Internet thoroughly.

One of the best general search engines is Google (**www.google.com**). It provides a basic directory of the web for beginners to browse through, while also offering you various different levels of searching. It also allows you to search the web solely for images, videos, or music.

Search engines are not very discriminating, and they won't be able to second-guess your intentions. Search for "star wars", and you'll find millions of pages about the science-fiction film, as well as related games and books. You'll also find documents about the Reagan administration's defence policies mixed in. But by using the special techniques detailed over the page, you'll be able to sift out the bits that you don't want.

It is a sad fact that even the most innocent of keywords can bring up links to a variety of potentially offensive websites, even when used with the best intentions. One way to deal with rude sites is to ignore them. Another is to use a security system (**www.netnanny.com** and **www.cyberpatrol.com** are just two examples) that will block out offensive sites. They are always obvious from the description and address shown by the search engine. Unfortunately, the site descriptions are usually exceedingly graphic, so parental guidance when using the Internet is definitely advised. The advantage of web directories is that they keep adult material in the adult material categories. Regular Internet search engines are not so discriminating. It's not their fault – the automatic indexing systems are easy to trick. See "Security on the Internet" on pages 304–6 for more details on avoiding the less tasteful parts of the Internet.

Surfing the Net 15

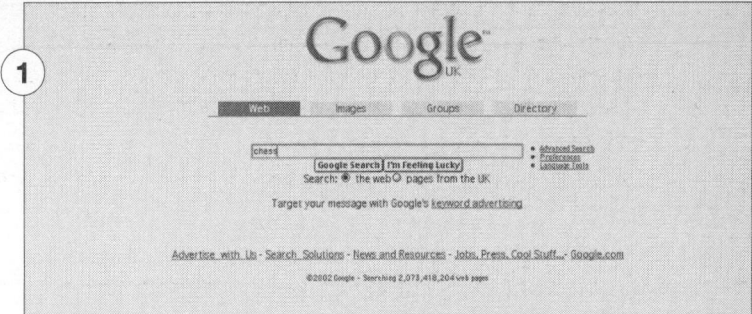

Start off with a general word or phrase before narrowing your search

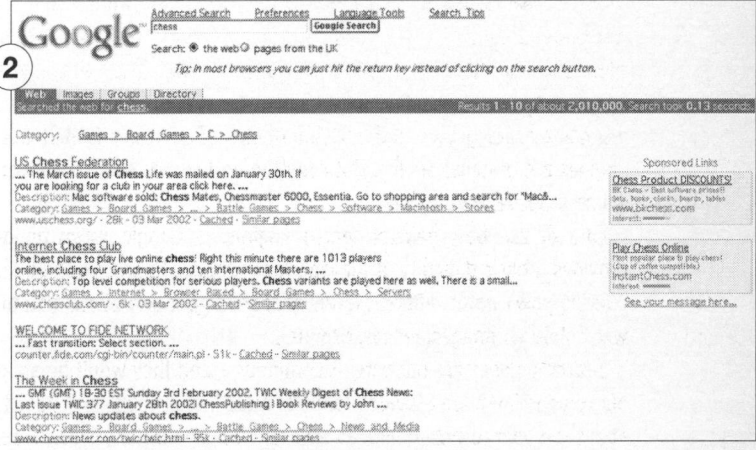

More than two million results, most of which are of no use

Searching with a search engine

We have chosen **www.google.com** as our search engine. If you want to search, for example, for coverage of the chess game between Garry Kasparov and the computer Deep Blue, type "chess" into the search box, and press the Search button (see step 1, above). An intimidating number of pages will appear, most of which will mean nothing to you (see step 2, above). Now try this: type "+chess +kasparov", and press Search. The plus signs mean that the search engine will only look for web pages that contain both of these words. You can see that the number of sites has decreased dramatically, and the chance of picking up relevant pages is looking more likely. But there are still thousands of pages listed. Now try "+kasparov + "deep blue"" (see step 3, next page). The inverted commas are needed when using a phrase containing more than one word, such as "deep blue". The more words you add, the more specific your search is likely to be, but be warned – do not use too many words or your search is likely to come up with no

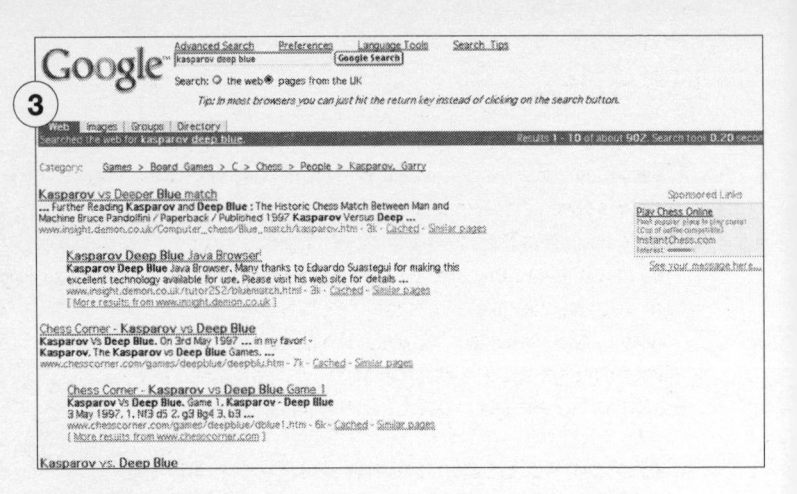

At last. Still nearly 1000 web sites listed, but the first few options should do fine

results at all. You can continue to use this technique to pare down the results until your list is of a manageable size, which you can then read through.

Advanced searching

You can really narrow your searches using a standard set of commands known as Boolean operators. The most common are AND, OR, and AND NOT. A search for "cocktail AND recipe AND NOT whisky" using capitals will save you a lot of time that you would otherwise waste trawling through useless pages. Some search engines support extra features such as NEAR, which will find key words that appear within a certain number of words from each other.

You can also try searching for exact phrases. If you are looking for a transcription of a speech, and you know a small quote, enclose it in inverted commas and give it a try. Search for ""i have a dream" AND "martin luther king" AND speech AND mp3", and the list you get is going to be very specific – probably including links to actual recordings of the event that you can listen to over the Internet.

Some search engines let you narrow the search to images, videos, or sounds. If you want to search several search engines at once, you can use a metasearch engine, such as **www.dogpile.com**. This will increase your chances of finding some hard-to-find information – remember that not all the search engines look at the same pages, and so the more search engines you use the better. However, this can be time consuming if you are conducting a more general search and, in these cases, one may suffice.

Many modern web browsers have a self-contained search facility, but these are limited in their scope, and it is therefore best to stick with using the professional search engines that are very easy to use.

Surfing the Net 17

Usenet

One of the most active parts of the Internet is called Usenet, which contains newsgroups. These are like electronic bulletin boards that people use to ask questions and post their opinions. There are certain rules within newsgroups – you would do well to have a look at the "Netiquette section" at the back of the book. You may not have the time to spend hours reading all the articles in a newsgroup, but you can still take advantage of other people's knowledge by using a web-based service provided by **www.google.com**. Visit the site and click on the Group's button. You'll find a store of online discussions, known as "threads", which can be searched using a powerful set of online tools.

Searching Usenet with google.com

Enter your keywords. We'll use "tree" and "fungus" in this example (see below). This brings up a list of discussions, rather than websites. You may well find people asking the same questions that you have, but with luck there will also be replies from other, well-informed individuals. Click through a few to see if they are on the right track. Your keywords will be highlighted where they appear in each message. If you need to narrow the search, there is an easy-to-use Advanced Groups Search option. Once you've found your answer, you can be on your way, but some people will want to ask more questions, or even add their opinions to a discussion.

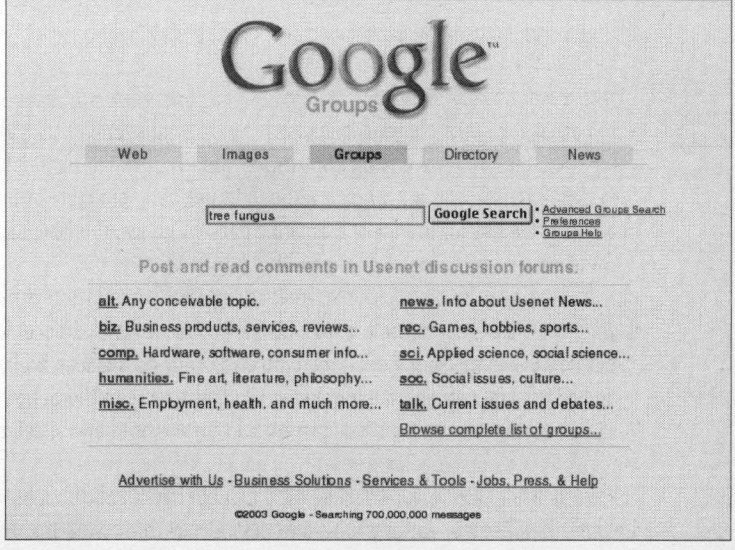

Visit google.com's Groups section to view newsgroups on your favourite topics

SHOPPING ON THE INTERNET

Using the Internet to buy goods and services has become very popular. Over the past two or three years, the number of online shops has exploded; no matter what you want to buy, it is very likely that there will be a website willing to sell it to you. Every high street and retail store that is worth its salt has its own website for you to buy from, almost certainly at discounted prices. You can buy prescription drugs, specialist food you would not find in your local supermarket, and rare records and CDs. By the start of 2000, it was estimated that 10 per cent of people in the United Kingdom alone had bought something over the Internet. More than 55 per cent of Americans have shopped online.

The online high street

You may be feeling left out. Perhaps you can't imagine why you'd want to buy something via a computer screen. And how do you even begin? You can't touch the merchandise, and any descriptive pictures are likely to be small and lacking in detail. Maybe you are worried about how you're going to pay for things. After all, surely there is an invisible army of hackers just waiting to pounce on your credit card number the minute you send it over the Internet?

The reality is that using the Internet to buy things is incredibly convenient and safe. Obviously, you can't squeeze fruit and vegetables to check that they are fresh before buying them, but, if you are buying commodities such as books, videos, and CDs, then you will already know what to expect anyway. And some music sites will even let you preview album tracks before you buy. In fact, if you have a mind to buy a particular item, the Internet provides an excellent way to shop around while saving on shoe leather and patience. It also means that you can avoid the Saturday crowds and browse through shops online in a fraction of the time that you could in the high street.

Shopping on the Internet

Buying from a website is like buying from a catalogue. If you're happy to spend based on a stamp-sized picture in a magazine, why not when it's on a monitor? The fact that the Internet is always up to the minute and up to date also means that prices can change every day. And competition between companies and the lack of overhead costs mean the prices usually come down. From a business point of view, running a shop on the Internet costs a lot less than renting, lighting, and heating a property in a city centre, and some of these savings are passed on to the customer.

Internet shopping

How do you dip your toe into the Internet shopping centre? Your best option is to start off small. Buy something that will fit through your letterbox, such as a book or CD. That way you won't be worried about sending money off into the ether, and you won't have to wait in to receive a large package. There are plenty of online shops that will sell you a single novel or album. You don't have to buy in bulk.

Shopping walkthrough

In this virtual shopping trip I will be looking for a cookery book. Because I spend far too much time using the Internet, the meals must be quick and easy – I don't want to waste any valuable time that I could use to be online!

I've chosen to shop at **amazon.co.uk**. As I don't know the title of the book I'm after, I'll browse the book section, rather than search for a particular title. Click on the "Books" tab to get the next screen (see step 1, above).

After negotiating a few subcategories, we come to the "Food & Drink" menu (see step 2, next page). The "Quick & Easy" section looks suitable, so let's have a look at it.

This one fits the budget, and other customers have rated it well. Press the "Add to Shopping Basket" button to select this title (see step 3, next page). If I find

20 Shopping on the Internet

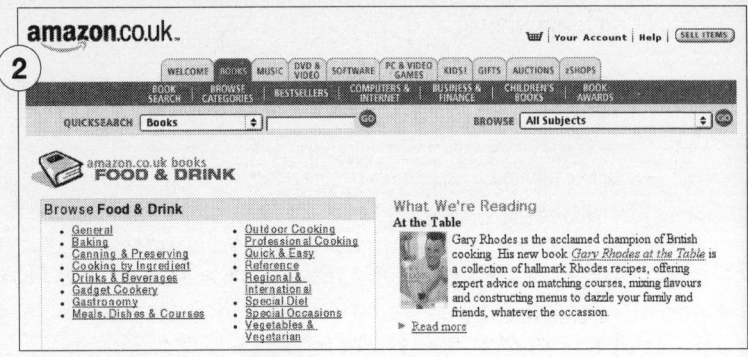

another book that I decide I prefer, I can easily remove this book from my Shopping Basket. We could continue shopping for other books at this point, or go straight to the online checkout to pay.

The next step would be to create an account with the online shop, as this makes it possible to track the order later on. It's only necessary to give them my address and credit card details once, though, as the shop will remember my details, reducing the tiresome job of typing it in each time I shop. It will also remember the items that you have shopped for and make recommendations based on the books or CDs that you buy from Amazon. You can also keep a wishlist of items if you do not want to buy an item on that particular e-shopping expedition, but might later. I can also ask for books to arrive at addresses other than mine, which is useful when sending last-minute birthday presents to friends and relatives. Some sites will even giftwrap an item for you!

A padlock on the bottom left of your window means that your details are encoded before they are sent.

Shopping on the Internet

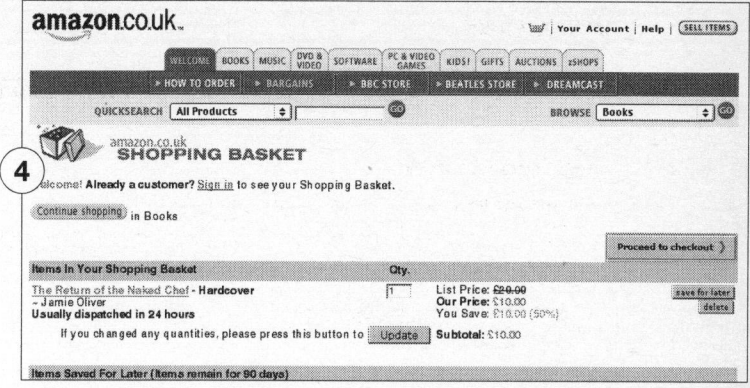

When you submit your details, you will notice a yellow padlock at the bottom of the screen. This means that the website is "secure" and that, until the transaction has been completed, all the information added to the forms will be sent in secret code to the shop.

When we are setting up the account, we will be asked to choose a password. This will have to be entered each time the account is used and so, in order to do this, we are asked to sign in (see step 4, above). It is important to remember whatever password you choose, or you won't be able to track your order.

The system will give us a final chance to check that all the details – address, list of purchases, etc – are correct before we decide to go through with the order. Postage and packaging, if not free, should be displayed at this point. When you are sure everything is correct, you can then press the "Place Your Order" button (see step 5, below).

When a parcel arrives, two or three days later, I guarantee you will be sold on the idea of using the Internet to shop. And I bet that the CD/DVD/bestseller you found was available at a discounted rate.

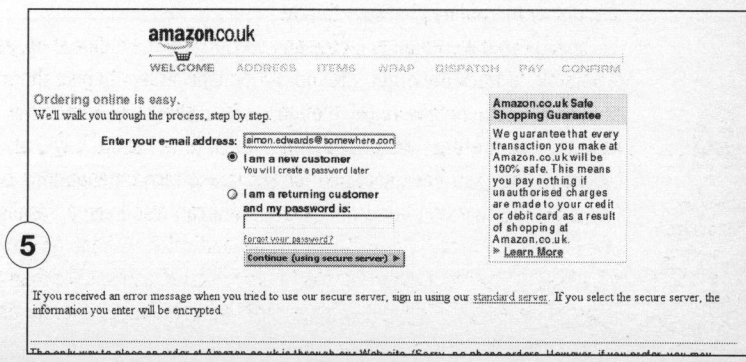

Order tracking is an interesting and useful feature you'll find on all the best websites. You identify yourself to the site using a unique user name and password, and the screen will tell you if your item has been placed into stock yet, whether or not it's actually been shipped out to you, and will possibly also give an estimated delivery date. Sometimes, when you order more than one thing, one item will be in stock while another needs to be ordered from the supplier. Companies such as **amazon.co.uk** will sometimes send the first item and forward the other ones as soon as they become available. You shouldn't be expected to pay extra postage charges for this service. If you use the order tracking facility, you will be able to see exactly what's going on without having to sit in a phone queue to speak to customer services.

What happens if the goods are faulty when they arrive? Or perhaps you don't like the colour of the shirt that looked so appealing on the web page. Maybe you've been sent a completely different item from the one you ordered! As with any business, an Internet shop will have a returns policy that will deal with any such problems.

Buying tips

Use a price comparison site, such as **www.kelkoo.com**, to get the best price on a product. These sites allow you to search for the best price on an item by searching a list of retail sites and giving you the biggest discount, including postage costs, and often telling you how long it will take to be delivered.

Given the choice, always use a credit card rather than a debit card. The former protects you when goods are faulty, or don't turn up, and the seller refuses to cooperate. You get your money back, and the credit card company chases the lost money itself. A debit card just provides a way to pay money from your bank account and can be useful for small purchases, but you don't receive any protection from fraudsters.

A good online shop will clearly publish its prices and include any tax you might have to pay. You should always be able to find out how much postage and packing will cost. Some Internet shops provide free delivery, but not all. Reading the small print can be painful – there's usually loads of it – but it is essential that you know what you're letting yourself in for.

Many stores will remember your details, so you won't have to type in your address and card number every time you buy something. "Cookies" are often stored on your computer by the store, so that each time you log into the site, it recognizes your details. If an online shop gives you a user name and password, make sure that you keep it in a safe place. You won't want to lose it, and you certainly don't want someone else to find it and go on a spree at your expense. That said, the worst that can happen is that you'll receive a massive package one day. Any customer services department worth its salt will be happy to sort the mess out. It's no different from someone finding your catalogue card and ordering goods with it.

A well-run business in the high street will have a nice, big shop with excellent displays and polite staff. An Internet site can be made to look equally fantastic by anyone with a computer, some cheap software, and a half-decent eye for design. So how can you tell if an e-shop is all it appears? Many major retailers recognize that Internet customer service needs to be of a consistently high quality, but this is no guarantee. Some sites join schemes where they agree to follow a certain code of conduct and, in return, are permitted to display a logo that certifies them as good traders. This is intended to instil confidence in consumers. Don't be taken in by any old certificate, though, as they can be falsely copied or created out of thin air. If in doubt, check the organization's website to see if the shop is listed.

Buying from foreign websites

You can buy things from websites in other countries very easily. There are bargains to be had and exclusive luxuries on offer. An increasing number of places will ship goods to anywhere on the planet and at reasonable rates. But please remember that you will probably have to pay duty and tax. Depending on what you have bought, you may be expected to pay VAT and some other local duty. The Post Office might also make a charge. Always expect to receive a bill from Customs when buying "bargains". That cheap CD could turn out to be more expensive than you think. UK shoppers should visit HM Customs and Excise (**www.hmce.gov.uk**) to get the latest details on import duties, while US customers will find the US Customs Service (**www.customs.gov**) useful.

Delivery

As with any mail-order transaction, the hardest part of Internet shopping is receiving the goods. Small items that come through the mail will pose little or no problem, but if you order a computer, freezer, or television, then you'd better make sure that you're at home when the courier comes knocking. This is no different from waiting for a delivery from a high-street electrical shop, though, and the prices on the Internet are almost certainly cheaper.

The problem of delivery is a bugbear to supermarkets, which desperately want to get on with the serious business of creating massive online stores. Unfortunately, having large, refrigerated delivery lorries hammering through urban areas every five minutes is neither practical nor desirable. As demand rises, we might see vans or even pizza delivery-style motorbikes fulfilling orders. Not yet, though.

Internet auctions

Online auctions can be a fun way to spend or make money via the Internet. Here's how they work. An online auction acts a bit like a classified advertisement page in a local paper. The seller puts up a price that he or she believes is reasonable for their item. If you want an item, click on it and offer an amount, which will be sent to the auction and published on the page – remember that you will have to be a registered user to do this. Other people will do the same, and the price will rise, as with a conventional auction. Online auctions run for a set period of time, possibly one day, but frequently a week or more, and the person who bids the highest at the end gets to buy. Sometimes there is a catch, though. Even if the offer price seems low, that probably means that a reserve price has been placed, so although you may be the highest bidder on an item, if that bid does not reach the reserve price, you can't buy it.

There are a few things to think about when taking part in one of these auctions. First of all, know who you're buying from. If it isn't the auction house itself, or a well-known, affiliated company, treat the deal as if it were a classified advert. Don't just send money off to a stranger because, should things go wrong and you end up without your vacuum cleaner/guitar/vase, the auctioneers won't help. Auction sites run self-policing communities, where naughty people are given black marks against their names, but this will be of no comfort to you if your cheque is cashed. Therefore, always check a user rating – if they have a number of dissatisfied customers, then refrain from buying from them. Continual offenders are suspended from trading, though there is no method to stop these people from rejoining under a different user name. Some auction sites are developing schemes where you send the money to them, and they release it to the seller once they know that you've actually received the goods. There are also payment schemes using credit cards. Companies such as **www.paypal.com** allow sellers to send the money to the seller electronically. This cuts out the need to send money through the post.

Also bear in mind how you will receive the things you've bought. Will the seller deliver, or will you have to pick them up yourself? Is this feasible if you live in different areas, or even different countries? What about warranties? Don't be blinded by the high-tech fun you're having on the websites. Anyone, including you, can sell through online auctions. And anyone can try to rip you off. Generally, though, honesty prevails, and auctions provide a great hunting ground – just be careful.

How to buy safely

Although your computer isn't being constantly monitored by electronic criminals, all good Internet shops still take serious security measures to make absolutely

Introduction 25

sure that your credit or debit card numbers remain safe. They do this by creating a special connection between your PC and their site, which encodes the information exchanged between the two. So when you send your name, address, and bank details, they are wrapped up in a secret code and sent to the shop, which can decrypt your details. You may see the abbreviation SSL (secure sockets layer) being mentioned. This is the technical name for a secure connection.

There is a simple way to detect a secure connection. Look at the bottom part of your web browser program. If you can see a small closed padlock, then it is safe to send your details. The website address will also begin https:// rather than the normal http:// – the extra "s" stands for "secure". Sites also provide information about how they will stop people stealing customers' details. If you're still not convinced, did you realize that it is much easier for waiters, shop assistants, and even refuse collectors to find and use your card number than it is for an unauthorized individual on the Internet?

Even though hackers may be a negligible threat, what about the companies themselves? This is where common sense comes in. We are yet to see a viable electronic equivalent to cash, so Internet purchases have to be made using a card of some sort. When you go shopping in town, you wouldn't (or at least shouldn't) give your details to every here-today-gone-tomorrow business. Sensible Internet shoppers only use online shops backed up by well-known businesses or at least ones with a genuine postal address and phone number. In the event that something goes wrong, it's easier to chase a company that exists in the physical world than one whose details only consist of a website and e-mail address. Be sensible, and I guarantee that you will enjoy the Internet shopping experience!

You can make or spend money at auction sites such as www.ebay.co.uk

ART, DESIGN, AND ARCHITECTURE

Whether you want to research a 16th-century printmaker or find out about the latest imaging technologies, these sites can help you locate and expand your visual interest. There is an extensive range of museum-based sites and a host of art galleries to sample from around the world. Alternatively, owners of crumbling old historic houses can also find help on the Internet, where the art of masonry restoration is documented, while potential visitors can locate said properties and arrange a viewing. Clothes fashions are equally well catered for, and you can click online to find out which pair of trainers is in fashion this week ...

Architecture

Architecture magazine online
www.architecturemag.com
An industry journal and art publication, this bright website gives you all that you might want to know about the world of architecture. Check out previous issues of the magazine, search through the ever growing database of architecture firms, and also consult the (very much US-based) events calendar. Very much like some modern architecture, this site is clean to look at, and I assure you, it will definitely grow on you.

Castles on the Web
www.castlesontheweb.com
This site pays homage to hundreds of medieval castles throughout the world. You can take virtual tours of castles, or take part in the castle question-and-answer area. The site is updated regularly and has a featured castle every day of the year. Marvellous.

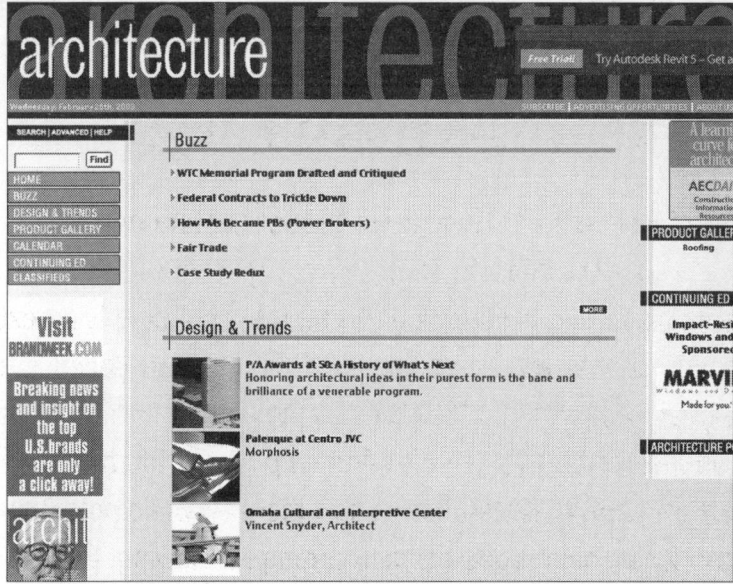

The professional architect's online magazine at www.architecturemag.com is a bright affair

Conservation of historic buildings
www.buildingconservation.com
If you own an old building in need of repair and want to either hire a professional to help or go on a course to learn about masonry or stone conservation, then the Building Conservation site is the place to try first. A good selection of online articles by leading authorities covers such areas as repairing reinforced concrete, and fire protection in historic buildings.

Database of buildings and architects
www.greatbuildings.com
Experience the world's best architectural feats with The Great Buildings Collection, which features a database that can be browsed by place, building, and architect. This handy resource includes a brief history of the constructions and the constructors, bibliographical sources, close-up photographs of buildings from different angles, and in some cases with 3D models. All this will certainly help to answer those awkward architectural arguments and aid with school projects.

The National Trust
www.nationaltrust.org.uk
The National Trust has a great website full of information about places of historic interest or natural beauty in the United Kingdom. Find one of its sites

28 Art, Design, and Architecture

a

through its searchable database by name or by area. A large educational site is also available, with a small photo gallery. Older students may find the Sites of Scientific Interest particularly enjoyable.

Art and artists

Art, artists, galleries, and exhibitions
www.artincontext.org
The stylish, minimalist appearance of Art In Context hides a complex work of reference, containing details of art galleries and dealers, exhibitions, and artists the world over (albeit with a large bias towards the United States). You can search for art by genre – every discernible style is listed here – and there is also an image database.

Art Bank
www.artbank-oldmaster.com
Browse through the biographies and bibliographies of more than 35,000 painters, drawers, and engravers who lived from the 10th to the 18th centuries, and feast your eyes on over a million works of art. The Opera Omnia section allows

The world's most famous auction house is far from antiquated online at www.christies.com

you to collate a complete archive or an artist and his works onto a CD-ROM. You can purchase the entire encylopedia on CD-ROM, too.

Art database and news
www.artcult.com
An up-to-date news service and a database of 30,000 paintings, complete with average auction prices, makes Artcult a compelling site for all art investors. The site also includes detailed advice for collectors on how to avoid fake goods and houses a comprehensive artist biography list. Don't be put off by the rather intimidating, ugly page design and the occasional irrelevancies here.

Art, design, architecture and media gateway
www.adam.ac.uk
This academic site aims to provide students in higher education with access to the highest-quality information on fine art, design, architecture, applied arts (crafts), film studies, and art history.

Art Lover's Guide to Britain and Ireland
www.artguide.org
This guide to the art collections of Great Britain and Ireland contains details of around 2000 "named" artists, more than 650 museums, and a large database of what exhibitions are currently on. There aren't any pictures here (try The Web Museum at **www.southern.net/wm** for those), but each artist's entry has a list of venues in the United Kingdom exhibiting his or her work.

Christie's
www.christies.com
The official website of the famous auction house that existed long before the likes of QXL has an auction calendar and a gallery of items, and you can view the sometimes ridiculous sums of money people will pay for old things. You can plan your next purchase or simply save your money and watch live webcasts of the auctions themselves, often at the New York auction house.

An introduction to art
www.southern.net/wm
Art students and amateur enthusiasts alike will enjoy WebMuseum's glossary of artistic movements, a thorough artists' index, and list of themes – from Picasso and Cubism to Japanese Momoyama art. The special exhibitions present very good reproductions of famous artists' paintings, listed by theme. In the past ,the site has featured the works of Paul Cézanne, as well as including an exhibition of the *Très Riches Heures* manuscript.

The Louvre
www.louvre.fr
This stylish official site contains a selection of exhibitions with photos and short descriptions, a virtual tour of the museum, and a list of events. You can also buy tickets for entry to the museum from the site, to help you avoid those lengthy queues. Whether you are interested in the ancient Egyptians, 14th-century prints and drawings, or even the history of the Louvre itself, you will be satisfied.

Mechanical sculpture theatre
www.cabaret.co.uk
Enter the eerie world of mechanical sculpture (automatons). Surreal and funny creations which you can bring to life yourself in the online exhibitions, or order your own kits or fully assembled contraptions from the site, which will be sent out to you wherever you are in the world. A useful education section and a shop on weird and wonderful things make this a great site for teachers, students, and fans of the bizarre.

The Metropolitan Museum of Art
www.metmuseum.org
This New York museum displays 5000 years of art from around the world, and almost 3500 objects are reproduced here on this site. You can view highlights from the collection of your choice, and by signing the Guestbook you can customize your own online calendar and Met gallery to display only those museum events and works of art that most interest you. Like the real thing, you could spend days here.

Museum of Modern Art
www.moma.org
View a selection of the collection from this New York–based museum, which includes more than 100,000 paintings, sculptures, drawings, and photographs. Films and books can also be found here. There is information about the museum's educational resources that will help you to appreciate and enjoy the works on display, and you can even purchase fashion accessories and furniture from the online store.

Online art gallery
www.artandparcel.com
This online art gallery sells paintings direct from the web page. You can view a directory of artists and see pictures that are listed according to their category. Aspiring artists are also invited to sell their works here. Some artists will work to your commission, and the site boasts examples from more than 100 of them.

Site for artists
www.nyfa.org
Aiming to bring artists together over the web, this site features links to members' own sites, as well as discussion forums, mailing lists, and exhibitions. Weekly news is available directly from the site, and an art-based jobs list (in the United States) can also be found here.

The Tate Gallery
www.tate.org.uk
Find out about the four Tate galleries (including the impressive Tate Modern), and buy prints, slides, and books from the online shop. Even if you don't wish to buy, you can browse plenty of images of paintings, which are all organized by artist and date. Tate in Space plans to take art even further with your help. Check it out!

Art on the Net
www.art.net
Experience the work of more than 100 artists from all over the world at this virtual art gallery. The featured pieces of art range from sculptures to digitally created pictures. Animations, music, and poetry are also available here. Art on the Net includes sites set up by many of the artists involved, so expect a varying degree of quality within them.

Worldwide arts
www.world-arts-resources.com
This all-in-one site tries to cover everything artistic, including antiques, dance, opera, and architecture. Even very modern techniques, such as Manga cartoons, are covered. It also has an artist portfolio that is changed daily. The massive, searchable database of links to other websites makes World Wide Arts Resources an ideal springboard to other parts of the Internet. Use it to compile a list of your favourite arty sites.

Fashion

The Museum of Costume
www.museumofcostume.co.uk
Anyone interested in the clothes of yesteryear will find the short tour a good introduction to what people were wearing up until the 1960s. Although it offers only a taster of what is available at the museum, you can search the database of 18th-century waistcoats and follow a sound set of links.

a

Find biographies of all your favourite designers at www.fashion.net

Online fashion magazine
http://ntouch.linst.ac.uk/
Claiming to be the future of fashion magazines, *NTOUCH* is designed and run by the London College of Fashion. You can read about the new wave of supermodels or just find out which trainers are cool this week. The site makes heavy use of Flash and so can be slow to download.

Suppliers' directory
www.whoapparel.com
Who? Apparel publishes a directory for suppliers to the fashion industry. Companies are listed in categories such as womenswear, menswear, and services including warehousing facilities. A news service, provided by an external source, has been tailored for people working in the clothes business, although stories from the world's headlines and general business news items are also given.

Vogue magazine
www.vogue.co.uk
Check out the daily fashion news to pick up on what's what in the fashion world. View virtual fashion shows and see the seasonal collections here. You can also view the online archives which go back to 1997. Short summaries of what was "in" make for interesting reading, as does "Who's Who", which gives you the low-down on the big fashion names. You can also buy clothing from the online shop,

enter competitions, and read some of the features that appear in the current month's edition. All put together impeccably, as you would expect.

The World of Fashion
www.fashion.net
If you really want to know about what is happening in every area of the fashion world, then this US-based site is the place to look. Fashion news is updated daily so you can read up-to-date profiles of the designers, models, stylists, etc, watch runway videos, and find out how to get a job in fashion.

Photography

Camera hints and tips
www.photo.net
If you want to know what sort of camera to buy, where to get it from, and how to take brilliant, colourful photos, then try this site. But be aware that the author's language can be colourful, too. Gear reviews are included, making your shopping expeditions for camera equipment much, much easier, and handy hints and tips on light and film usage help you take that perfect picture. Once taken, you can post it on the site to be entered for "Photograph of the Week".

Digital photographs
www.ofoto.com
If you own a digital camera (and if you own a computer, it might make sense to get one), then this site will help you improve those pictures. Follow the online tutorials and, once you are happy, why not store the results online, create your own album of pictures, order prints, or even create your own postcards. If you are confident enough, visit the frame gallery, see others' photos, and add your own!

For professionals
creative.gettyimages.com/photodisc
This is a helpful site for the lens professional, with almost 100,000 high-quality downloadable images from some top photographers. You can buy CDs of stock images in its store. Registration is required to access the full site.

Kodak
www.kodak.co.uk
Kodak's site acts as an introduction to both traditional and newer imaging technologies. You can learn how film processing works and discover what you'll

need to create digital pictures you can store on CD or send by e-mail. Kodak Picture Service Online lets friends and relatives see your efforts or order reprints, even from overseas. If you you live in the United States, try the US site at www.kodak.com.

The photographs of Life Magazine
www.life.com

Some of the world's greatest photography has been taken for *Life* magazine – and here is a selection for the world to see. It's worth returning on a regular basis to check out the picture of the day and see what was going on in the world on "This Day in Life". You should also take an extended visit to marvel at the 20th-century's best pictures selection, which are each accompanied by an audio commentary from one of the magazine's photographers.

see also...

As I have shown, there is a wide selection of art galleries available on the Internet, and The Art Canvas (www.artoncanvas.com) can often be a good place to start, with its high quality, scanned images of works from a variety of 19th- and 20th-century painters and sculptors. For paintings and sculptures specifically from the Gothic, Renaissance, and Baroque periods, you should try the Web Gallery of Art (www.gallery.euroweb.hu). Artinfo: From Russia With Art (www.artinfo.hu) provides access to information on more than 1000 high-profile Russian artists. The Official Magritte Site (www.magritte.com) provides a biography of the artist, as well as books and CD-ROMs to buy. A wider selection of virtual galleries is available from Mark Harden's Artchive (www.artchive.com), which also contains extracts of critiques and CD-ROM reviews.

The London National Gallery (www.nationalgallery.org.uk) has plenty of information on its collections, as well as an exhibition history and details of those coming up in the next year. It has a job competing with the Fine Arts Museums of San Francisco (www.thinker.org), though, which features more than 75,000 images. The Detroit Institute of Arts (www.dia.org), one of the largest fine arts museums in the United States, has a site featuring information on its collections, video lectures, and a bit of online shopping to boot. For a more European flavour, visit the Uffizi Gallery's official site (www.uffizi.firenze.it). Within seconds you can also explore the National Museums of Scotland site (www.nms.ac.uk). The Smithsonian American Art Museum (nmaa-ryder.si.edu) features art collections, event calendars, and a study centre.

ArtMag (www.artmag.com) contains listings of art galleries, artistic events, museums, and photographic galleries all over the world, while dedicated

Art, Design, and Architecture 35

photography fans can view the works of a number of skilled photographers at Masters of Photography (**www.masters-of-photography.com**). You should also check out FocalFix (**www.focalfix.com**), an online photography community where you can browse galleries or submit your own pictures for general viewing. The rather strange Secret Garden (**www-personal.umich.edu/~agrxray**) exhibits extraordinary floral radiograph images, where flowers have been photographed using an X-ray machine.

If sculpture's your thing, then check out the International Sculpture Center (**www.sculpture.org**) as it should satisfy your desire for conference listings and details of artists and their works. View a selection of British sculptures at Sculpture at Goodwood (**www.sculpture.org.uk**). Some of the exhibition examples are also for sale. You can buy from the selections of international goods on sale at the Folk Art and Craft Exchange (**www.folkart.com**), too. You can buy the gargoyles at **stonecarver.com/gargoyles**, and more dark stuff at **gothic-creations.com**. Equally weird is **www.maskmakersweb.org**, where you can find out about mask-making artists and cultural masks. Art students might enjoy the Art Comics Syndicate (**www.artcomic.com**), with its stylistic cartoons (that would love to be thought of as avant-garde). Frieze (**www.frieze.co.uk**) is a magazine on contemporary art and culture, which includes visual arts, design, film, and fashion. Traditionalists will feel more at home visiting a tribute site to the graphical satirist William Hogarth at (**www.haleysteele.com/hogarth/**). You might also appreciate d'Art (**www.fine-art.com**), where you can browse through virtual art galleries, find out about student organizations, and see the work of some very talented people. Axis is a national database of UK-based artists and worth a look if you feel like commissioning something contemporary (**www.axisartists.org.uk**) Real art swots will love Aesthetics On-Line (**www.aesthetics-online.org**), complete with articles on aesthetics and art philosophy, theory, and criticism.

Fashion lovers should visit *Elle* magazine's official site (**www.elle.com**), where you can have a look at the famous magazine's worldwide presence. Or, if you fancy buying some fashion, then you should try **www.fashionmall.com**, a US-based fashion shop with some of the top American high street names. Probably one of the most famous websites is boo.com. This was one of the most famous dotcoms to crash, but it has since been revitalized at **www.boo.com/boo**, and Miss Boo is still your host around the shop.

Professional and amateur photographers alike can visit any one of Nikon's worldwide sites from its portal at **www.nikon.com**. Once you have all the information to purchase your camera, learn to take better pictures with advice from the professionals at **www.betterphoto.com**.

BOOKS

Some of the most successful businesses on the Internet have started off selling books – the market for the bestsellers is fiercely competitive, and shopping around can bring discounts of up to 50 per cent. There are dozens of sites selling books, and it would take a book to name them all, but we do list some of the best. The turn of the millennium has seen the first tentative steps towards e-books (notably by major author Stephen King), by which you download the author's work from the web. There is also plenty of academic information available, from critical works to specialist dictionaries. Rhyming dictionaries may help writers out of a block, while book reviews could tempt you to try using the online shops. Online literature magazines are to be found, as is plenty to encourage younger readers.

Author sites

Agatha Christie
www.agathachristie.com
The official site of one of the 20th century's most popular writers. It contains lists of her books, plays, and films based on her work. A must bookmark site for the mystery book lover. For avid sleuths, we recommend **www.mysterynet.com** where there are dark doings aplenty for you to solve online. There may be a prize in it for you, too.

British greats
www.incompetech.com
For those looking for a bluffer's guide to the greats of English literature, you couldn't get a much better start than here. Included are short, pithy biographies of 26 major authors, from William "The Over-analysed" Shakespeare to Charlotte

"Jane Eyre" Brontë. Writers are categorized by colour-coded symbols denoting poets, novelists, playwrights, essayists, and journalists. The biographies have obscure and interesting facts to impress your more literary friends.

Danielle Steel
www.randomhouse.com/features/steel
The queen of romantic fiction is an author who takes an active interest in her website. She writes regular letters to her fans, with some quite astounding honesty. There is also a personal scrapbook on the site, the opportunity for visitors to read excerpts from her books, the obligatory, exhaustive bibliography, and a trivia contest, too.

Harry Potter
www.bloomsburymagazine.com/harrypotter
The biggest worldwide literary phenomenon of recent years has hundreds of fan sites, but the official one is definitely worth a visit for wannabe Hogwarts students. Playfully interactive (you can enter the site as a muggle and a wizard), there is also an interview with his creator JK Rowling, reviews, and gossip. For those of you who know how, why not scare your friends and send them a howler ...

Roald Dahl
www.roalddahlfans.com
The most exhaustive site on the topselling children's author to be found on the web, this has resources for students, teachers, and fans. It is filled with meticulous biographical information, plot info on all his stories, and movies based on his work. Sadly, excerpts from the man's work are limited, but this site still makes for an excellent read.

The Shakespeare Birthplace Trust
www.shakespeare.org.uk
This site, based around the great bard's historic birthplace in Stratford, is full of biographical detail from Shakespeare's life. Mini online tours are available of the houses in which the playwright lived, together with details for visitors who wish to see them in actuality. There are several educational resources.

Stephen King
www.stephenking.com
Few famous writers are brave enough to venture onto the web in person. Not so bestselling author Stephen King. This stylish official site deals with the facts behind the fiction – King answers rumours and criticism, and provides insights into his motivation and influences. Enjoyable, well-written articles will delight

aficionados and may even whet the appetites of newcomers to the man's work. You can read about his work – past, present, and future – and there is even an opportunity for you to post any comments you have on the web.

Underground authors of America
www.instantclassics.com
Instant Classics reads pretty much like a treatise on the strange. Art, comics, poetry, fiction, non-fiction, and the general outpourings of American underground culture are jumbled to amusing effect. Links take you to authors' own websites. Note: the site contains some adult-oriented material.

What a tangled web they weave ...
www.twbooks.co.uk
An excellent site for lovers of all crime, mystery, and fantastic fiction. Inside the obligatorily creepy design is a huge book section, profiles of over 300 authors, reviews of the latest titles, and essays on mystery fiction.

The world of underground writing
www.levity.com/corduroy
This exquisitely named site, Bohemian Ink, is devoted to "underground writing". A broad range of cult figures is covered with brief biographies, and snippets of the authors' work are included. Every entry comes complete with a raft of links for those keen to shed a little more light on these literary obscurities.

Browsers

Browsing by genre
www.bookbrowser.com
Stuck for what to read next? BookBrowser (now under the wing of Barnes & Noble) makes the task easier by grouping books by genre, identifying the next title in a series you've read or suggesting a similar or related author. Selections are largely middlebrow US titles, but extensive. You can find out more about the authors you like and fill those gaps in your bookcase.

The Online Books Page
www.digital.library.upenn.edu/books
Contains links to over 17,000 (mostly academic) titles in all fields, all available as e-texts, searchable by author, subject, or title. Foreign titles from countries as far afield as Spain, the Czech Republic, and Denmark are covered, and the site

Find out what's new in cult fiction at www.levity.com/corduroy

boasts special features on subjects of interest from women's writing to censorship. This site is hosted by the University of Pennsylvania and is updated almost daily.

For book lovers

The Conservation Centre
www.ccaha.org
Specializing in the treatment of art and historic artefacts on paper, the Conservation Centre for Art and Historic Artefacts offers a wealth of advice through online tutorials – from treatments for mould invasion of your favourite books to salvaging precious photographs from water damage. The tutorials are for sale, but you can browse the highlights for handy hints.

Directory of antiquarian bookshops and dealers
www.biblion.co.uk
Biblion is trumpeted as a "bookshop of bookshops": in practice, it's a directory of specialist second-hand and antiquarian book dealers worldwide. This professional-looking site enables you to join as a dealer and search the stock lists of a wide range of participating dealers. It also offers secure online purchasing, so you can get your hands on that hard-to-get title without even leaving home!

Liven up your day with a piece of poetry from www.poems.com

The Gutenberg Bible
http://prodigi.bl.uk/gutenbg/
This site outlines the exhibition of a reproduction of the famous bible printed by Johannes Gutenberg in 1455. Gutenberg is credited with being the father of modern printing, and this informative site provides in-depth biographical information, together with sample pages from the book to download and links to other book resources on the web.

History of Reading Codes for the Blind
www.nyise.org/blind
The New York Institute for Special Education here provides you with a fascinating insight into books and reading systems that are used by blind readers, from Louis Braille onwards. Hypertext links take you on to illustrated resources on the various systems that are in use around the world. The site is also available to view in large print form.

Your daily poetry break
www.poems.com
Need a piece of poetry to liven up your day? This is the perfect site with a great anthology of modern poetry. You can check out the featured poet and journals, or subscribe to the free e-mail newsletter. If your tastes verge on the classical, then try **www.netpoets.com**.

For writers

Advice for writers
www.writersbbs.com
In this cozy place you'll meet fellow writers and find many resources of interest to authors, poets, and journalists. Meet other writers for writing workshops, conferences, or just to talk in more than 50 Writers' Discussion and Critique Forums covering both fiction and non-fiction, with topics ranging from poetry to politics, and almost everything in between. (Check out their chat rooms, too.)

Hints and tips for writers
www.fictionwriters.com
FWC provides help with novel writing, as well as information on finding agents and editors and getting published. If you join up you'll be able to have your hard work critqued, get all the hot news and storm warnings (reports of less than reputable or downright fake publishers), tips and Email courses. It can be tough getting a deal. Don't get ripped off along the way.

Poetry resource
www.poetrykit.org
UK-based site The Poetry Kit is an archive of features, interviews, listings, and links of use to aspiring poets and published writers alike. It also lists the various poetry readings and events going on in countries around the world. Okay, so the features are thin on the ground, and it is definitely not the most pretty of sites, but the extensive collection of links makes it the perfect springboard to poetry resources on the web.

Publish your own book
www.iuniverse.com
Get past the slightly self-important and verbose intro and you have a site that lets you publish your own book. The site offers potential publishers information on rights management and website hosting. Its services even include the e-book cover design.

Writing for the Internet
www.ebookweb.org
Under the slogan "Home of the eBook community", optimistic the Electronic Book Web is dedicated towards the success of the general-purpose Open eBook file standard. Not only does it include in-depth articles for readers of e-books, but it

is also aimed at those people writing them. Articles on writing and designing e-books as well as business information and general e-book news will put you in the picture. A lively read for all those interested in new technology and the future of the printed word.

News and reviews

Arts and Letters Daily
www.aldaily.com
With links to high-brow debates on literature, philosophy, and high culture, Arts and Letters Daily has an excellent news resource with links to all the major world broadsheets, magazines, and journals.

BookEnds
www.bookends.co.uk
UK magazine *BookEnds* is a great place to catch up with popular titles. It's also packed with interesting (and often satirical) spin-off articles on topics relating to featured books, so it's also a leisurely means of keeping track of current affairs. A search engine helps you to locate items of interest that you can then buy online. The site offers exclusive fiction from well-known authors, as well as interviews with rising and known stars, reviews, excerpts, and competitions.

The BookSeller
www.thebookseller.com
Book enthusiasts and publishing types alike will want to check out the United Kingdom's leading book trade journal. As well as the dry industry-related news, you'll find author profiles and special features, as well as a publishing jobs list and links to virtually every major publisher website. Handy services such as the twice-yearly "Buyer's Guide" are available to subscribers. An archive allows you to search articles from the magazine dating back to 1995.

Books unlimited
books.guardian.co.uk
The online book arm of the award-winning *Guardian* newspaper website follows its mother site's lead and so is clean and easy to read. The usual extensive reviews and bestseller lists are here, along with an author database and the chance to read the first chapters of the more literary books on the market. If you don't fancy reading a whole novel, why not glance over the "Digested Read" – the latest releases condensed into 400 words.

BookWire
www.bookwire.com
This spin-off from the publishing industry is a great place to keep up to date with the latest releases. BookWire provides US bestseller listings, as well as news and reviews. Special features provide an informative take on book genres and issues, while famous authors talk you through their picks from the world of literature.

New York Times reviews
www.nytimes.com/pages/books
A regular online publication from *The New York Times* stable, incorporating new reviews every day, split into easy-to-navigate categories, plus access to the entire catalogue of reviews published since it went online in 1996.

Journalists' dream
www.allyoucanread.com
A vast searchable database of more than 23,000 magazines and newspapers from 200 countries makes this site an excellent resource for budding journalists. All You Can Read is free to join, so whether you are looking for something from *Time Magazine* or a feature from a Mongolian weekly this is where you come.

Publishers Weekly
www.publishersweekly.com
All the latest news reports for publishers and booksellers from the (mainly) US book world are here. Read interviews past and present, and find out when your favourite author will be making an appearance in your town.

Book List
www.ala.org/booklist
Bored with the limited selection of reviews available in daily newspapers and mass-market magazines? Here is your source for more current, more concise information on a wider range of new books rom the American Library Association. Over 8000 titles reviewed and added every year.

Online shops

Amazon
www.amazon.com
Probably the most famous site on the web, with mirror sites all over the world (the UK site is found at **www.amazon.co.uk**), it has now expanded into more areas – music, auctions, DVDs, computer games, and toys to name but a few. You can read

reviews written by other customers, locate every book in print in the United States or United Kingdom, and have your selected books delivered within a few days. The postage charges unfortunately remove the sweet taste of discounted prices, but at least you can shop from your chair – and its customer service is second to none.

Antiquarian bookshop
www.shapero.com
Bernard J Shapero is an online antiquarian bookshop specializing in maps, travel literature, and illustrated and colour plate books. Its services include the ability to order over the Internet, plus regular mailing lists of catalogues and acquisitions via e-mail. Subscribers can submit a detailed account of their interests to pinpoint titles that should interest them quickly.

Book clubs
www.booksdirect.co.uk
If you feel that your interests would be best served by a specialist book club, then try out www.booksdirect.co.uk. For example, if you are interested in food, then why not join the Taste Book Club? Or if you are more of a Pratchett fan, then join the Fantasy and Science Fiction Club. Whatever your taste, this site has links to more than 20 book clubs, with unbeatable joining offers to entice you.

Borders
www.borders.com
Borders Online, Inc. and amazon.com have teamed up. You can still buy books, CDs, DVDs, and videos through the Borders teamed with amazon.com site. You'll also find plenty of exclusive content, including information about Borders store locations and events, as well as amazon.com's award-winning online store, reliable shipping and delivery, and renowned customer service.

Waterstone's
www.waterstones.co.uk
Another bookstore to cozy up with the mighty Amazon. Best buys here are the front-page bestsellers, with many tempting discounts. Shopping here, like all Amazon sites, is a simple matter of filling a virtual basket with books and heading for the "checkout".

WH Smith
www.whsmith.co.uk
Not just a newsagent and bookshop, WH Smith has really embraced the Internet and turned its site into a place where you can not only spend your money on books, videos, CDs, and stationery, but also search the Internet, look things up in

Online booksellers dominate the web – and www.borders.com is better than most

an online encyclopedia, and even sign up for the company's own brand of free Internet access.

Online texts to download

Anthologies of English verse
www.bartleby.com/verse
Project Bartleby is the University of Columbia's e-text archive. Here, at BartlebyVerse, you'll find six of the most authoritative anthologies of English verse, including the *Oxford Book of English Verse*, in electronic format. A perfect introduction to poetry.

A world of literature
www.gutenberg.net
This is the last word in electronic books. The US Project Gutenberg team has been converting texts to electronic formats since 1971, so the library's catalogue is now absolutely vast. Entire, copyright-free book titles are presented – completely free of charge – as text files that can be downloaded and then printed out for your perusal. The titles offered cover fiction and non-fiction alike, and they are drawn from all over the world.

Penguin has many authors under its wing and plenty of good web stuff. Visit www.penguin.co.uk

Publishers' sites

Dorling Kindersley online
www.dk.com
The company may have been taken over by Penguin, but the still-adventurous publisher, which was one of the first to venture into computer-based publishing, continues to be a leading web-publishing presence. The site provides much more than online shopping, with plenty of content provided free – one unique feature is the ability to look inside any book before buying.

HarperCollins
www.fireandwater.com
Browse the books published by HarperCollins in dozens of subject areas, read the interviews with their authors, and enter the competitions. The US-based site can be found at **www.harpercollins.com**.

Penguin and Puffin
www.penguin.co.uk
An impressive site, it is incredibly high on content, with many well-designed mini-sites for its major authors, such as Alex Garland and Nick Hornby. It also includes the Puffin Books (**www.puffin.co.uk**) site, which is a visual treat for kids and provides many fun activities, too.

Reader's Digest
www.readersdigest.co.uk
Find all sorts of interesting articles and mildly amusing jokes, and discover the magically abridged world of condensed books that you can buy online. There are also top tips for travel and health, and a prize draw on this publisher's site. You can access other Reader's Digest sites from around the world, too.

Writers' prizes and libraries

The Booker Prize
www.bookerprize.co.uk
A striking, Flash-heavy site, this is the authorized site of the United Kingdom's most prestigious literary award. It features lists of previous shortlists and winners, together with details of winners over the past 30 years. Reading the quotes from Booker winners and other authors about the award will keep you entertained, and you can also check on last year's bookies' odds.

The British Library
www.bl.uk
Now relocated to London's Euston Road, the British Library has made a determined push towards digital media. And the venerable institution takes its online service very seriously: its book-resource database, BLAISE, contains over 150 million entries – and the list is growing all the time. Its new service "Inside" will deliver journals and texts to its users via PDF and other formats – an invaluable tool to researchers. You'll also find details of the library's collections and special exhibits, as well as information about visiting the library.

Library of Congress
www.loc.gov
This is the fascinating homepage of the US Library of Congress. The site offers beautifully illustrated guides to special exhibits at the library, plus web-based research materials. Online exhibits on ancient written cultures, from the Dead Sea Scrolls to the Vatican Library, are particularly worth a look.

The New York Public Library
www.nypl.org
Here you can find opening details of all the different branches and details of all the collections. Through the site's online services, US residents can even place reserves on items of their choice found in the library's catalogue, as well as review

the status of books checked out. The Teenlink takes you to other Internet sites for homework help, sports information, and advice on college and careers.

The Pulitzer Prizes
www.pulitzer.org
This is the official site of the world-famous American prizes for journalism, and it features articles on winners, as well as a comprehensive archive containing original works – words, pictures, and sound – from previous winners back to 1917. An interesting "History" section details the life of founder Joseph Pulitzer and the development of the prizes.

— see also...

With so many book websites on the Internet, one of the most difficult tasks is simply to decide which ones are actually worth a look: **www.whitbreadbookawards.co.uk** gives you the low-down on which books impressed the Whitbread judges. High-brow literary review *The Times Literary Supplement* also has its presence on the web at **www.the-tls.co.uk**.

If you get hooked on an author, what then? **www.catharton.com/authors** provides links to sites on many major writers, while Charles Dickens has his own site at **www.geocities.com/Athens/Styx/8490**, as does Sir Arthur Conan Doyle at **www.sherlock-holmes.co.uk**. For the lovers of sci-fi writer Terry Pratchett, there are numerous sites, including the *Discworld Monthly* site (**www.ufbs.co.uk/dwm**). The Brontë Parsonage Museum has a website at **www.bronte.org.uk**, where you can read about the three sisters and the inspiration behind classics such as *Wuthering Heights*. If poets are your thing, this German-based site on British poet Ted Hughes is one of the best (**www.uni-leipzig.de/~angl/hughes/hureview.htm**). Lovers of rhymes, meanwhile, should venture to the RhymeZone rhyming dictionary and thesaurus (**rhyme.lycos.com**) to release their inner poet. They might soon join the 2.4 million poets reputed to be contained at **www.poetry.com**, although, if a browser, just stick to the 100 greatest poems. if you have a novel in you yourself, **www.writersservice.co.uk** may well help you to get it out and onto the shelves.

But what of lesser known figures? Read their words in webzines such as **www.zetnet.co.uk/oigs/gazet**. Or perhaps you should get involved yourself? Don't be shy – submit your own work to **www.oneofus.co.uk**, to Maybe Later ... (**www.illyria.com/webzine.html**), or to the more high-minded **trace.ntu.ac.uk**. And from the obscure to the unintelligible, dedicated lovers of the Beat Generation should make a beeline for **www.charm.net/~brooklyn/LitKicks.html**.

Books 49

The online bookshops are phenomenal, and the competition means that there are a lot of them out there... Here are just some of them, all with their own merits: **www.bol.com**, **www.barnesandnoble.com**, **www.bookpeople.com**, and **www.streetsonline.co.uk**. More academic books can be found at **www.blackwells.com**. Most of these will draw a blank if a book's out of print, but that's not a problem for The BookFinder General. You can visit him at **www.nwnet.co.uk/BFG**.

Soon, though, books won't just go out of print. According to some people, there will be no print at all – which is where sites such as **www.openebook.org** and **eserver.org** all come in, spreading the gospel of non-print. And owners of palmtop computers can even download software which reads e-texts from **www.mobipocket.com**.

Print may not yet be history, but there's certainly some history behind it. For an insight into the rich history of the printed words, see Printing: Renaissance and Reformation at **www.sc.edu/library/spcoll/sccoll/renprint/renprint.html**. And if that whets your appetite to discover more of the forgotten art of bookbinding, seek good advice from **www.cs.uiowa.edu/~jones/book**. Of course, some books don't die without a fight – **www.ala.org/bbooks** commemorates titles and authors past and present that have fallen victim to the censor. The rogue's gallery includes *Huckleberry Finn*, *Harry Potter* and Roald Dahl's *The Witches* would you believe?

It doesn't have to end on the last page. If you've just found something a bit special you can spread the word at the rather unique **www.bookcrossing.com**. You can commit random acts of literacy by registering your favorite read and a glowing report then leaving it somewhere out there for browsers to discover and who knows, maybe get back to you with enthusiasms of their own.

Finally, fans of the late, great Spike Milligan can view some of his lesser known serious poems at **www.geocities.com/broadway/booth/2009/milligan.html**.

COMPUTERS

A very large chunk of the world wide web is devoted to computers because the Internet was originally the domain of the nerd and, also, because it is the ideal way to share computer-oriented knowledge and files. You will find technical help, free programs and utilities to make your computer work better, and low-cost add-ons from the many online shops. You don't have to be a genius to understand much of the available data, though, because a large part of the information is aimed at less experienced users. But if you want to get techie, you can find things that will really challenge your brain and make you spend far too much time away from your family ...

Computer reference sites

All your questions answered
www.experts-exchange.com
Don't suffer the frustrations of a broken computer, erratic printer, or a wonky word processor. Quiz the experts available at this site, or browse through the answers to other people's queries. The site works on a points system. The longer you are a (free) member, the more points you have and the more difficult and frequent your questions are allowed to be. Earn extra points by answering other people's questions. The most popular topics are listed on the front page.

Computer graphics and multimedia
www.multimedian.com
Why spend hours wading through reams of information and technical specifications when Multimedian promises to cut to the chase? Offering clearly presented and objective information on web/graphic design, video production, and music software, this will put you on the right track whether it's all new to you or you're a hardened techie. The best software is reviewed and rated, and web news and articles provide

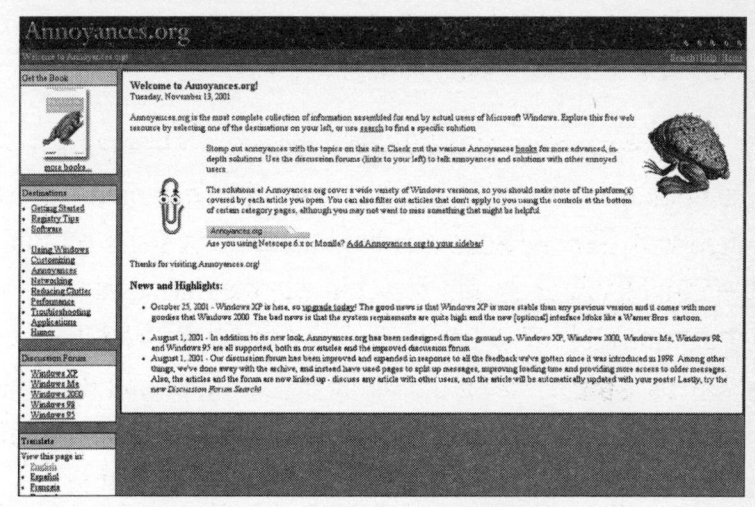

Get relief from the frustrations of your computer at www.annoyances.org

links to all-important multimedia concerns. Originally started life as pcartist.com, pcvideomaker.com, and pc-musician.com – now same content, different name.

The Computer History Museum
www.computerhistory.org
Follow the thrilling (sometimes) history of computers, robots, and the Internet, with the well-constructed and colourful timelines within this site. The museum itself is based in California, but here you can view its online archives and exhibits. Do beware of the online photo collection, however – it frequently crashes.

Computer support site
www.annoyances.org
You will find so much information about optimizing and fixing your Windows software here that you may not bother with any other Internet offerings – and that includes Microsoft's technical support section. The Annoyances site includes help on Windows 95, 98, 2000 and Windows XP. Book versions of the help given are available, with titles covering Office 97 and other Microsoft programs.

Computing dictionary
www.webopedia.com
The *Webopedia* is an online dictionary of computing and Internet terms, and very useful it is, too, if you want to understand any of the technical websites that abound. You can educate yourself by traversing the categories and finding the meaning to such terms as "BLOB", "nibble", and "FAQ".

Computer geeks will be kept goggle happy at www.geek.com

For all techies, geeks, and nerds
www.geek.com
As if the Internet didn't have enough nerdy websites, Geek.com is dedicated to those who spend a large amount of time online, can program a VCR without the manual, and would only consider using PCs they'd built themselves. A technical glossary will help you through the tough times, and there are hints on the technical necessities to consider when buying a laptop or PC. Tips, tricks, and technology news all add up to a winning result for nerds everywhere.

Internet etiquette (netiquette)
www.albion.com/netiquette
The Internet is a wonderful resource allowing everyone equal access to each other's opinions. However, sadly not everyone is equally as nice, and touchy individuals can become offensive if you display what they consider to be bad Internet manners. Avoid nasty e-mails by reading the Netiquette Home Page and following its advice.

Online business initiative
www.ukonlineforbusiness.gov.uk
Small businesses can receive advice on how to use technology effectively to compete in their particular market. Find your nearest UK Online for Business

centre and organize an appointment, browse through the free booklets (in Adobe Acrobat format), and read case studies of competitors who have already taken the plunge into the 21st century. For the serious, there is an outline of the UK Government's Policy for the Information Age, too.

Online dictionary of computing
www.foldoc.org
This site enables you to search for the meanings of the immense number of often baffling computing terms there are out there. Links to other sites are included in the relevant places, making this an ideal resource for learning about computing. If you find yourself returning frequently, which, let's face it, is quite likely as it is so useful, consider downloading the text version of the site to your PC to save your phone bill.

Using the web anonymously
www.anonymizer.com
I'm sure that you have nothing to hide, but there is a principle behind using the Internet anonymously, and this site goes some way towards letting you visit websites without giving away too much about yourself. All you need to do is visit the Anonymizer and enter another website's address on its page. You'll then be completely secret and safe thereon in when you are exploring the wonders of the Internet.

Hardware

Getting the best out of your PC
www.hardwarecentral.com
If you want to gain every last drop of performance out of your PC, then follow the advice on this site to fully optimize your system. The extensive forums should answer any questions about your desktop PC that you might have. There is extensive advice on overclocking, a technique that can be used to turbocharge your PC's processor (and reasons why this may be dangerous).

Guide to hardware
www.tomshardware.com
If you'd like to become more familiar with the contents of your PC, then read the German doctor Tom Pabst's findings. He regularly puts the latest hardware through performance tests and offers his comments in no uncertain terms. With his help, you'll become a PC guru in no time.

Literature/articles

Computer Buyer Magazine
www.computerbuyer.co.uk
The online presence of the UK magazine is packed with reviews of the latest PCs, hardware, and software, and is an indispensable site for anyone wanting to buy a PC or upgrade an existing model. The Top 50 award (based on opinion) ensures that the equipment listings are always up to date. The daily news service and an active chat forum make this an essential visit.

Finding technical books
www.oreilly.com
For details of some of the most useful and technical computer books, try the site of the book publisher O'Reilly & Associates. If you want to find a book about simply using the Internet or writing a letter using a word processor, though, look elsewhere. Only hardcore nerds wanting to learn about HTML, Perl, and Linux need apply – and if you are feeling extra lucky, then why not ask Tim O'Reilly a question, although you should make sure it is complex enough.

Maximum PC Network
www.maximumpc.com
Home of the US *Maximum PC* magazine, this mini-network of technical sites aims to educate wannabe nerds in the ways of building fast PCs, creating home networks, and running performance benchmark tests.

News for nerds
www.slashdot.org
This is a great place to visit if you want the latest computer-based news. The scope of this site isn't limited to computers, though. World issues, comics, music, and games are all covered. Anyone is allowed to submit articles, so if you have an opinion or specialist knowledge of Linux, then let them know.

News on technology
www.theregister.co.uk
The Register is an online technology newspaper that is full of tasty gossip, supposition, and speculation. It's frequently right, too. This site is a must for the budding techie entrepreneur. Visit *The Register* regularly if you want to feel yourself at the heart of the so-called "IT industry", although to get the real experience you should actually spend a few hours in the pub first …

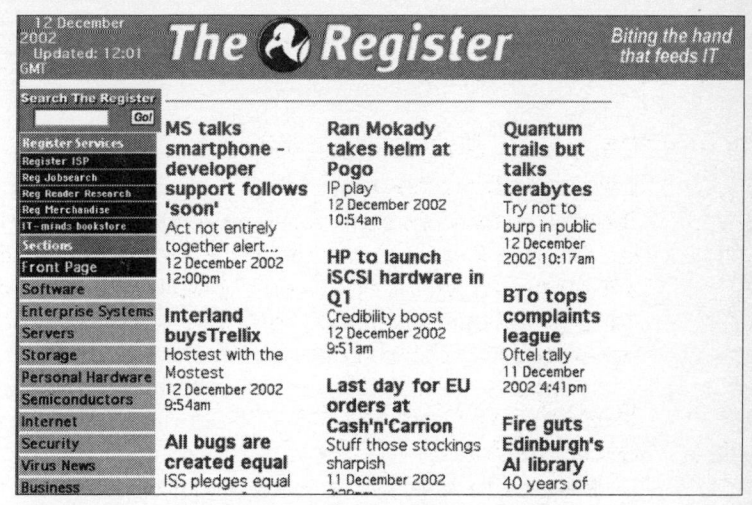

www.theregister.co.uk is a site with no thrills, but mountains of information

Ziff Davis: reviews and advice
www.zdnet.com
Hardware and software reviews, hints, tips, and help – it's all published on ZDNet, the enormous website run by computer publishing monster Ziff Davis. The websites of all Ziff's computer magazines are available at a click, although much of their content has already been absorbed into the main site.

Major manufacturers

Advanced Micro Devices
www.amd.com
Intel's main rival in the PC processor market publishes details here of its new products and benchmark results of its performance, and offers software to make certain programs run faster if you have an AMD chip in your machine.

Apple Computer
www.apple.com
Learn all about Apple's home computers, including the resurgent iMac and the PowerBook, and the software you can run on them, and download updates to the Mac operating systems. You can also read the latest news about technical developments, find out where you can buy a computer, and learn how to fix problems as they occur.

Dell Computer
www.dell.co.uk
Buy a PC from one of the most successful manufacturers in the world today direct from its site. You can choose a base model, then customize it to suit your needs, adding more memory, bigger hard disks, or a better monitor, and the price changes are reflected. If you want to talk through your choices with a salesperson, just enter your phone number during office hours and they will call you back.

IBM
www.ibm.com
The original PC manufacturer is still going strong, and its website contains details of the current ranges of computers. You can customize their configurations, if you know what you are doing, then buy the products online. Even if you're not sure how much RAM you'll need, or how large your monitor should be, the online help aims to guide you through the purchasing process.

Intel
www.intel.com
Check out Intel's latest PC processors, home networking hardware, and digital cameras. There are press releases published online, as well as very detailed technical information about the company's different microchip products. A buyer's guide aims to help you choose the specific processor you should have in your PC. Intel also has an impressive line in streaming media.

Microsoft
www.microsoft.com
Find out about the latest software products from arguably the world's most successful software publisher (the UK site is at **www.microsoft.com/uk**). The technical support section is second to none. If you have a problem with the software on your PC (and let's face it, most of it will be Microsoft software), check here first, before calling your computer's manufacturer and spending hours on a phone line talking to teenage techies. US residents can buy Microsoft products from this website.

Palm
www.palm.com
Lovers of handheld gadgets, such as the executive's current fave, the Palm Pilot, should browse this site. Get help with which type of Palm organizer you might need and the various, often expensive, peripherals that go with them. The site has mirror sites all over the world, so it is easier to see which products are available in your particular market.

Psion
www.psion.com
This website is home to the little pocket computers, beloved of nerds and well-paid businesspeople the world over. A new online store means that you can now buy tasty items such as the Series 5mx and Revo here if you're feeling the urge to splash out.

Search sites

AltaVista
www.altavista.com
One of the best search engines on the Internet, AltaVista offers varying levels of searching, which differ from its rivals – you can search by region or by type of media (image, video, sounds). The most basic screen will get you started, though you will need to learn how to narrow your search (see pages 14-16). If you aren't sure what you're looking for, browse the categories.

Ask Jeeves
www.ask.co.uk
This web search engine doesn't ask its users to scramble around with complicated forms and database languages. Instead, you pose questions in plain English and the resulting lists of sites are supplied in the form of answers, rather than meaningless web addresses and page titles.

Best use of search engines
searchenginewatch.com
After reading the handy notes in the introduction to this guide, learn how to use Internet search engines to their maximum efficiency, whether you are looking for sites you need or are trying to get your own ones noticed. There are lists of specialist engines that concentrate on certain types of page or file, such as MP3 music files, and reviews that evaluate just how good they are.

Dogpile
www.dogpile.com
Probably the best of the metasearch engines, the very simple interface of this site in fact hides a complex search tool. Like most search engines, it is best for making specific searches, otherwise you might end up barking up the wrong tree. Dogpile has a huge directory, and you can localize in various ways, by type of media, or even to find jobs.

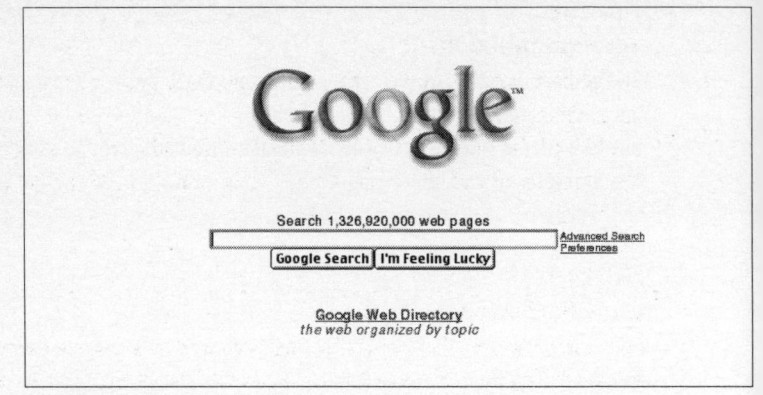

Appearances are deceptive – simply the best search engine on the net is www.google.com

Excite
www.excite.com
Search the entire Internet, or localized areas of it, using this well-designed search engine. You can restrict searches to sites in the United Kingdom, Europe, or plain news sites. There are also categories of sites to browse through, if you're not quite sure what you're looking for. News headlines and stock quotes are included to encourage you to return frequently. You can even get WAP content, as well as text message to mobile phones. You do need to register first.

Freeserve
www.freeserve.co.uk
Freeserve, the Internet service provider that changed the face of Internet access in the United Kingdom, has a generally helpful website that offers a web searching facility, news headlines, auctions, broadband info, and a shortcut to the Scoot business search engine. If you want to create professional web pages, you'll find an Internet domain registration service, and there are also plenty of advertisements to entice you.

Ghost Sites
www.disobey.com/ghostsites
Discover the fascinating world of the dead website. Ghost Sites searches for other sites that haven't seen an update in a long time, possibly because of a failed business or perhaps a loss of interest from the original author. A good piece of technological history. A sobering lesson on the ephemerality of the web. For any real ghoul hunters that stumble onto this site by mistake, there are helpful links to real supernatural sites to put them back on the right track. Well worth a look for web designers or anyone with a passing interest.

Google
www.google.com
Giving the appearance of just about the simplest web page you can imagine, this site's minimal design belies the powerful search engine that lies at its core. Enter a search phrase and you have two options – "Google Search" will give you the lists of results, or try "I'm Feeling Lucky", which will take you straight to the first on the list.

HotBot
www.hotbot.com
Both a web directory and a search engine, Hotbot offers a few interesting features such as the ability to create a list, then search that same list for other keywords. This could help the less experienced Internet explorers to refine their web searches, although it has to be said that sites such as AltaVista are generally still more powerful in the long run. This site also has the almost obligatory free web access. Worth checking out.

InfoSpace
www.infospace.com
This web directory has an interesting feature in the shape of special software that you download and customize to provide an Internet experience designed around your specific interests and, possibly, business needs wherever you are in the world. The Yellow Pages business finding service works in the United States, Canada, and the United Kingdom, thanks to regionalized versions of the site.

Lycos
www.lycos.co.uk
This Internet search engine distinguishes itself by providing "webguides". These are small groups of related sites, which are sometimes accompanied by articles. The overall theme could be privacy on the Internet, tax advice, or surviving as a student. Inexperienced web users, particularly those in the United Kingdom in some instances, will find this a handy way to start exploring the Internet. It also happens to be home to one of the most extensive mp3 search engines available at the moment (**www.music.lycos.com**).

SeniorSearch UK
www.seniorsearch.com
This is a comprehensive directory of links of interest to older web users. SeniorSearch is far from being as exhaustive as regular services such as Yahoo! or AltaVista, and the site lacks a keyword search – but resources are more likely to suit the specific needs of senior citizens.

WebRing
www.webring.org
Communities and organizations on the Internet are no less "real" than their non-virtual counterparts. Directories such as WebRing enable you to locate people on the web with whom you share common interests. The site provides categorized links to web rings – groups of sites linked by a common theme – and the sites are navigable from one to the next. If you have your own website, this is an invaluable way of increasing traffic to it.

Yahoo!
www.yahoo.com
This top searchable web directory beats most others hands down, with its comprehensive coverage of almost every area of the web. There are also other features, including news headlines, TV listings, and sections dedicated to health, movies, and local events – they have their information "fed" from a number of reliable external sources (Reuters among them) to ensure its high quality. Available in many regionalized flavours, people from China to Sweden will be able to feel at home on the Internet (the UK version is found at **uk.yahoo.com**). Its other features are too numerous to mention – go see for yourself. Needless to say, this should be one of your first stops on the web – not for nothing is it the world's most popular site.

Software and downloads

All about drivers
www.driverguide.com
If something within your PC used to work and it has now started failing, then you'll probably need a device driver (software that talks to printers, scanners, etc for the uninitiated). DriverGuide lets members download drivers, as well as access chat forums aimed at helping locate software for discontinued hardware. You can help others, too, by sending in the drivers for your own gadgets via e-mail.

Computer downloads for free
www.freedownloadscenter.com
With more than 20,000 software titles available for free download, you can't go wrong. From business programs and e-mail tools to games and multimedia and graphics packages, it's all here waiting just a click of the mouse away. A simply laid-out site with useful reviews of freeware and shareware, it may mean you never want to buy software again.

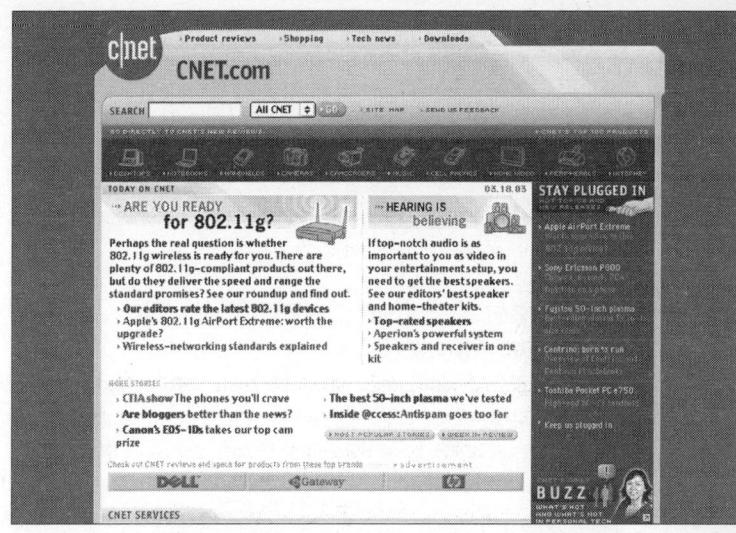

Find out about the latest software and download what you need at www.cnet.com

Computer programming
www.geocities.com/progsharehouse
This resource for computer programmers contains tutorials, articles, FAQs, and codes that can be used in your own software. Just about every programming language under the sun is included, as well as some unearthly ones, too! Articles from seasoned, and sometimes embittered, programmers can be eye-opening.

Drivers, hardware, news, and reviews
www.windrivers.com
More than just a place to download hardware drivers for your PC's bits and pieces, Windrivers collates help and news bulletins from other websites and even publishes some reviews. The most ingenious part of this site is that you can search for any piece of hardware you desire, even if you only know its FCCID code (printed on almost every piece of electronics in the world). It even has a FTSE-type table which lists the latest prices for pieces of hardware and shows any fluctuation in price.

Free software
www.download.com
Download all the free software your computer and your spare time can handle from this well-respected and easy-to-use site (it is part of **www.cnet.com**). It caters for most common types of computer, including Windows PCs and Mac computers – you can search through a quarter of a million shareware files.

More free software
www.cnet.com
No matter what you want to use your PC for, someone will have written a free or nearly free program to help you. CNET is a massive, easy-to-use archive containing software, neatly organized into different categories, such as e-mail updates, Windows shareware, and bugs and fixes. So if you want to mount a web cam in your garden pond or create your own home network, then this is the place to try first.

Privacy/encryption software – PGP
www.pgpi.org
Read about and download some of the most powerful and controversial encryption software available. Its strength rivals anything available to the military and, as a result, it has been the centre of legal action in the United States. If you have something to hide, or wish to exercise your rights to privacy, start using PGP (Pretty Good Privacy) – it's a lot easier to use now than it used to be.

Stores

Buy discounted goods
www.buy.com
Computer hardware and software can be bought here at discounted prices – digital imagery, networking, and other peripherals are all catered for. You can also track your orders. Look out for the excellent buy.com vouchers that are often offered at other sites (spend £20, get £10 off is just one good example).

Dabs
www.dabs.com
Dabs.com is the place to buy the bits and pieces that you'll need to upgrade your PC. There is more than just memory and hard disks in the online catalogue, though. There are branded PCs from all the big names, as well as printers, monitors, and software. Web orders have free delivery to UK addresses, and you can track your goods to see if they have come into stock, been sent out, or are temporarily unavailable. Note: it will not deliver outside the European Union.

Insight
www.insight.com
Whether you live in the United States, United Kingdom, Canada, or Germany, Insight provides an excellent outlet for all things Mac- or PC-based. The prices

have traditionally been very competitive, besides which it is always easy to shop around online. Delivery is free for orders made over the web, and you can save a price quote for three days if you're not ready to make a decision straight away.

The Outpost
www.outpost.com
Outpost will sell you anything to do with PCs or Macs, networking, software, and home electronics. It also has a large selection of toys, video games, kitchen and home products, and stuff for the office. Although based in the United States, the company will ship internationally for a very low charge.

— Web page construction help —

Creating a successful web page
www.anybrowser.org
Anybrowser is another great site for website authors to add to their list of favourites. For the technical reasons explained on the site, not every computer reads web pages in the same way. Follow the advice supplied and your pages will be universally readable – well, nearly. And if you are forever frustrated by websites designed only for specific browsers that you don't have, then join the Campaign for a Non-Browser Specific www.

Creating and developing your website
www.wdvl.com
If you're interested in writing your own web pages, and want your efforts to be available to everyone on the Internet, you should read what this site has to say. The Web Developer's Virtual Library starts at the beginning and takes you right through to very advanced topics, providing something for everyone. If you are writing a small homepage or creating a killer commercial site, come here regularly. Exhaust yourself and take yourself through the Top 100 tutorials. There is a great "History of the Internet" section, too.

Monkey around with your site
www.hotwired.lycos.com/webmonkey
This arm of the Wired website is an essential bookmark for those who want to learn how to create their own pages. Some of the best designers have donated their time to put together tutorials that are easy to follow and are annotated with pictures that show you exactly what to do. The makers of the site have done their best to demystify the complexities of webpage design.

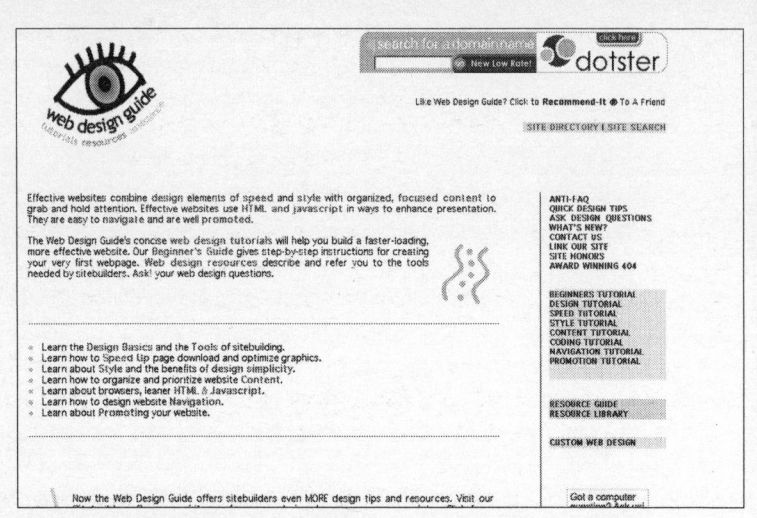

Why learn the difficult stuff when www.dreamink.com will create your pages for you?

The Web Design Guide
www.dreamink.com
The Web Design Guide offers concise tutorials to help you build your own fast-loading, eye-catching website. Web design resources point you in the direction of the tools that you will need.

Running your own website
www.webdevelopersjournal.com
The Web Developer's Journal aims to take some of the pain out of administering your newly created website and is neatly divided into different sections, for suits (businessmen), ponytails (designers), propheads (programmers), and something called a "javascript weenie". If that sounds like you, this could be right up your modem, dude.

Watch your web design
www.webpagesthatsuck.com
A novel approach to learning good web design from Vincent Flanders – use the badly designed pages of others. Find out which are the suckiest sites around at the moment, nominate your own or take advantage of the free site survey. Just make sure you don't end up back on this site with your own disasters.

Up-to-the-minute articles about the web
www.webreview.com
Once you've decided to create your own website, and realized that you'll need to know at least a bit about HTML to achieve the results you want, you absolutely

must visit WebReview. There are articles on all the subjects you don't yet realize that you'll find interesting. See what's there now and, when you want to do something clever, you'll remember where to go for help.

For computer game sites see Games, pages 119–21.

see also...

As you can imagine, there are still hundreds more computer news sites on the world wide web, so if the ones listed earlier do not suit your needs then try one of the following – the informative **www.thestandard.com**, **www.linux.com**, and Tucows (**www.tucows.com**), which also offers games and music to download.

The first Internet stores sold computer gear, and this tradition continues with Computer Warehouse (**www.computerwarehouse.co.uk**), where you'll find printer cartridges, extra disks, and other bits and pieces at competitive prices. Crucial Technology (**www.crucial.com**) will also be happy to do business with you, provided you only want to buy computer memory at ridiculously low prices. These stores will all undercut each other with certain products. You can never have enough online stores on your list. Make sure that you add SMC Direct (**www.smcdirect.com**), Software Paradise (**www.softwareparadise.co.uk**), **www.jungle.com**, and Watford Electronics (**www.savastore.com**). PC World (**www.pcworld.co.uk**) is also worth a look, if only to verify buys from other places as bargains.

For advice on what you should spend your money on in these places, make use of the educated opinions of computer magazine websites. *Computer Shopper* (**www.computershopper.co.uk**) is one of the biggest PC magazines, while computer magazine publisher VNU's site (**www.vnunet.com**) offers news, reviews, and comment – some of which is valid. PC Pro (**www.pcpro.co.uk**) is aimed at the "high end" of the market. Future Publishing (**www.futurenet.com**) is home to many popular computer and technology-led magazines, including *PC Plus*, *Mac Format*, and *Official PlayStation2 Magazine*.

In the market for a new computer? Try a range of manufacturers' sites, then check out the reviews with your favourite computer magazine's website (**www.comp-buyer.co.uk**) and purchase online. Mesh (**www.meshplc.co.uk**) and Evesham Technology (**www.evesham.com**) aren't as well known as some others, but will often offer better value for money when buying a computer for home use or for a small business. Giants Time (**www.timecomputers.com**) and **www.pcworld.com**, a subsidiary of International Data Group, are always ready to offer some interesting deals. Big players that are also worth a mention include Hewlett-Packard (**www.hpl.hp.co.uk** and **www.hp.com**), Gateway Computers (**www.gateway.com**), NEC Online UK (**www.nec-online.co.uk**), Fujitsu PC Corporation (**www.fujitsu-pc.com**), and Viglen (**www.viglen.co.uk**).

Inevitably something will go wrong with your PC at some point. You should check out Computer Incident Advisory Capability (**www.ciac.org**) to learn how to detect hoax e-mail alerts and Symantec's AntiVirus Research Center (**www.symantec.com/avcenter**) for information on real threats. When everything has been sorted out, relax by playing a few games. Find out which ones are the best at PC Zone (**www.pczone.co.uk**).

Finally, once online, you will already have an extensive list of search engines to find whatever it is that you want to locate, but there are also many search and metasearch engines that you should try out – **www.ixquick.com**, **www.profusion.com**, and **www.go.com** are just three others to try if you cannot find what you want from those listed earlier in the chapter.

EDUCATION

Students, teachers, and parents alike can find a wealth of information on the Internet. Homework can be made much easier by searching online encyclopedias (see pages 245–9) and trying online tutorials, while parents can find out how to help educate from home. There are ideas and lesson plans for the wired-in teacher and tailored news for those with an interest in the latest UK government reforms. The amount of help for those in higher education is staggering, with advice ranging from coursework to CV writing and job applications. There are puzzles for geniuses, help for those with special needs, and adult education resources. And there are even sites for the youngest of children, providing educational games.

Alternative teaching sites

Home tutoring
www.learninfreedom.org
This site advocates giving students the choice to use teachers and schools voluntarily when required. It explores the issues surrounding teaching children in their homes, rather than in a recognized classroom, and what taking on that responsibility means. There are college ratings, including details on which ones have accepted home-tutored students, and numerous articles – some including anti-school quotes from the likes of Albert Einstein and George Bernard Shaw. A booklist and resources guide will also help to steer you in the right direction.

Introduction to home schooling
www.homeschool.com
Providing a thorough look at teaching a child from home, this informative site includes the "Ten Most Important Things To Know about Homeschooling", a list of useful reference books, and online courses – including a "click learning" section

for children. A resource guide to curricula and other commercial products, as well as a handful of interviews and articles, completes this introductory site.

Steiner Waldorf Schools Fellowship UK
www.steinerwaldorf.org.uk
Find out all about this alternative method of teaching, and browse the directory of schools in the United Kingdom and the Republic of Ireland that offer it. There is also a list of kindergartens and, for American readers, an alternative site at **www.awsna.org** provides a similar service for those that are living in the United States, Mexico, and Canada. Further links list worldwide schools.

For graduates

Jobs and career fairs in the United States
www.jobweb.org
The site of the National Association of Colleges and Employers has news for both job seekers and employment professionals in the United States, publishing a calendar of careers events fairs. The news is almost entirely optimistic, but that's hardly surprising – graduates won't want to feel more insecure than they already do. In any case, there are dozens of articles to help the recently graduated find their place in the job world.

Universities and Careers Worldwide
www.hobsons.com
Dedicated to empowering students all over the world to make the right course and career choices, and aiming to bring students together with the universities and companies that want them. Choose where in the world you want to study, then a list of learning programmes and study information is available from which you can make an informed choice. A very useful place to start.

Vital information for all graduates
www.prospects.ac.uk
So utterly useful; if UK graduates only ever bother with one site after finishing their exams, this should be it. There are available jobs listings, vacancies for graduates of the coming year, job-seeking strategies, and free downloadable software to help with filling in a standard application form. "My Prospects" is a great system that automatically searches for the kind of job that you are after and sends you e-mail messages or texts your mobile phone when it finds ones that match your criteria.

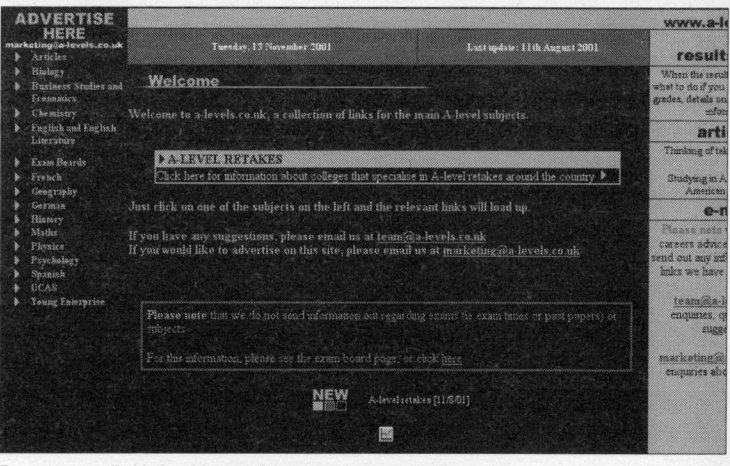

Teenagers can find help with stressful exams at www.a-levels.co.uk

For students

Advice from other young people
www.uni-survival-guide.freeserve.co.uk
If you've decided to go for higher education, but are feeling a bit apprehensive, calm yourself with this semi-humorous guide to student life. Written for students by students, this will give you some idea of what to expect in the terms to come, from day-to-day living and making friends to study tips and more.

A-Levels
www.a-levels.co.uk
Easy to navigate, this site cuts to the chase for teenagers in the final throes of their secondary school education. It lists texts that are relevant in most subjects and, of course, gives students the chance to buy the books. Contact addresses and e-mails for the various (confusing) exam boards are also listed, and advice is offered on taking a gap year.

Discount booking service for ELT students (UK)
www.gouk.com
Aimed at international students studying in the United Kingdom, this site offers information about available schools and colleges. It operates a free discount booking scheme and also features tourist information for that popular between-lectures time. There is general advice on how the Brits live and an accommodation list.

Guide to everything a student needs
www.bigwideworld.com
Aimed largely at the teenage student population (who see themselves as babes or blokes with attitude), hence the hipper-than-normal page design, this site offers guides to universities, colleges, and careers, as well as the lighter subjects in life. There are areas where you can find out about cars, where to go travelling, and what films are worth watching. The latest gadgets and gizmos are reviewed. Goodbye student loan.

Information for students of disability services
www.abilityinfo.com
The information on this site is aimed at students and professionals studying or working in this field of expertise. There is a news ticker that can push the latest headlines onto your screen, job listings, and a bookshop. Discussion forums are also provided, and there are loads of links to a whole range of other sites.

Letts Education Guides
www.letts-education.com
Letts, makers of the highly respected revision guides, has moved online and has something educational for everyone, ranging from reception to higher education. The site has a breakdown of each age group and answers all your questions. Curious about what is expected at Key Stage 3? This site will answer your questions – and will, of course, sell you its guides as well.

National Union of Students
www.nusonline.co.uk
The colourful site of the NUS is never going to be as "hip" as some of the other less institutional student sites, but it is a font of information with the latest news, advice, useful links, and, most importantly, lots of discounts and special offers.

Online student magazine
www.juiced.co.uk
Juiced is a youth electronic magazine published on the Internet by the electronic *Telegraph*, and it contains film, music, sport articles, horoscopes, and news. There are also sections on travel and, more importantly, careers. Special offers and competitions are listed for use in that rare student commodity – leisure time.

Open University
www.open.ac.uk
Discover which of the enormous number of available courses suit you best and reserve yourself a place. You can also find out which of those late night "Learning

Zone" programmes will appeal to you and order a copy of the listings if you wish to browse offline. You can find out what the Open University has to offer in your area as well.

Studying worldwide
www.studylink.com
StudyLink publishes CD-ROM directories of so-called learning opportunities in both the United Kingdom and Australia. There are directories of courses for school leavers and business/management and postgraduate programmes around the world. A special post-grad site regularly features "schools", meaning "universities".

Universities and Colleges Admissions Service
www.ucas.ac.uk
If you want to go to a UK university or college, this is the organization to apply through. This site offers advice to UK and international applicants, mature students, and even referees. There are tips on filling in your application form, and financial advice is offered with information on how to apply for help.

The Year In Industry (UK)
www.yini.org.uk
It may be slow and unnecessarily flash, but the Year in Industry site aims to help talented students into industrial placements during their gap year at university. Graduate opportunities are listed alongside information for students, parents, and teachers. Case studies aim to encourage students along this path.

For teachers and parents

Catholic Teachers Gazette
www.e-ctg.co.uk
Choose between a Flash and non-Flash offering from the publishers of the free newsletter of the same name. The latest job vacancies are available in schools from state primary, middle, and secondary levels, as well as independent schools. Administration vacancies are also listed, and details of the saint for the week are listed here, too.

Department for Education and Skills
www.dfes.gov.uk
Receive the news hot off the government's press, complete with spin. More importantly, there is a quite comprehensive online database of DfES circulars and

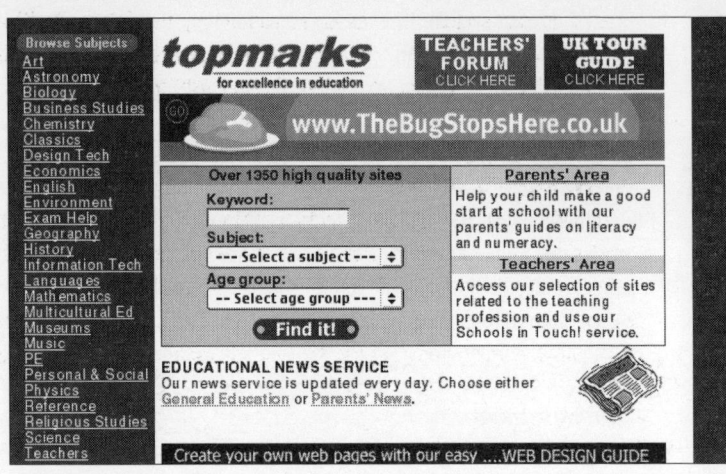

Teachers and parents alike can learn from the informative www.topmarks.co.uk

publications, which is ever expanding. The department runs an electronic communications service, which can alert you by e-mail whenever a new document is posted on the site. There are links aimed at young people and job seekers.

Educate the Children
www.educate.org.uk
Now part of Schoolsnet, Educate the Children covers the whole of the National Curriculum for primary education – it has over 2000 lesson plans, worksheets, and articles available to download. The site also gives advice on assessments and provides pictures and suggestions for lessons. The Teacher Forum is a web-based affair and includes a staffroom area where gossip and complaints are welcome. Subscribe to the informative e-mail newsletter. The Parent Zone helps primary school parents understand their child's education and gives activity suggestions.

Education Unlimited
www.education.guardian.co.uk
The *Guardian* newspaper's educational supplement features stories for students and those working in the academic world. Issues such as national debates and the curriculum are all covered, next to university league tables and reports on, among other things, teachers' pay. Or just find out what the mot risible degree is.

European schools network
www.en.eun.org
The European Schoolnet (EUN) has been designed to help school networks all over Europe work effectively together, sharing ideas and projects. Of particular

interest is the section that looks at combining the Internet with education, especially within lessons in primary and secondary education. Help is available online for teachers wishing to explore this new(ish) technology.

Parents Online
www.parents.org.uk
Designed to help parents with children of primary school age, this site contains articles on government policies, book reviews, readers' letters, and a weekly activity idea. There are sections on education, health, leisure, and an "Ask an Expert" forum. If you have Adobe Acrobat, you can even download sample pages from home learning books. There is a free ads column for grown-out-of clothes.

Library in the Sky
www.nwrel.org/sky
The Library in the Sky is a database of interesting and useful educational websites for those involved in education. Find the information you want through the search, user tabs, by department, or by materials. With more than 1600 educational websites listed, this should prove invaluable to teachers, students, and parents.

Times Educational Supplement
www.tes.co.uk
Take part in heated debates in the virtual staffroom, choose from lists of schools with websites, and peruse the online job vacancies in the teaching world. The links are a good mixture of official UK government curriculum and policy ones, as well as academic study-based offerings. Read some of the latest extracts from this newspaper supplement online as well. There is a separate site for Scotland: www.tes.co.uk/scotland/news.

Top Marks
www.topmarks.co.uk
A site for teachers and parents alike – for parents it has articles and features by practising teachers to help with education. There is also the UK Tour guide, which gives teachers the opportunity to publish their pupils' work about their local area. The search engine allows you to search the site for relevant articles in subject areas, from science to the classics. It even gives you the particular audience (Key Stage etc). A must-see site.

Up My Street
www.upmystreet.co.uk
If you really want to find out the truth about your local area, or an area that you are possibly about to move into, then this is the site to check out – and it does

cover local schools. It gives the highest scoring schools in the area and also has a table of the results within the schools in the area, with average results and much, much more.

Intelligence sites

American IQ Test
www.iqtest.com
Take a free, timed, IQ test and, if you want deep analysis, spend a few dollars and receive a report. Unfortunately this one is for Americans only – unless you feel you are particularly familiar with quarters, cents, and dimes. Do you dare risk your self-confidence?

Exercise your brain
www.mindtools.com
Get your brain into ship shape with the online tutorials at MindTools. You can also "plan and live an excellent life" with a piece of shareware software and read self-help articles on planning skills, improving your memory, learning time management, and learning how to manage stress effectively. I can personally recommend this last chapter, especially to any authors out there that are under the pressure of deadlines ...

Mensa International
www.mensa.org
Learn about this famous organization for clever people and take an interactive test online, which sadly won't count as an official admission test. The benefits and details of membership to Mensa groups worldwide are listed, as well as ways for "Mensans" to communicate, including e-mail and Internet news groups, but, strangely, not telepathy.

Online business courses
www.cyberu.com
Sign up to a host of business-based online courses on subjects ranging from accounting and finance, dealing with tax and insurance to taking on human resource management, e-business, marketing strategy, leadership, management, and web design. Clearly set out and catering for the small businessperson that wants to learn at his or her own desk, there's plenty to get your teeth into here. You can even become a partner and start up a Small Business Training Centre of your own. Spread the knowledge!

Dictionaries are just one of the handy tools for learning languages at www.travlang.com

Language sites

Bilingual Research Journal
brj.asu.edu
Concerning itself with issues surrounding bilingual classrooms and teaching, this online journal offers practical information, as well as research articles that could prove useful for those studying this area as an academic subject. There are also book reviews and case studies, available online or as downloadable files in Adobe Acrobat. The site itself can be adapted to suit your computer, with a choice of two versions – text-only or graphics – and two formats. Archives allow you to access back issues, although you can also order the paper version online.

Language database for teachers and students
www.travlang.com
Interested in learning a new language, or are you just wanting to brush up on old skills? Travlang is an essential language resource for both students and teachers alike, featuring free translation dictionaries for 24 languages including German, Spanish, Norwegian, and Czech. For example, there are English-French, French-English, French-German, and German-Afrikaans versions. Amazing. Brush up on

your foreign language skills with a quick lesson in the basics such as numbers, shopping, and directions. A pronunciation guide will also help you on your way. The site provides travel information and facilities. And subscribe to the "Word of the Day" e-mail to receive and learn a new foreign word each day.

Learning

BBC Schools Online
www.bbc.co.uk/schools
This site has a healthy mixture of education news, learning resources for primary and secondary level students, and a special "Home Learning" section that will help keep teachers and scholars in touch with their jobs/studies. There is also a guide to the best education websites which, although not comparable to the excellent book you're now reading, is still very handy.

Campaign for Learning
www.campaign-for-learning.org.uk
Promoting the worthy ideal that we should all be learning away to our brain's content, Campaign for Learning is a charitable organization that publishes details of awareness days and articles discussing the issues surrounding education of the masses – impressive names, including former Education Secretary David Blunkett, have been drafted in to get the message across. The National Learning Forum has a discussion page here, but you'll have to join the NLF first to be able to join in.

Database for teachers, students, and parents
www.schoolzone.co.uk
Teachers, students, and parents should benefit from this site, which contains thousands of links to hundreds of subjects. They vary from Welsh resources to the weather and climate, and all are to be found on other websites. However, the links have been selected by teachers, so you should be able to trust them.

Educational exhibitions
www.learningcurve.pro.gov.uk
Part of the Public Record Office (www.pro.gov.uk), this site displays a large number of educational exhibitions, including political cartoons. There is information on the Domesday Book and a discussion of 19th-century political change, covering subjects such as white slavery, the Luddites, and the suffragettes. The excellent "Snapshots" section takes a look at moments from history based on sources from the National Archive.

Educational Web Adventures
www.eduweb.com
Access a large number of interactive educational web games, exploring the worlds of art, science, and history. This site even includes a simulation where you design a marine reserve to protect the ecology of the Channel Isles. Eduweb actually writes these mini-sites for educational institutions, so the links are external, but, if you want it to produce something similar for use in your school, their rates and contact details are available.

Interactive learning
www.sparkisland.com
This is an interactive learning site, based around the fictitious Spark Island, which relies heavily on Flash, with a lot of curriculum-led activities for primary school children. Special characters lead the children through the site – it can be confusing, but given that the site is relatively new it is likely that these problems will be ironed out.

Learning to use the web
www.virtualfreesites.com
Jump straight to the Virtual Internet Tours, where you will find a basic introduction to the web, or, alternatively, use one of the categorized links to more than 50 Internet search engines to find what you are looking for on the Internet. Be warned, though. You'll have to negotiate an extremely annoying commercial each time you try a new site.

www.sparkisland.com is a great interactive site – kids will love games like the word spinner!

Education

Lessons online
www.learn.com
Enrol in a few online courses (what they call the Instant Learning system – 80 per cent faster than normal courses) from an almost surreally varied list and change your life. For example, you can learn and remember the Ten Commandments, learn how to change a flat tyre, or make a Japanese-style sponge cake. There is no doubt that you will find a course that is tailor-made for you. You do need to join to access the lessons, but membership is free.

National Grid for Learning
www.ngfl.gov.uk
You can join discussions with teachers and other education professionals on all manner of educational subjects, but best of all you'll find here some well-organized links to, and summaries of, important but often quite well hidden sites that may be of help to your lessons or studies. For example, there are a few governmental sites worth checking out, and the museums and libraries are also a worthy inclusion, as well as links to sites for higher education.

Online educational encyclopedia
www.spartacus.schoolnet.co.uk
Approved by both the US Education Department and the UK's National Grid For Learning, the Spartacus Educational Home Page provides an Internet encyclopedia that spans the Norman Conquest through to the Vietnam War, via the emancipation of women and the slave trade. (American history from 1840–1960 receives special treatment.) Articles are accompanied by great illustrations.

PLAY – Project Literacy among Youth
www.kidsplay.org
Raising children's awareness of the media and advertising is the name of the game here. The hope is that teachers will educate younger members of society to evaluate the ever present constructs of newspapers, television, and other forms and not accept them entirely on face value. Just what our cynical youth needs …

Mathematics sites

Geometry Center
www.geom.umn.edu
This maths research and education centre has a number of useful and fun puzzles and tools. The graphics archive has 3D images, fractals, and tiling puzzles, while

the web applications include a rainbow builder and an advanced curve calculator. Geometry formulae and facts are available, too, along with some free maths-based software.

Mathematics made fun
www.c3.lanl.gov/mega-math
This site helps teachers and parents turn crusty old maths concepts into colourful, fun stories and projects. The Hotel Infinity is a story that explains (sort of) the paradox of infinite numbers, and there is a machine that eats words and attempts to try untangling the mathematics of knots. Phew! Print some of these out and annoy your kids.

Maths Net
www.mathsnet.net
This excellent site is updated daily. It includes interactive puzzles, many of them Flash-based (and therefore more fun). It also explains spreadsheets, graphs, and even fractal zooms and has a huge resource centre. You can also follow the Maths Net Trail where you surf the Net to find the answers to questions it poses to you and build up your score – this is a riveting way to learn about mathematics. Show this site to your children!

School revision

GCSE answers
www.projectgcse.co.uk
The plain design of the site belies the useful information contained within. Subjects covered include English, Geography, Maths, History, and French GCSEs and many others (roughly Grade 10 in the United States). There are also resources for GCSE sciences such as Physics and Biology. Project GCSE offers many resources for panicking students revising for their GCSEs, including revision notes and practice questions, a GCSE bookshop, help and advice, and a take-a-break section to provide essential light relief when it all gets a bit too much.

SAT Math
www.satmath.com
This excellent site for students in the United States provides online tutoring on math- and SAT-related questions and topics. There are interactive lessons and quizzes, but best of all is the built-in analyser that provides students with the chance to see exactly which areas they need to improve in the most. Membership

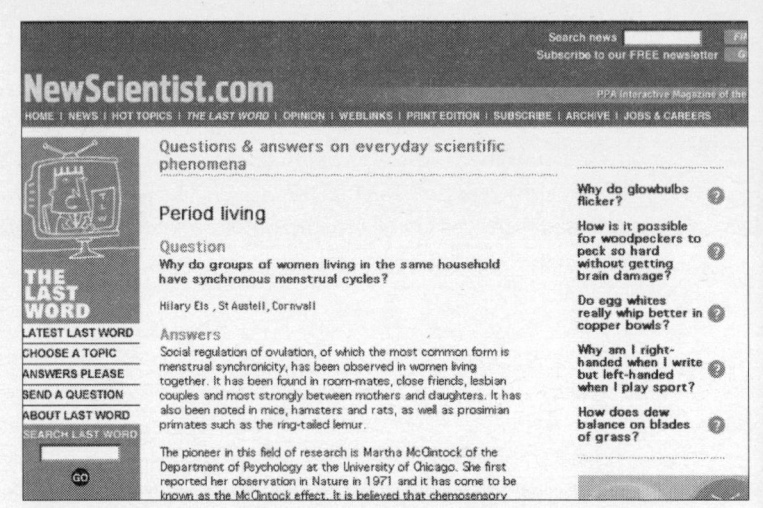

There are answers to all kinds of scientific phenomena at www.newscientist.com/lastword

does cost, although you will receive an individual study plan and an interactive CD of math tests 1 and 2 (United States only). Alternatively, you can e-mail your query to the support section for free and receive an answer within 24 hours.

Science sites

All your science questions answered
www.madsci.org
If you have a scientific question, post it here and one of the "collective cranium" will answer you. Past postings have solicited some very in-depth and serious but clear explanations. The "Random Knowledge Generator" can find a few assorted examples for you, so you can see what sort of questions are being answered before posting one of your own.

CHEMystery: An Interactive Guide to Chemistry
offchemmath.roshd.ir/thinkquestchem/
This "virtual chemistry textbook" is aimed at US high school chemistry students, although its depth is roughly equivalent to the UK chemistry GCSE. For example, you can learn about mixtures, compounds, and states of matter. This all makes the site a good starting place for revision for US and UK students alike. They also have a brand new physics site entitled "Fizzics Fizzle", which can be accessed at **hyperion.advanced.org/16600/**.

How Stuff Works
www.howstuffworks.com
An award-winning online destination for anyone who wants to know how anything works. Ever wondered how a light sabre works or what rust does? From the obvious (how does a plane work?) to the slightly mundane (have you ever really wondered how a store gets its money back from coupons?), it's all here and guaranteed to get you out of a jam next time a small child begins that familiar wail, "But how …?"

NASA
www.nasa.gov
This extensive site nearly demands a book to itself. Follow the Mars Odyssey mission, find out what is happening with the Gravity Recovery and Climate Experiment, and read about how to become an astronaut for real. With its own "NASA Education Programs", this could be a potentially great teaching aid. There are pages for kids, students, educators and the press.

New Scientist's help page
www.newscientist.com/lastword
The *New Scientist* has this great offshoot site that explains all things scientific in a language that children can easily understand. The archive contains 600 questions on scientific phenomena, with answers provided by the readers – this is a perfect place to find out the answers to difficult questions.

Pupil Researcher Initiative
www.shu.ac.uk/pri
Encouraging communication between scientists and schools, and with an aim to make GCSE and Standard Grade science "more real, more relevant, and more motivating for pupils", the Pupil Researcher Initiative (PRI) also hopes to involve schools in undertaking science projects with each other. There is information about its scheme on the site, as well as an article that describes the skills that are necessary in order to write technical reports.

Science directory
www.scicentral.com
This comprehensive web science directory is aimed at professional scientists from a large number of disciplines. There are categories for biological, health, engineering, physical, chemical, and earth and space sciences, as well as a dedicated policy and ethics section. The online news stories are drawn from various respected sources. You can also customize your own science news alerts from the site.

Social sciences sites

Encyclopedia of philosophy
www.utm.edu/research/iep
This Spartan-looking affair contains some serious, classical philosophical texts in a number of formats so that you can download them. There is also a timeline, outlining the different schools of ideas throughout the ages. A list of keywords is provided, and the search facility makes the database instantly accessible.

Environmental issues and information
www.envirolink.org
The EnviroLink Network is, it claims, one of the world's largest environmental information "clearing houses". An online library is stocked with activist resources, facts and material on nuclear issues, and links to government agency sites and other organizations. There is also a large section on sustainable business, including a specialist bookstore. A mailing list, which is how this site originally started, is available. (For other environmental sites see "The Natural World", pages 214–18).

History database
www.historychannel.com
The search facility on this site makes isolating a specific historic moment a piece of cake. So if you can't quite remember what year one of the Apollo launches was, and it's not on the timeline provided, you can dial the details up. There is a "This Day In History" page and video clips for those special sporting moments. If you fancy yourself as the new AJP Taylor, have a go at the History IQ quiz.

Origins of Humankind
www.versiontech.com/origins
The Origins of Humankind webiste is a comprehensive Internet resource for the human evolution community. This site gives you a one-stop place to efficiently locate, research, interact, and share information. Recently updated to include a database-driven bookstore and research centre, it now allows you to review books or pick over the bones of paleontological debate to your heart's content. Or see if you can get on an expedition.

Sociology
www.digeratiweb.com/sociorealm
SocioRealm is an excellent, high-gloss site bringing together information from diverse disciplines such as sociology and criminology, and aiming it at a general

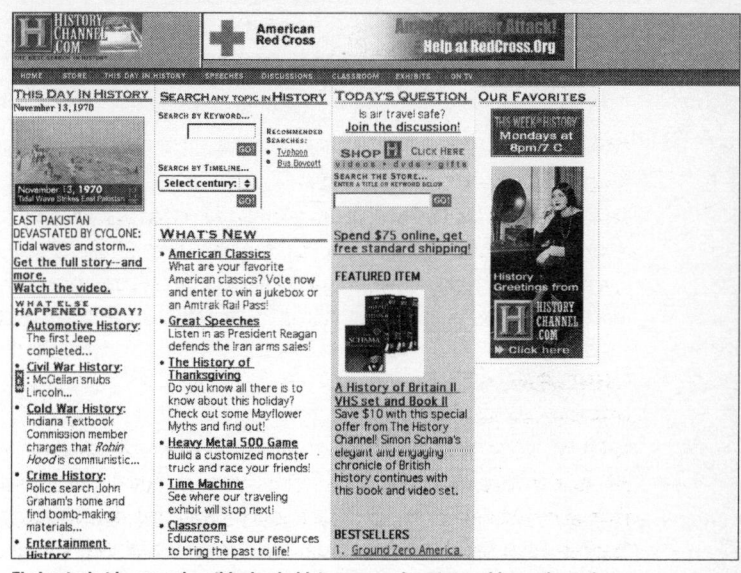

Find out what happened on this day in history every day at www.historychannel.com

audience. You'll also find in-depth discussion of the work of luminaries such as Durkheim, Marx, and Weber – names that will strike fear in the heart of many an undergraduate – together with pieces on terrorism and September 11th, and rated links to other resources on the various subject matters.

Statistical Abstract of the US
www.census.gov/statab/www
This is a slightly dull but extremely useful site. It has gathered together a vast number of statistics on social and economic conditions in the United States, including state rankings. One section can present you with the various figures on health, employment, and social welfare "in brief". However, throughout the rest of the site, you will have to use Adobe Acrobat to access all the other figures that it offers to you.

The world around us
www.worldbank.org
Gain a better understanding of the world that is around us, particularly in terms of developing countries, and make and maintain links to schools from all over the Earth. There's plenty of in-depth information and statistics on subjects including AIDS, food, pollution, and urbanization. The site also welcomes articles that are submitted by students on the subject of sustainable developments.

see also...

Whether you are a student, teacher, or concerned parent, there is an enormous amount of relevant websites. Parents will find the DfES School and College Performance Tables (**www.dfes.gov.uk**) of interest, as it allows you to judge the performance of your child's school. You can also check up on the guardians of the UK educational system by visiting the Office for Standards in Education – Ofsted (**www.ofsted.gov.uk**). The illustrated guide to every school in the United Kingdom, which includes exam results and inspection reports, is available at Schoolsnet (**www.schoolsnet.com**).

Geographers will find Geological Maps on the Web (**geomaps.geo.ukans.edu**) a handy place for project material, while mathematics students will definitely find **www.calculator.com** useful as well.

If you need a bit of competition to get you stimulated, try the American Mock Trial Association (**www.collegemocktrial.org**), where American students can engage in a simulation of the United States' fine tradition of litigation.

LearnPlus (**www.learnplus.com**) at the moment gives online lessons in Spanish and German, although other courses are planned for the future. Perseus Project (**perseus.tufts.edu**) will help you to discover the history of the ancient world with this art, archaeology, and teaching resource.

Teachers are equally well catered for. Education Week (**www.edweek.org**) has news, special reports, and extracted articles from the US magazine of the same name, and the Society for Promoting Christian Knowledge (see "Society, Politics, and Religion", page 264) has set up a new site with assembly material for primary schools at **www.assemblies.org.uk**. The British Association for Open Learning (**www.baol.co.uk**) promotes distance learning and provides an online journal covering technical issues and coverage of the education industry. English teachers and their students will find the articles and links at EFLWEB (**www.eflweb.com**) invaluable. Keep an eye on the National Curriculum by regularly visiting the Qualifications and Curriculum Authority (**www.qca.org.uk**). The Reading Online (**www.readingonline.org**) electronic journal of the International Reading Association aims to keep professional educators up to date with current developments, too. The Bilingualism, Languages and Education Network (**www.rmplc.co.uk/orgs/blen**) provides news and education resources for teaching English as a second language.

Preparing for university? The US site Education Testing Service (**www.ets.org**) is the gateway to information about college and graduate school. Find out about two of the world's most famous learning institutions – University of Cambridge (**www.cam.ac.uk**) and University of Oxford (**www.ox.ac.uk**) – or, if you are in the United States, visit Harvard University at **www.harvard.edu** or Yale University at **www.yale.edu**. SearchGate (**www.searchgate.co.uk**) provides everything a conscientious student could want, including guides to courses, colleges, shows, and student issues. A more fun site can be found at Student UK (**www.studentuk.co.uk**), which has lots of advice and entertainment news, too. After the fun, though, you'll need to think about employment. College Grad Job Hunter (**www.collegegrad.com**) will help you have something to do (and hopefully some money to spend) after leaving college. MonsterTRAK (**www.monstertrak.com**) will try to locate the job that suits your interests, while the University of London Careers Service (**www.careers.lon.ac.uk**) provides help to anyone studying at an institution affiliated to the university. If you are currently working and want to find out about evening courses in London, then **www.floodlight.co.uk** is your best bet.

And finally, what about those old school chums you've lost touch with? Ask yourself if there is a reason for this and, if you still want to re-establish contact, visit UK Alumni (**www.alumni.net**), which provides a directory of the people who have bothered to register.

ENTERTAINMENT

The entertainment industry is big money, so it's no surprise that there is a huge number of sites vying to supply you with the ultimate in television, film, and music services. You'll find TV listings, film guides, equipment reviews, and, of course, shops where you can buy all of these things. We have included other fun things in this category, such as theme parks, toy shops, and sites for sci-fi fans. However, if you are looking for much more detailed sites about the music world, then you will find them listed in their own, dedicated Music section (see pages 197–210). Books have also been given their own chapter (see pages 36–49).

Cartoons and comics

Aardman Animations
www.aardman.com
This is the home of Peter Lord and Nick Park and the award-winning Wallace and Gromit/*Chicken Run* team. You can watch animated clips from your favourites, including the whole of *Creature Comforts* and Morph. Catch up on their latest news or send an electronic postcard.

Animation Blast
www.animationblast.com
This e-zine offers a unique blend of news and commentary, with the focus firmly on animation artists and their art. It is serious stuff, but well worth a look.

Animation World Network
www.awn.com
If you foster a serious interest in animation, this is the place to come for a world view. There are profiles of artists, articles on animation technologies, and information on commercial studios and film distributors. Multiple magazines and e-mail newsletters are available, and there are sections for job-seeking animators.

Wallace and Gromit, and Morph, can be found at the excellent site www.aardman.com

Comics galore
www.marvel.com
This is the electronic home of cult classics such as the *X-Men* and *Spiderman*. Updated every two or three days, Marvel's website is full of new comic content. There is also a free-subscription chat forum and resources, as well as a comprehensively stocked online shop. This is a must for comic lovers.

Comic shop online
www.comicshack.uk.com
The Comic Shack provides a list of more than 30,000 titles, from *The Incredible Hulk* to *Batman* – all available on its website. Graded according to the condition they are in, you can either buy from or sell to the site. A "Wanted" section tells you which copies of what comic they are looking for in particular at any given time. The London-based shop's owners are real devotees of comics and graphic novels, and they promise that all titles are shipped speedily to each of their customers with reasonable postage charges.

Directory of cartoonists
www.pipemedia.net/cartoons
If you need a cartoon drawn for your local newsletter, headed notepaper, or promotional material, then pay a visit to The Cartoonists' Guild online directory.

Find out all you want to know about the latest DVD film releases at www.dvdworld.co.uk

Cartoonists are categorized, so whether you need a caricature or a web page illustration you'll be able to locate an appropriate person.

For all sci-fi comic fans
www.swapsale.com
From vintage comics from the 1930s to the 1980s such as *Space Cadet* to independent titles such as *Amazon Woman*, there's a lot to get stuck into here. Also available are animation cels, books, and a whole assortment of memorabilia. Disney gets a look-in, as do dolls and movie-related collectibles and sci-fi toys.

Internet Cartoons Forum
www.cartoonsforum.com/index.ssi
Updated nearly every day, this site is dedicated to exploring the inky underbelly of the world of cartooning – from art and business, to collecting and the fan phenomenon. Innovative amateurs and professionals, animators, illustrators, designers, writers, and publishers all get a look-in here, and all aspects of cartoons on the Internet and beyond are given a sound probing. You can add your own scribblings to the ToonZone library for widespread acclaim or general derision. Better start practising.

View popular comics
www.comics.com
Probably the most sought-after comic address on the web, United Media's comic collection includes office geek Dilbert and the famous Peanuts strip, as well as

newspaper regulars Garfield and the Wizard of Id (all of these have their own sites – www.dilbert.com, www.snoopy.com etc). Images are presented at fairly decent quality, and you'll find a 30-day archive for each strip. And, of course, United Media has not missed the opportunity to offer books for sale.

Electronic equipment

Dixons
www.dixons.co.uk
The high-street electronics chain has its own online presence, from which you can buy the usual selection of cameras, binoculars, computers, and games. You can find out where your nearest store is located and consult a buyer's guide that explains home cinema and the fundamentals of the many other gadgets and accessories available to purchase.

DVD World
www.dvdworld.co.uk
An excellent site, with lots of great DVD films and player offers, not to mention a PlayStation 2 section. The simple, uncluttered design makes the site easy to navigate and its goodies very tempting to buy.

Gadgets galore
www.firebox.com
This site could also be called "where men buy stuff". It is the supreme site for buying gadgets – a site to suit mostly upwardly young mobile males who desperately want a new electrical toy to play with during rush hour. As if to push the point home, the site is split into categories such as "Boys Toys", "Expensive Stuff", "Bachelor Pad" and "Gadgets". From ice shot glasses to £36,000+ powerboats, this site has something for every man.

Home entertainment gadgets and systems
www.home-entertainment.co.uk
Find out about the latest gadgets that will change your world forever (in your spare time, at least). If you have yet to catch up with the DVD revolution, or want to know which particular subwoofers are the best, then check out the reviews section. If you are not sure what you should purchase, then go to the useful buyers' guide section for advice. All the latest developments in home entertainment systems are announced on this site, and you can also buy older technology in the classified section.

Home entertainment magazine site
www.homecinemachoice.com
Home Cinema Choice Online has published reviews of equipment, answers to DVD questions, and a decent number of ways to "hack" your DVD player to be able to play differently regionalized disks. Sometimes these include using soldering irons and so are only suitable for experts or the foolhardy.

Quality Electrical Direct
www.qed-uk.com
Not the prettiest of sites, but one of the best for buying electrical goods in the United Kingdom. Its delivery service is impeccable and more to the point is free (for goods over £100). You may not be able to access your account details, and it is frustrating having to fill in your details each time, but for these prices it is worth it.

Events

Festivals database
www.festivals.com
Whether your idea of bliss is to chill out to the smell of incense while having your palm read or you prefer to partake in the World Championship Duck Calling Contest, you'll find details of hundreds of festivals and events all over the world at this site. Browse through categories or search for your favourite subject.

Miss Universe
www.missuniverse.com
Home of Miss USA and Miss Teen USA, as well as Miss Universe, this site offers information about the contenders, lists success stories, and covers the history of the pageants. Do visit if you are interested in this sort of thing.

Night-Out Magazine
www.night-out.co.uk
This entertainment guide contains a magazine with listings of new clubs and a small photo gallery of parties in clubs. The most useful part is the venue directory, which lists clubs all over the country and will keep you informed of special events.

Plan It For Kids
www.planit4kids.co.uk
If you are stuck as to how to entertain your demanding children, then visit this site. Simply select the area (or country) that you want, and it will make some

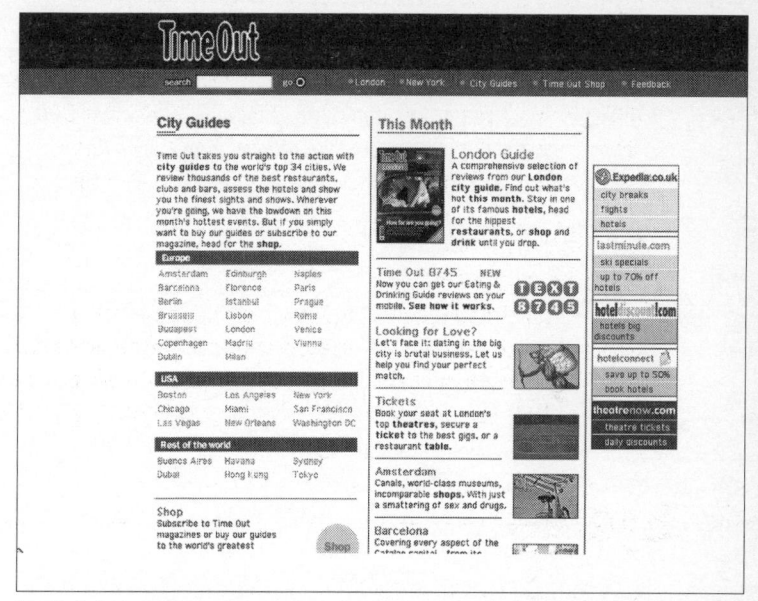

New York, Paris, London... find out what is happening in the world's cities at www.timeout.com

suggestions to keep the whole family happy, from museums and galleries to theatres, shows, and other activities. On rainy days, check out Bizarre Stuff You Can Make In Your Kitchen at **home.houston.rr.com/molerat**.

Time Out
www.timeout.com
Based on the magazine of the same name, this site give you details of the clubs, bars, galleries, restaurants, museums, and music venues in all the world's major cities. Events to come are reviewed, along with venue information and admission prices. You can also learn about the world of fame from the celebrity interviews that have appeared in the magazine over the past 30 years.

Worldwide Events Guide
www.whatsonwhen.com
This is an attractive site, colour coded for ease of use, that tells you what is going on in each major city all over the world. The permutations of categories – which allow you to search by theme or by country, just take your pick – mean that you can either find out what is happening in the city you want to visit or just browse to find something interesting. The site also offers flights, accommodation, insurance, and other travel services, making this site a future serious rival to **www.timeout.com**.

World Wide Events
www.wwevents.com
Aiming to help you enjoy (or even avoid) major events around the world, this excellent resource lets you choose the country then the region to find out where and when a specific show is running. You can also submit your own event, or one you've heard of, to the listings.

— Films ——————————————

All about movies
www.hollywood.com
The strength of this film site, and the reason it is included here along with several other possibly better ones, is that it has an excellent multimedia section where you can choose a film from the menu and select from images, trailers, video footage, and notes. Beware of the intrusive adverts.

British Academy of Film and Television Arts
www.bafta.org
Find out which films, TV programmes, and interactive entertainments are in the running for the next awards ceremony. You can see who was nominated and won last year and find out about this month's events programme of film screenings and workshops. A press release area lets you in on the official line that is fed to entertainment journalists, although you will miss out on the boozy lunches, of course.

Empire Online
www.empireonline.co.uk
Read the latest entertainment news and buy videos, DVDs, and books from the online shop. Box-office figures are available and, just so you know what you're missing, the contents of the paper version of the magazine is listed. You can also watch trailers from forthcoming films.

Reviews for Parents
www.screenit.com
Created to give parents a way to access the content of popular entertainment their kids are exposed to, this is not intended as censorship. Rather, it is designed to allow parents an informed choice on the films videos and music that are out there, giving more information than normally supplied by vague rating systems It even tells you if the music's a bit scary or there are some "tense family scenes."

Film personalities
film.guardian.co.uk
Coming from *The Guardian* and *The Observer*, Film Unlimited offers insights into the world of the most important or interesting actors, producers, and those other individuals involved in enticing us into stuffy cinemas. Video releases, an A–Z of British personalities, and a mood-matcher section that chooses a film for your current state of mind make this a must-see site.

Film plots, images, and reviews
www.darkhorizons.com
Are you after images, clips, and reviews of the latest blockbusters? You won't be disappointed with the spookily named Dark Horizons site. Films of the year are organized along with their plot lines, cast details, and links to trailers and other resources, while a "News and Rumours" section should keep you bang up to date with the world of Hollywood. You can also check out episode guides to your old cult TV favourites.

Film previews, listings, and merchandise
www.filmfour.com
Previews and reviews of all the latest film releases, find out where they are showing or just stay home and check out DVD availability. Channel 4's site has a host of delights for cineasts, including a screening room with video downloads, features on movie news and film-making, banned films and extreme cinema, and their own often wonderful productions (sadly, now no longer being made).

Film reviews and news
movie-reviews.colossus.net
Sit back, and let the opinionated advice of one James Berardinelli guide you through the tidal wave of Hollywood blockbusters and art-house classics that will be coming soon to a screen near you. From the latest releases to archive reviews and the all-time top 100 films and videos, you'll find that there's a lot to get your teeth into here.

Internet Movie Database
www.imdb.com
Containing probably the most comprehensive list of films in the world, the Internet Movie Database lets you search through actors, directors, and genres. What's more, its rating system is based on your views, not the critics. It is ideal for solving those trivial arguments about who played who in what movie, and it provides an unbiased view in disputes over which video to rent on a Saturday night. The UK site can be found at **uk.imdb.com**.

Jokes

Joke database
www.lotsofjokes.com
This is a huge database of jokes, some clean, but most are likely to offend someone. There are rude song lyrics, oxymorons, and lists of things not to say to "her when she's pregnant" or "a-naked-man". There are some funny jokes, but it'll take some exploration to find them. As, no doubt, the actress said to the bishop.

Online comedy publication
www.netfunny.com
Originating from an Internet news group rec.humor.funny, this website has a large archive of jokes and provides random chuckles, lists of favourites, and a selection of the best jokes posted on the site. To get the most out of the site, you'll need special software, but there's plenty to keep the unadventurous happy.

Magic sites

Introduction to the world of magic
www.allmagicguide.com
There are loads of links here to different magic sites, including ones where they give the game away, and the site also features step-by-step instructions on how to perform. There are also book and video reviews, and a list of dealers. Learn a few tricks from here and one of the exclusive clubs might take you on ...

The Magic Circle
www.themagiccircle.co.uk
Find out a limited amount about this famously low-key magician's society, and apply for an application form. As a mere member of the public, you'll be restricted to a limited photo gallery and a history of the club, but should you be allowed to join you'll be privy to the "Members Area". It also includes information about public shows and forthcoming events.

The Society of American Magicians
www.magicsam.com
Download details of how to join this old society for conjurers from a very "corporate" and uninviting website. For example, you can buy SAM luggage tags and read

about the conventions and magic shows to come, but if you want to learn how to do tricks – forget it! However, there are links to members' websites, some of which have archives of tricks. Become a member and get the M-U-M magazine, which will keep you up to date on lectures, performances, and news.

Movies and television

Entertainment Online
www.eonline.com
This good, all-round entertainment site covers movies, music, and television, with features on the latest blockbuster films, this week's favourite actors, and a section containing games and quizzes. E! Online also includes gossip on which projects celebrities are currently involved in and transcripts of online chat interviews.

New films and reviews
www.aint-it-cool-news.com
Written by self-proclaimed film nerd Harry Jay Knowles, Ain't It Cool News is THE film site to read if you want to know what films are coming up and, more importantly, if they're any good. His film reviews are so spot on that producers invite the guy to pre-previews. Like films? Visit here.

Rotten Tomatoes
www.rottentomatoes.com
This US-based site will give you the critical lowdown on all the latest films. It has a vast review database, taken from newspaper and website sources. It then accumulates the reviews and gives them a rating (either fresh or rotten using the complicated-sounding Tomatometer). Subscribe to the weekly newsletter to find what has been said about the latest US releases. It has great news and gossip areas as well – one of the best.

Shaken, not stirred
www.jamesbond.com
As befits the dashing 007, the official site is flashy and suave. Catch up with the latest news about the next Bond film, watch the trailers, and see the posters as and when they are ready.

Star Wars
www.theforce.net
Don't head to the lacklustre official *Star Wars* site (**www.starwars.com**), go here

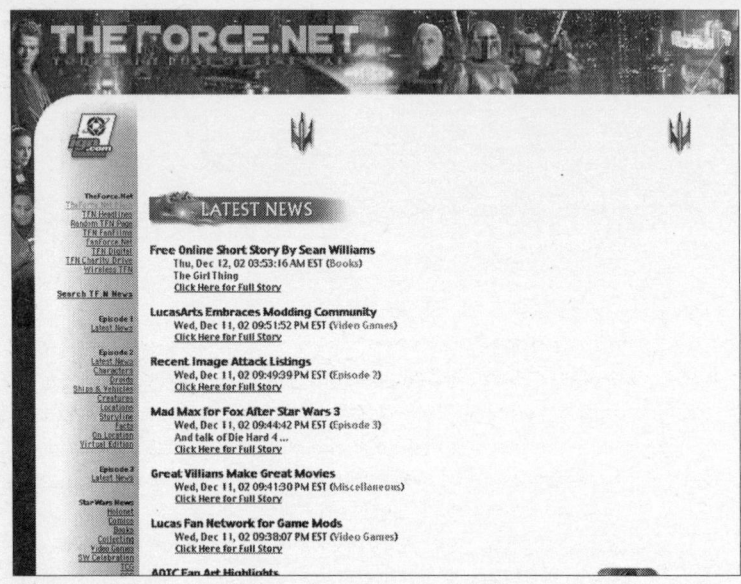

Star Wars lovers will be in heaven at www.theforce.net – all news, however trivial, is listed here

for all the information you might need on George Lucas's epic series of films. All the insider knowledge that you might need about the next *Star Wars* films, currently being filmed in Italy. And you cannot leave this site without watching *Star Dudes* and *The Bad Dude Strikes Back* – hilarious Flash animated movies condensing the first two *Star Wars* films into about four minutes each (if you can't find them easily, go to **theforce.net/theater/animation**).

The world of Disney
www.justdisney.com
This isn't an official Disney site, but is still packed with in-depth information about the company's history, as well as that of the man himself. There are pictures, quotes, and sounds, while the links section caters for visitors, providing access to review and guide sites.

Music, sound, and video

BlackStar videos and DVDs
www.blackstar.co.uk
One of the very best places to buy your European videos and DVDs, BlackStar will

hunt down rare titles for you and pre-order near future releases. Not only that, the site offers most items at a discount. Pre-ordering will get you some serious money off, and the postage is free. Its loyalty scheme is called Star e-wards, which allows you to receive anything from a free video to a DVD player when you spend over a certain amount of money.

British Video Association
www.bva.org.uk
Find out about up-and-coming releases, and read in-depth about the video industry at the site of the organization that is concerned with representing video publishers. There are also links to some of the major players in the industry, including regulatory bodies. See where the law stands on tape and disk copying, and visit the British Board of Film Classification for news on recent decisions.

CDs over the net
www.cdnow.com
Aside from selling music CDs and movies on DVD and video, the US-based CDNOW has an innovative way to provide music that you pay for then download straight to your computer over the Internet. You can also buy custom-made CDs here that contain just the tracks that you want from any number of albums (these can be shipped all the way to Europe, although it is often expensive to do this). There are also interviews with various artists on the site to keep you up to date with the music world.

DVD Town
www.dvdtown.com
One of the best of many, many sites, DVD Town has all the normal features that you would expect, but possibly the most innovative is its rating system pop-up on the main featured titles on the home page. Marks out of ten are given for each DVD – for sound quality, picture quality, entertainment, and extra features (which appear nowadays on almost all DVDs). What's more, you can personalize the site to your own tastes.

HMV
www.hmv.co.uk
This high-street music store provides a very useable Internet version of itself, which is organized into musical categories, with separate sections for games, DVD, video, and spoken word tapes and CDs. You can find out here when releases are due out and how much they'll cost you. It's a shame that you can't pre-order on the site, but the low prices (well, less than the prices in its shops anyway) should soften this blow ...

After Phil or Bootsy Collins? You can find music, videos and more at www.towerrecords.com

Music, video, book, and games shop
www.101cd.com
You can never have enough music and video shops on your list of favourite sites. Try 101cd.com when shopping around, and compare its often surprisingly low prices with other online stores, although the focus is more on the mainstream. You can also choose from a large catalogue of books and computer games.

Online store
www.jungle.com
This online store stocks music, computer games, computers, software, and movies in both VHS and DVD format that it can send to you wherever you are. When it began, the site came under heavy criticism for its slow customer service, but it has since become one of the best and quickest sites to buy from, helped by the easy, and fun, navigation. It also provides an e-mail service that you can call on any phone and have your messages read to you by a computer. The prices include VAT, and delivery is free.

Tower Records
www.towerrecords.com
Much improved since it began, this popular record shop's online effort features articles as well as the usual shopping areas. You can download music from the

site, as well as browse through the video, DVD, and book departments. A slightly lighter UK version of the store is available at **uk.towerrecords.com**.

Sci-fi sites

The Actors of British Science Fiction
www.tnelson.demon.co.uk/cult/index.html
Spend happy hours following these links to discover favourite and revered British actors playing third alien in some hokey, long-forgotten episode of a long-forgotten science-fiction, fantasy or cult TV show. Almost 10,000 entries make this quite an exhaustive site, listing cast members from *Ace of Wands* to *UFO*, and taking in such eternal classics as *Dr Who*, *Blake's 7*, and *Quatermass*. Some other cult titles are also included on this site, such as *The Return of the Saint* and *Dempsey and Makepeace*.

The Borg Collective
www.theborgcollective.com
Make sure that you have time to spare before visiting this *Star Trek* fan site. Not only is there a huge amount of information through which to navigate, but the large graphics also make the site extremely slow to download as well. You can send Internet greeting cards from the site, learn about the Borg's history, read various character profiles, and play a game of *Star Trek* trivia. You can also visit the official site at **www.startrek.com**.

Sad Geezer's Guide to Cult Sci-Fi
www.sadgeezer.com
Fans of *Red Dwarf*, *LEXX*, and *The Hitch-Hiker's Guide to the Galaxy* will have fun here at this aptly designed site. There are episode guides to these, and other, TV shows, as well as tests to make sure that you really know your science fiction facts. Links to similar sites are available on the site, and these are packed with so much detail that you won't even need to watch the programmes ... A must-see site for science-fiction fans.

The X-Files
www.thex-files.com
Explore the archives of the official *X-Files* website and uncover past episodes. You may not find definitive answers to all the mysteries, but you might be able to dig out a few clues. The vault contains a huge amount of merchandise that you can spend your cash on, too.

Entertainment

Luvviness abounds at www.theatrenet.co.uk – find out all about plays in the West End and afar

Theatre

News, reviews, and tickets
www.theatrenet.co.uk
Join TheatreNet's ShowSavers club, and you can make savings when attending shows both in and out of London. Hotel rooms, merchandise, and books are also in the list of special offers. The site also offers the latest theatre news – all the major shows have their own well-designed mini-sites within the larger whole.

Playbill online
www.playbill.com
Check out the listings of the newest Broadway, and off-Broadway, shows. The categories include London and US national tours, and you can buy your tickets online. There are articles and interviews, as well as links to gift shops. Fancy treading the boards yourself? The casting section may help.

The Royal Shakespeare Company
www.rsc.org.uk
Find out what the next performances from the company will be, where the venues are, and the tour dates. You can also buy gifts, books, and other Shakespearean

bits and pieces from the online shop, and a separate box-office section will gladly sell you tickets for any of the up-and-coming shows online.

Theme parks

Alton Towers
www.alton-towers.co.uk
Find out about the rides, prices, and facilities at one of the United Kingdom's most popular theme parks on this brilliantly designed site. You can take a 360-degree panoramic view of some of the hotel rooms directly from your screen, and tickets are available to buy during the park's open season. If you need scaring, you can find out details of the latest big ride, including the Hex, which shakes the screen when your cursor goes over it, or view footage of Air.

Chessington World of Adventures
www.chessington.co.uk
Do a quick reconnaissance of this UK theme park using the online map and you can hopefully avoid queues or losing your kids when you are actually there. Zoom in to find out about each ride. The "Thrillometer Readings" and height restrictions should also help you to avoid disappointments when you visit. It also includes opening times, directions, prices, and booking details. Play the Tomb Blaster online game to get a taster of the real thing, but be warned – it's pretty dire.

Disney online
www.disneyinternational.com
The official Disney website has information on its CD-ROM games, films, cartoons, musicals, and videos. However, you can also find out about the Disneyland resorts in the United States and Paris. While you're waiting to visit, you can keep the kids occupied with the online animated stories and games.

See also "Universal Studios" in Travel, page 295.

Treading the boards

Dancer Magazine
www.danceronline.com
Covering all aspects of professional dance from the latest news to the latest

fashions. Subscribers are treated to everything dance-related, whether it be jazz or ballet or the best yoga exercises. There's even a Dance Dad's Diary to give a fresh perspective on it all.

Salsa
www.salsabeat.freeserve.co.uk
Stay up to date with the increasingly popular UK salsa. Find out when special events are to take place, download salsa tunes, and get the low-down on various salsa bands. There are also links to similar sites all over the United Kingdom and the world, so this is worth a visit even for those not living in the Big Smoke.

Showbiz kids
www.startips.com
If you want to put your son or daughter on the stage, follow the advice offered by this Hollywood site, which is aimed at helping parents promote their children as young stars. It includes tips on getting started and signing with an agent, as well as the best ways to present photo CVs.

TV, radio, and ads

The Advertising Standards Authority
www.asa.org.uk
You might wonder why you would visit a dry-sounding site like this, but there is much entertainment to be had in reading about the latest ASA adjudications. You can find out which ads have received complaints and what the ASA recommends as a result of those complaints.

Children's BBC
www.bbc.co.uk/cbeebies
Fun and games are the order of the day at the BBC's site devoted to kids' television. There are stories, things to print out, birthday cards, prizes to win, and a gallery of kids drawings. Popular TV characters dominate. Old favourites such as Bill and Ben, and newer arrivals such as the Fimbles are all present and correct. Guaranteed to keep the little ones away from the telly for an hour or two ...

Coronation Street
www.coronationstreet.co.uk
Pop into the Rover's Return to take an "exclusive" look behind the scenes of this long-running UK soap opera, have a go in the competitions and win yourself

Corrie memorabilia, and download images with which to decorate your computer. You can also chat with the stars of *Coronation Street*, follow the video diary, and watch the interviews provided.

EastEnders
www.bbc.co.uk/eastenders
If you find yourself at a loose end between episodes of this soap, you can spend time with classic clips of "Ricky!", sour Pauline, or Dirty Den. Take a tour of Walford, express your opinions (remember, it's not real!), and catch up on the storyline, if you cannot wait for the Sunday omnibus.

Episode guides
epguides.com
This remarkable set of episode guides (some of which have plot summaries and guest stars) covers US TV series as diverse as *Jeeves and Wooster*, *Ally McBeal*, *King of the Hill*, and *Manimal*. Cast lists are linked to the Internet Movie Database site (**www.imdb.com**), so you can visit there to find out what else your favourite TV star has been in.

Fox
www.fox.com
The mother site of *The Simpsons* hosts a lot more than our yellow friends. The site is huge, with features on all its hit shows including *Ally McBeal*, *The X-Files*, *Futurama*, and *King of the Hill*. Simply scroll down the right-hand menu and take your choice. It also has TV listings for the United States.

Independent Television Commission
www.itc.org.uk
Has digital television passed you by already? Catch up with the introduction and technical appraisal published on the ITC's site. You can also read about which UK TV stations are in trouble for breaching the code of conduct and which Channel 4 documentaries have allegedly misled viewers. If you are particularly interested, you can also find out how the ITC regulates programmes, advertising, and sponsorship, as well as follow complaints made against programmes in the past.

Media UK
www.mediauk.com
Fancy turning your computer and Internet connection into a radio? Find out where you can "tune in" at this large list of online radio stations, TV shows, and one-off broadcasts (webcasts). There are media UK forums focussing on Internet radio stations and an Internet Directory listing websites, addresses, and phone numbers for online media.

Online TV Guide (US)
www.tvguide.com
This US TV guide publishes programme listings for all the cable, broadcast, and satellite channels. You enter your zip code or choose your time zone and it works out what's available in your area. Catch up on the soaps – any questions you have about them can be answered by "The Expert". News and gossip are readily available here, and a chat forum is provided to fill in time between episodes of *The Simpsons*. (See also **radiotimes.co.uk** for UK listings).

Sitcoms
www.sitcomsonline.com
The ultimate site for the sitcom fan! Included in this site is the latest news in the world of sitcoms, with hundreds of links from A–Z, message boards, and merchandise links for sitcom videos, books, and CDs. There are also downloadable theme songs for hundreds of sitcoms from the 1950s, 1960s, 1970s, 1980s, 1990s, and present.

Soap Opera Central
www.soapcentral.com
Breathless coverage of the bizarre and surreal world of daytime and primetime (mainly US) television soaps. It includes all the latest news, soap scoops, spoilers, awards, ratings and recaps. Who's in? Who's out? Who's contract is up? All the insider industry gossip is here.

TV Century 21: The Gerry Anderson Home Page
tvcentury21.com
Dedicated to the producer of shows such as *Torchy the Battery Boy*, *Fireball XL5*, *Thunderbirds*, and *Captain Scarlet and The Mysterons*, this site has news and almost too much detail on the models used in his programmes. Interviews with all the personalities involved in the shows are also included. Get those sought-after pieces in the trading zone.

What's on?
www.yack.com
Yack is one of the most comprehensive guides available to what's streaming away out there. You'll be able to find movie trailers, music videos, MP3s, celebrity interviews, online films, radio, sports webcasts, and much, much more. There are also speciality guides to games, animation, online films and sport, and radio. Give it a go, it's all out there.

See also the "Radio" and "TV" sections in News, beginning pages 236 and 238.

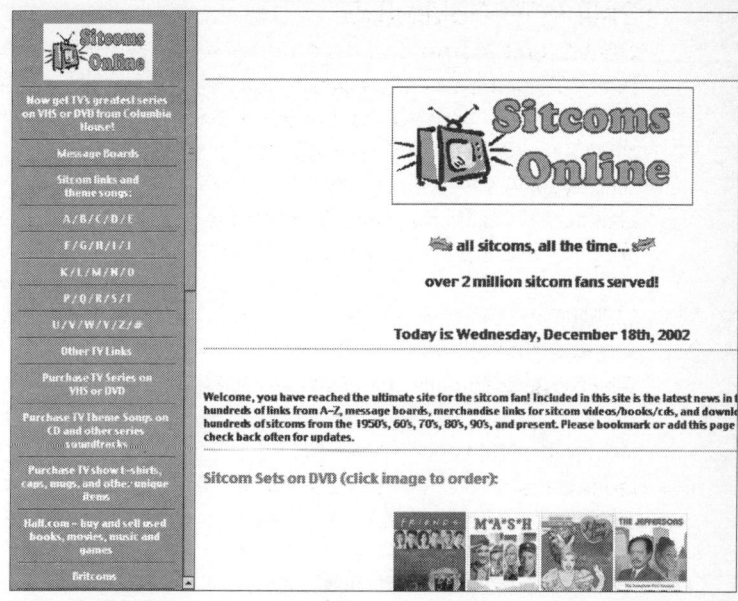

The goggle-eyed should visit www.sitcomsonline.com for the latest on sitcoms worldwide

see also...

Science-fiction sites are a dime a dozen, but you could be in heaven at **www.scifi.com**, which has all the news that you could possibly want. Fans of the nihilistic 1970s sci-fi show, *Space: 1999*, will be happy at **www.space1999.net**.

One strong characteristic of the Internet is the presence of personal tributes to favourite films, stars, and even cartoons. The Big List of Movie Mistakes (**www.movie-mistakes.com**) dissects famous films and ruins them all for you, pointing out filming mistakes that are so obvious once you know they're there – they have a Top 25 and, would you know, *The Matrix* is at the top. Another great way to spoil a film you haven't seen is to visit the Movie-A-Minute site (**www.rinkworks.com/movieaminute**), where you'll find ultra-compressed summaries of popular movies. For those who already know what they are getting (in far too much detail), there are pages devoted to films such as *Star Wars* (**www.starwars.com**). Going back in time, you'll find dedications to silent movies at The Silents Majority (**www.silentsmajority.com**), while homage is paid to yesterday's Hollywood stars at Bombshells (**www.bombshells.com**). As for the Oscars, you can find out all you want to know about the ultimate movie prizes at **www.oscars.org**.

Today's stars are definitely of the animated variety. You can say hello to the online presences of the cult cartoon *South Park* at South Park Central (**www.comedycentral.com/tv_shows/southpark**). The latter is found in the United Kingdom on Channel 4, and so is one of hundreds of shows featured on the site **www.channel4.com**. As you would expect, *The Simpsons* (**www.thesimpsons.com**) are also connected, even providing a free Internet access service to those in the United States. If "Ren and Stimpy" mean anything to you, read the terrible saga of their rise and fall from grace at Nickelodeon at **www.yesterdayland.com/popopedia/shows/saturday/sa1620.php**. A warning for independent animators everywhere. For the sanitized approach, try Nickelodeon (for UK residents at **www.nick.co.uk** or for those in the United States at **www.nick.com**), but you'll only "get" the site if you regularly tune into this children's TV channel. Most people, however, will "get" the Cartoon Network site (**www.cartoon-network.co.uk**), as it is the home of the marvellous Scooby Doo (and Shaggy, too). For classic comic lovers, you can visit the colourful *Beano* website (**www.beano.co.uk**) to see Dennis the Menace and other old favourites. *Viz* (**www.viz.co.uk**), on the other hand, tends to appeal to the somewhat ruder person, as shown by the Roger Mellie Profanisaurus, the definitive reference guide to sexual euphemisms.

Other cult-viewing essential sites include current media darlings the Osbournes (**www.mtv.com/onair/osbournes**) and the very odd *League of Gentlemen* (**www.leagueofgentlemen.co.uk**) – a local site for local people. And for the lovers of the doll world, visit **www.barbie.com** for a surreal online experience. For those keen on the online TV experience, go to **www.virtuetv.co.uk** to watch concerts, music videos, interviews, live sport, and short films on your computer.

There are absolutely hundreds of sites from which you can buy your goods to watch the entertainment that is detailed in this chapter – some of the best of the rest happen to be Empire Direct (**www.empiredirect.co.uk**), Unbeatable (**www.unbeatable.co.uk**), and Richer Sounds (**www.richersounds.com**). All are in competition with each other, which means that prices are often much lower than on the high street.

Alternatively, do you want to know what all those couch potatoes at home are watching? Try the Broadcasters' Audience Research Board (**www.barb.co.uk**) to find out how many people share your taste in soap operas, using the data from this audience analysis site. If British sitcoms and sketch shows are your thing, have a look at **www.phill.co.uk**.

There are also various quiz sites such as Trivia Bytes (**www.triviabytes.com**), where you can take part in the online trivia quizzes, using sound and other multimedia elements as questions. For the ultimate challenge, why not visit *Who Wants to Be a Millionaire?* (**www.itv.com/millionaire**), although unfortunately you won't actually win any money at all. Assuming you haven't been a successful participant there, you might want to resort to Free UK Stuff (**www.ukfreestuff.net**), which will find the free things in life for you – but only if you live in the United Kingdom, of course.

Find out what's around the corner in the world of entertainment with sites such as **www.dvhs.co.uk**, where the new digital video tape format that will no doubt revolutionize our lives is outlined. Technology-based TV programme *Tomorrow's World* (**www.bbc.co.uk/science/tw**) should also keep you up to date with the latest innovations – even if they never actually materialize in the real world.

FOOD AND DRINK

Your taste buds will doubtless be tickled by the tempting array of recipes, luxurious items, and exotic cocktails detailed on these foody websites. You will also find information on GM foods, fast food outlets in your area, and cuisine from around the world. Whether your interest lies in basic home cooking or creating a killer Thai banquet, you will find hundreds of different options, plus advice on what to drink with your chosen feast. You'll be making space by the toaster for your PC in no time.

Drink

All about tea
www.tea.co.uk
Discover those elusive tea facts, including the average daily consumption per person, what percentage of the UK population are avid tea drinkers, and what the future holds for the tea market. A directory of suppliers, importers, and other specialized services is available, as is an overview of the history of the drink.

Beer and where to drink it
www.goodguides.com/pubs/search.asp
Not really fêted for their cuisine, the British do excel at a good pub, and this site has them all. You can search by region, but not just for what alcohol each pub serves. For every one they tell you whether it serves food or has accommodation, and its general value. The pub descriptions are detailed and informative.

Cocktail party planner
www.hotwired.com/cocktail
Browse the archives of cocktail recipes or use the pain-free "Virtual Blender". Once you have specified one or more ingredients, it will search for you, then pinpoint the recipes that you should like. Or, even easier, just go to the "Drink of the Week" (hic ...) to find a recipe to try out. The party planning page will help you keep record of all those important planning points: the number of people

Food and Drink 109

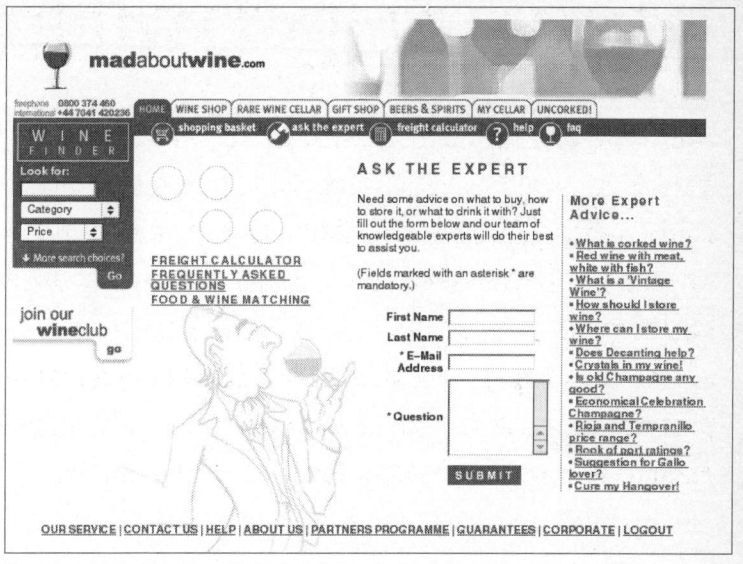

If you fancy buying your favourite tipple in bulk, www.madaboutwine.com is sure to help you out

you're having around for your party, what glasses you have to use for the event, the time of day it is to be held at, and how formal you intend the event to be.

Cocktail recipes
www.cocktail.com
Access a massive database of cocktail recipes, submit your own speciality, and read a few book reviews. The editorial section might be a little stronger than some of the drinks, but we're all entitled to our opinions. The shopping section takes you to the site's store, where you can buy everything from glassware to spirits.

Learn more about wine
www.winespectator.com
Learn to be a wine buff, and put your lesser friends to shame when the next bottle is cracked open. Features include a wine school, a database containing wine reviews, and a worldwide wine retailer directory. The library will take you through the basics of wine appreciation. To get the most from this site, you'll need to subscribe for a fee, although a cheaper trial is available.

Mad about Wine
www.madaboutwine.com
This excellent site entices you to stock up your cellar with a variety of wines. There is no snobbery here – the wines vary from the cheap and cheerful to the more

expensive and rarer vintages. The site promises to deliver its readily available wines within 10 working days, longer for the rarer tipples. You can ask the experts for advice and can even put your personal preferences in your account through the "My Cellar" area. You can also tell their experts what you are having for dinner, and they will suggest a complementary wine for you.

Oddbins
www.oddbins.com
Avoid the sly smiles when you fail to pronounce posh wines correctly by buying directly off the web, using the services of the award-winning Oddbins wine merchant. You'll find special offers, a "Fizz Finder" to help select a nice bottle of bubbly, and a no-nonsense (well, nearly) guide to the gassy wine.

Whisky in depth
www.scotchwhisky.com
Whisky lovers are predicted to spend far too much time on this highly detailed effort of a website. The "Malt Whisky File" is a searchable database that asks you to express your tastes in order to tell you what your perfect dram is. Pour yourself a glass, and settle down to learn how whisky is made, the regional differences, and just about anything else you'll ever want to know.

The world of beer
www.realbeer.com
Keep up to date with what's happening in the world of beer – including how to make your own. Find out about beery events, and discover the best places in London and other major cities to visit for a good pint. Play drinking games and enter the odd contest, while a good selection of recipes will keep you locked in the garage "working" for some time. The list of equipment and ingredients suppliers can only act as encouragement.

— Luxury food

Cheeses from around the world
www.wgx.com/cheesenet
Refer to the "World Cheese Index" to find how fatty each cheese is, where it comes from, and which wines are likely to best accompany a snack. You can find out how cheese is made and even ask "Dr Cheese" any cheese-related questions that you think of. Beware, though, of the cheese-related poetry and prose, unless you've the stomach for a true taste of the dark side.

Dean and Deluca
www.deananddeluca.com
The famous New York deli store has its own immaculately designed website. The site sells delectable-looking food, from tupelo honey to foie gras, kitchenware, and corporate gifts (but be warned that it is all very expensive). You can also request their catalogue in order to salivate over the goods on offer, but only if you live in the United States, unfortunately.

Fortnum and Mason
www.fortnumandmason.com
This most prestigious of grocers, famous for its luxury goods and hampers, offers a tastefully designed online shopping service within its beautiful site. This is complemented by a smattering of recipes and short pieces on cigars, wine, and cheese, as well as other elegantly unhealthy pursuits. And they say that you can't buy class ...

Gastronomic delights
www.camisa.co.uk
Fratelli Camisa has been supplying some of the finest foods to delicatessens throughout the land for the past 70 years. Now you can feast your eyes on its online shop and order up outlandish cheeses, wild mushrooms, cakes, wines, fine pastas, and olive oils – all ready and waiting to be delivered straight to your kitchen. Absolute luxury.

Le Gourmet Français
www.gourmet2000.co.uk
Order the finest ingredients for your gourmet creations from this continental online grocery store. There are all sorts of interesting products on offer – from wild mushrooms and truffles to wild boar pâté. There is also a small selection of organic, British, and Italian food.

Online chocolate shop
www.chocexpress.com
Send your loved one, or potential loved one, a box of chocolates or sweets (and even the occasional bottle of bubbly) by way of this online gift shop – it is a free service throughout the United Kingdom. Enrolling someone ensures that they will receive monthly packages of chocolates to scoff. A scoring card for them to fill in will helpfully steer future selections towards their specific tastes. ChocExpress also runs a chocolate tasting club – wonderful. What the ensuing weight gain on both sides will do for your budding relationship is another matter completely, of course. But isn't it worth it to be able to buy chocolate on tap?

Recipes

All about cheese
www.ilovecheese.com
The ultimate site devoted to cheese, I Love Cheese is both amusing (just check out the cheesy photography) and informative. This site will find the perfect cheese for your tastes and offer recipe ideas. Do you consider meltability when you visit the shops? Well, then. The site is run by the American Dairy Association and offers a free bi-monthly e-mail newsletter.

Barbecue hints and tips
www.barbecuen.com
Give your summer barbecue a boost by following some of the tips and recipes provided here. You can find out what the perfect cooking temperature is, what utensils you'll need, and how to achieve that unique smoky taste without the accompanying charring. An online store is also available.

Food and Drink
www.bbc.co.uk/food/foodanddrink
Check out the latest recipes featured on television, and remind yourself of the drinks that Jilly and Oz bang on about most eloquently. Unfortunately we are not treated to transcripts of their opinions, but you will get a rough idea of the prices, which are probably more informative.

Ideas for meals
www.mealsforyou.com
Come here not just for recipes, but also complete meal plans. The recipes are listed by ingredients, as well as the dietary requirements they fulfil. You can store the recipes that you like in your online cookbook. You can use "Meals for You" to choose an entire menu quickly. It will show you exactly how long the meal will take to prepare and how good (or fun) it will be for you. Measurement units are available in US, British, metric, and antipodean.

Internet Chef
www.ichef.com
Full of handy tips and good advice, iChef is one of the best culinary websites around at the moment. For example, if you cannot think of a recipe, why not tune in to the Radio Kitchen— ingenious (although cooking while listening may prove a bit tricky). The recipe categories scroll down the page forever, so that you will

Food and Drink

Impress all your friends and cook something up from what is on offer at www.allrecipes.com

never need to be short of delicious meals for guests or family again. The spotlight on particular food items changes regularly, so, if you are wondering what to do with those green beans in the larder, this site will enlighten you and give you plenty of mouthwatering ideas. With free samples thrown in and a weekly cartoon, too, iChef is hard to beat.

Recipe network
www.allrecipes.com
This is the ultimate resource for all home-based chefs. The site acts as a gateway to a number of its own other sites, which include **cake.allrecipes.com**, **cookie.allrecipes.com**, **pie.allrecipes.com**, and **vegetarianallrecipes.com**. There is, of course, a reason behind this well-organized philanthropy. An online cookery store, **allrecipes.com/shop**, sells a large range of kitchen equipment and, of course, is just one click away ...

Star Chefs
www.starchefs.com
Don't be put off by the home page and the poor navigation, as it is still worth visiting. Where it differs from the many other food and drink sites is its section on celebrity chefs, which includes biographies, recipes from them, and interviews. There are also numerous features and articles on all types of food and drink.

Reviews

Coffee Review
www.coffeereview.com
Overwhelmed by the selection of coffees in the supermarket? Then why not let the experts do the tasting for you, once you've read about how to interpret their tasting results. Different types of coffee bean, with details about their country of origin, are listed. Categories include espressos, dark roasts, and organics, to name but a few. US residents can buy some of the reviewed products at www.greatcoffee.com.

Eating in – and out
www.foodtv.com
This site has been brought to the public by the Food Network. It has all the information that you will need on culinary entertaining and details of programmes on the television channel. The categories to be found on the site include recipes, wine, celebrity chefs and hosts, holidays, gatherings, and other gastronomic escapes. Food 911 is there to sort out your kitchen dilemmas, and you can read about the lives of your favourite chefs.

No food lover with an Internet connection should forget to visit www.eat.epicurious.com

Zagat's restaurant reviews
www.zagat.com
At this site you can find over 20,000 reviews and ratings of restaurants that can be found in the United States, London, Paris, Toronto, and Vancouver. Categorized by Zagat ratings, cuisine, cost, or location, the paths to find the restaurant of your choice are easy to follow. Once found, you can pull up a handy map telling you how to get there. It also gives you a chance to vote on your favourite venue.

Safety and other issues

Everything about food
www.eat.epicurious.com
Whether you want a hand equipping your new kitchen, have forgotten how to mix a Singapore Sling, or want to mellow the taste of garlic, then this site will suit. There are a staggering 13,000-plus recipes here to choose from, if you so desire. In fact, there are so many articles that, once tried, no other food site will satisfy.

Food safety and preservation
www.foodpres.com
If you are not quite sure how long that cheese has been lurking at the back of the refrigerator, how do you find out if it's still safe to eat? The advice on this site will help, although its main emphasis is on food preservation.

The Vegan Society
www.vegansociety.com
Find out what it means to choose a vegan lifestyle, and use the information sheets to learn about staying healthy while eschewing animal products. You can locate vegan cookery courses, discover the truth about diabetes and other disorders, and find out what kinds of alcoholic beverage are "safe". You may be surprised ...

The Vegetarian Resource Group
www.vrg.org
Maybe you are trying to raise a vegan family or want to know where to buy specialist vegetarian goods. Is kosher gelatine vegan? This site will give advice and explain things that the most fastidious veggie might be unsure about. Vegetarian teenagers have a section all to themselves, with help on how to reassure worried parents that they won't break in the next gust of wind.

See also "Food and Drug Administration" in Health, page 145.

Supermarkets

Jewel-Osco
www.jewelosco.com
Browse this US food store by category, and pick up the latest bargains from your armchair. Place your orders online for pickup at your local store, and search the menu database for ideas on turning your goods into great-tasting meals.

Sainsbury's
www.sainsburys.co.uk
Work out what you can make from the ingredients already in the larder or get some more food in by shopping online. Sainsbury's runs a home-delivery grocery service that costs £5 each time (it's called Sainsbury's to You). It has links to its banking service as well, and you can build up your recipes from the site (there are more than 6000 to choose from).

Tesco
www.tesco.com
Tesco's online shopping service is available to a growing number of households throughout the United Kingdom — and this is the place to access it. It no longer offers just food supplies, but will also deliver sofas, televisions, refrigerators, and crates of wine. It is certainly easier to navigate this simple and effectively designed site than to push a wonky trolley along countless busy aisles.

World foods and restaurants

Curry info and shopping
www.curryhouse.co.uk
All you'll ever need to know about curry making is contained in the Curry House's electronic pages. You can also order specialist ingredients from the Chilli Willie Spice Emporium and learn about the potentially life-saving gadget called the CurrySafe, which stops your takeaway curry tipping over in the car!

Taste of Ireland
www.tasteofireland.com
Find guides to restaurants in Ireland, food shops where you can buy classic Irish fare (smoked salmon and cheese, it appears!) online, and a recipe book containing traditional dishes. Most of the site's efforts are directed at the

restaurant guide, which has detailed listings including sample menus and the occasional featured recipe.

US restaurant reviews
www.dinesite.com
Imagine the scene – you are on a trans-America car journey and you're starting to flag, but which roadside diner should you opt for? If you've planned properly, you'll have read the reviews on this site and know where to go for the best burgers or something a bit fancier. More than 12,000 US towns are covered, and they even throw in some tips on table manners. Tasty!

— see also...

There are plenty of websites that offer recipes from all over the world. Global Gourmet (**www.globalgourmet.com**) is a long-established site that features delightful food and wine from various countries all over the world. Asia Cuisine (**www.asiacuisine.com.sg**) offers a full Asian culinary experience, with a useful e-zine and recipes. For a more limited range of recipes and ingredients that are popular in Thai restaurants, try Thai Cuisine (**www.thaicuisine.com**). A veritable feast of recipes for lovers of Indian food, as well as shopping tips and references, may be found at **www.daawat.com**, while Indian recipes abound at **www.sanjeevkapoor.com**.

Gastroscout (**www.gastroscout.com**) is a comprehensive guide to restaurants across Germany, Switzerland, and Austria by state and city. Try **www.france.com/gastronomy** for information on regional French products and recipes, and order delicious products from the online shop of the Italian delicatessen Valvona & Crolla (based in Scotland) at **www.valvonacrolla.com**. For French dessert and side dish recipes, visit La Cuisine de Véronique (**www.cooking-french.com**). And lovers of great Italian chocolates and lots more simply must head to **www.carluccios.com** at once.

Good American food sites include Webicurean (**www.webicurean.com**) and Recipe Source (**www.recipesource.com**). A good example of a regional US food site can be found at FoodStop (**www.foodstop.com**), which takes you on a gourmet tour of New Orleans. For a more personal viewpoint, check out **www.gastronomer.com**, with guidance on eating and, amusingly, advice for young men on dining with young ladies.

Fast food is everywhere and that includes on the web. Burger King (**www.burgerking.co.uk**), McDonald's (**www.mcdonalds.com**), Domino's Pizza (**www.dominos.co.uk**), and Wendy's Restaurant (**www.wendys.com**) can all be found online. Before visiting any of these restaurants, check out Food Finder (**www.olen.com/food**), a US nutrition guide for some of the best-known restaurant chains in the world. The truth revealed!

Maybe you're trying to cut down on burger sessions. Try Cyberdiet (**www.cyberdiet.com**) for recipes, food facts, exercise plans, assessments, and motivation for a healthier lifestyle. Get back to basics with the Wheat Foods Council (**www.wheatfoods.org**), which provides nutritional information, news, discussion, and recipes for grain foods. And if you are worried about genetically modified food, hopefully the issues will be cleared up for you at **www.newscientist.com/hottopics/gm**.

Vegetarians are well catered for on the web, as proved by the excellent Living and Raw Foods (**www.living-foods.com**), a site which is dedicated to providing comprehensive information on vegetarian food, as well as recipes. Go Veg (**www.goveg.com**) is a bit less subtle, with news of current activism. Tarla Dalal (**www.tarladalal.com**) is a good source of vegetarian recipes from India and around the world. Political veggies should visit the Vegetarian Society of the United Kingdom (**www.vegsoc.org**), which features vegetarian news, as well as recipes and online shopping facilities. Discussions are held at Veggie Life (**www.veggielife.com**), where the forum is accompanied by recipes, press articles, and online shopping.

Expand your drinking horizons at the Joy of Sake (**www.joyofsake.com**), which provides product information on Japanese rice wine. Wines and Food from France (**www.frenchwinesfood.com**) carries some good basic information on French wines, as well as interesting recipes and the lowdown on cheeses, while **www.winedine.co.uk** is an online magazine for lovers of, unsurprisingly, wine and food. Or, if you just want wine, then check out the great deals on cases at Virgin Wines (**www.virginwines.com**).

GAMES

What the web doesn't "know" about computer games just isn't worth knowing. You'll find reviews, walkthroughs, cheat codes, and pictures of games that aren't even finished yet. If staring at a screen isn't your cup of tea, you'll be pleased to hear that there is also a huge amount of coverage provided by the Internet on board and card games. Resolve poker disputes with rules guides, and buy the latest *Star Wars* version of Monopoly to keep the family happy. There are cerebral sites for chess players, too many places for people interested in role-playing games, and plenty of online shops that will sell you anything from a PlayStation 2 to a set of dice.

Computer games

All about games
www.gamespot.com
GameSpot deals with computer games for the PC, Nintendo 64, Xbox, and PlayStation. There are reviews, strategy courses, news items, and features on games developments, hardware upgrades, and game artificial intelligence. Previews of up-and-coming games are also published regularly, and there is a calendar of approximate release dates for those long-awaited games, including an already impressive array of PlayStation 2 reviews. Cheat codes are provided, too, for those who can't win fair and square.

Avid about Xbox
www.xbox.com
Get the inside information on this games console from Microsoft. There are previews and reviews of the latest games and news stories covering all things Xbox, with opportunities to become part of the Xbox research team, community forums and technical support. Now with some great games under its belt, Xbox is finally giving the PS2 a run for its money.

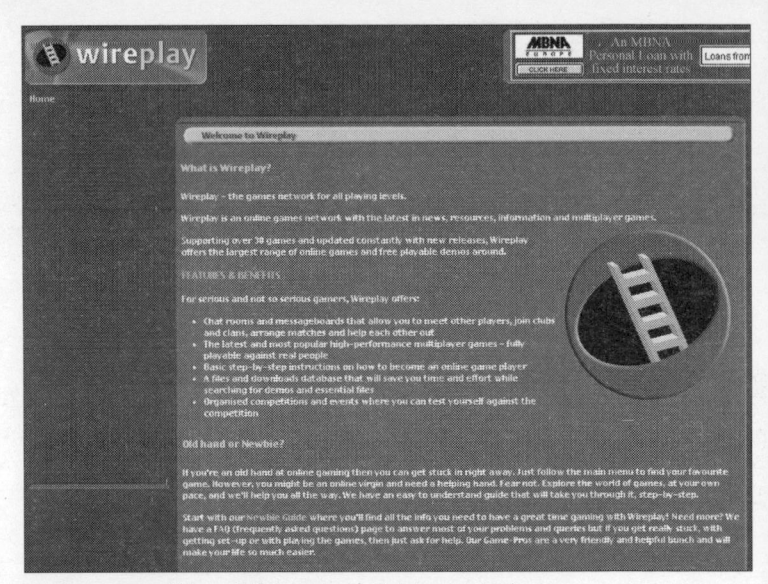

Hardcore gamers will have all their needs supplied at www.wireplay.com

GameBoy hints and tips
www.gameboy.com
Find out which are the essential GameBoy games, and seek help on the chat forums – or just go straight to the downloads section for previews and e-cards and other goodies. Release dates for the next load of games are available, and you can submit your own feelings in the Life Advanced section ...

Wireplay
www.wireplay.com
Wireplay is the free online games service – just download the software and play. There are lots of demos, patches, and more – in fact, everything that you would want from an online gaming environment. You can play by yourself or join a multiplayer free-for-all, then check out the community pages to talk about your experience. There's plenty of support and newbies are welcomed in gently. What are you waiting for?

Inside Mac Games
www.insidemacgames.com
As with many computer games sites, Inside Mac Games errs on the technical side, assuming that you know what an Unreal Tourney and MacMAME is. If you are in the market for such a site, you should visit this one. It's got all the news, the usual reviews, sneak previews, and some interesting views in the chat forum.

Kids' games
www.surfmonkey.com
Go on a voyage to the deep sea or a virtual trip to the desert, vote for your favourite pop star or get a sneaky preview of the newest Muppets movie. Designed to be a safe and fun place for kids to play online, this site offers a special web browser that keeps nasty Internet pages at bay, gives info to parents, and also provides great online games. The shop's stock includes toys, video games, and sports gear, and a chat forum lets kids run up their parents' phone bills.

UK gaming
www.ukgames.com
Not as pretty as other sites, but you are almost guaranteed to find out about every game released here. The home page shows the release dates of all the latest games and sells them at discount prices. Cheats, charts, demos, and discussion groups can all be found here, too.

News and software

The Adrenaline Vault
www.avault.com
Read the latest news about up-and-coming computer games, and download software fixes for the ones you bought last weekend, but cannot finish (because of the software bugs). You can check out the demos or get patches to improve your gameplay with your current games. You'll also find cheats and hints for those games that seem impossible to finish.

PC games news and updates
www.bluesnews.com
For real PC gamers who know their TNT2 from their MODs, this techie website publishes the latest news (updated daily) on 3D games, including software updates, as well as features on optimizing your mouse (really) and where the next network game party is happening. There are links to similar sites, God help us.

PlayStation
www.absolute-playstation.com
Claiming to undergo updates three times a day (you're never going to visit that often, now are you?), Absolute PlayStation offers a seriously large archive of games reviews, previews, and tips. You can choose to find out what is new either in the United States or Europe for the PSX or PS2.

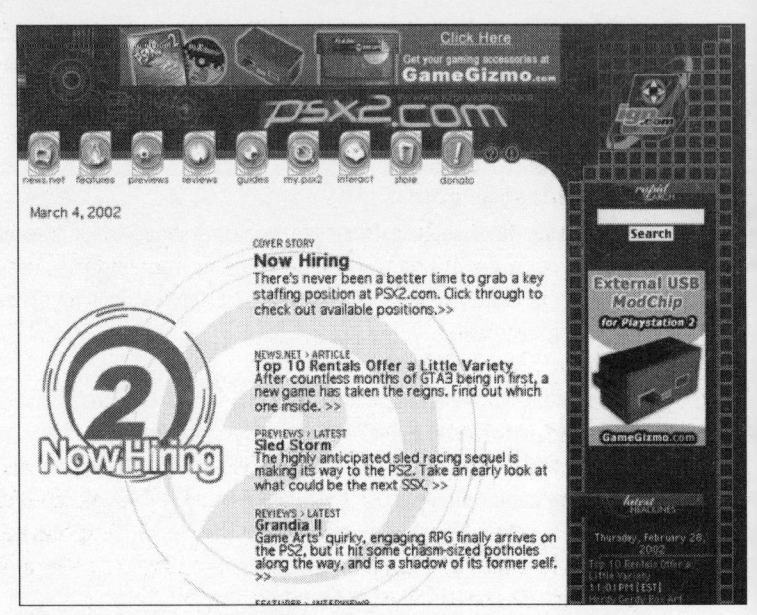

Hints, tips, and reviews for PlayStation 2 games can be found at www.psx2.com

PlayStation2 in depth
www.psx2.com
Find out everything there is to know about the PlayStation2, including cheat codes, game guides, previews, reviews, release dates, hot deals, and the latest accessories. Swap cheats and tips, and chew the fat with fellow gamers on the busy chat forum.

Old favourites

The annals of toy history
www.historychannel.com/exhibits/toys
Trace the development of toys and games from 4000 BC to today with the History Channel, and learn about some of the milestones along the way. Favourites such as the yo-yo, Barbie, and Monopoly are featured, along with their inventors.

British Chess Federation
www.bcf.org.uk
This most uncomplicated of sites contains a huge amount of information, including details about local UK clubs, tournaments, and news articles from the

national press. National Club Championship rules are published, as is the monthly newsletter. There are no playing tips, which is extremely disappointing, although a few links may take you to sites where you can play the game.

Foosball/table football
www.foosball.com
Refine your table football technique with the library of tutorial images and movies, learn the official rules inside and out, discover trick shots, and even discover the history of the game that revolutionized sixth-form common rooms absolutely everywhere.

The Game Report
www.gamereport.com
This is the online version of a quarterly magazine by the same name. It concentrates on card, dice, and board games, and reviews the latest arrivals. The site has a partnership with an online games shop and hosts games auctions, too. Extracts from the paper magazine are sometimes published online as well. Leave your comments on its various news features.

Mr Potato Head
www.mrpotatohead.com
Nearly everyone has had a Mr Potato Head, so he needs no introduction. Follow his life, using the "Tater Timeline" and the scrapbook, or just visit the fun corner and, among other things, construct your own spud head online.

North American Tiddlywinks Association
www.tiddlywinks.org
You'll be eating, sleeping, and drinking tiddlywinks by the time you've finished absorbing the information held on this wink-flicking site. You can learn the rules, advanced strategies, and how to talk like a bona fide winker. There are international tournaments to take part in, too, details of which are all here. So start practising!

Online games and puzzles

Board games and mental skill exercises
www.msoworld.com
Providing coverage of the Mind Sports Olympiad, as well as a set of message boards for like-brained people to chat, this site is a hub of cranial activity. There is a free puzzle section where you can download favourites such as tic-tac-toe or

draughts, and new puzzles are posted on the site every day, and there is also an area where you can play games online. There are a host of IQ tests and a massive network of links to other "mind sports sites", too.

Family favourites
www.hasbro.com
Home of an extraordinary range of family game favourites that include Monopoly, Scrabble, the Game of Life, and Risk, Hasbro's site also provides free online games in the "Fun Area" that you can play right from your web browser program. So now you can easily play ActionMan Avalanche Extreme or Mr Potato Head. Don't let your boss catch you, mind ...

Gamesville – bingo and other games
www.gamesville.lycos.com
Play multiplayer, online games such as bingo, pop trivia quizzes, and American football pools, and you may even win prizes or cash. These games are free to join in with. Just make sure that you carefully read all the small print on the site, and also check that gambling is legal in your country/state before you start playing any of the gambling games.

Lexigrams
www.lexigrams.com
This site is a bit disturbing if you don't understand what a lexigram is, and, as no online dictionaries or encyclopedias I've found provide adequate explanation, I'm afraid you're on your own! Suffice to say, you'll only enjoy Lexigrams if you like clever word play. Very weird place (that's one).

Playnet
www.playnet.com
Register here and begin online gaming – you can win prizes at games such as Wild Card (find out the rules on the site!) as well as take part in the chat forums. All game types are covered, from RPG to shoot-'em-ups.

Zarf's List of interactive games on the Web
www.leftfoot.com
Want to know who's playing the latest web-based, multiplayer interstellar space conquest game and how to join in? Or maybe you fancy exerting your influence over an online web village. Whether it's role play or a trivia quiz you're after, Zarf is a good place to start, offering links and advice on a wealth of games resources, as well as other online strategy and adventure power struggles going on right now in far-flung corners of the web.

Everything for the 'triv' fan at www.trivialpursuit.com

Telegraph Premier League
www.telegraphpremierleague.com
Play *The Daily Telegraph's* online fantasy football game at this site and have all the information that you could possibly need at your fingertips. You can set up any number of teams here and log on as regularly as you like to administer to them. Give the game a try, then compete against the hundreds of other bored managers out there ...

Trivia challenges
www.puzzles.cwc.net/trivia-index.html
There's no escaping it – playing trivia games is one of the most popular pastimes on the net. Take your pick from SoYouThinkYouKnow ..., played for a multitude of prizes; TRIVIA BLITZ, played for cash prizes; or a selection of challenges, played just for the fun of it! From the Simpsons to Shakespeare, you'll soon be a pub quiz expert or the world's biggest bore!

Trivial Pursuit
www.trivialpursuit.com
Discover the multitude of versions of this popular game, as well as its origins. An online version is available, where you play against other people for prizes. Downloading the necessary file may take a long time, but, if you're going to play a whole Triv game over the Internet, then this won't bother you, will it? As long as you have unmetered access of course ...

Budding Merlins should find all the info they need at www.wizards.com

Word games and puzzles
www.thinks.com
This is an odd, mixed-up site that offers "brain games, puzzles, and pastimes". It actually contains a large number of links disguised as content. However, there are a good section on words and wordplay, a plethora of online web games, and some interesting fractal images and generated music.

For other mind tests see "Intelligence Sites" in Education, page 74.

Role-playing games

Fantasy games
www.games-workshop.com
Official home of the Warhammer role-playing games, Lord of the Rings and many other fantasy pursuits, Games Workshop publishes sets of rules and special offers. There is information here on painting, collecting, and playing. You can also browse through a few of the countless Citadel miniature figurines available or download icons for your mobile. No Lord of the Ringtones yet, though.

Online multiplayer game world
www.avalon-rpg.com
Avalon is an online game, the likes of which many of us just don't have time to

encounter. It is a multiplayer role-playing game that runs in real time and works in an evolving online world where your actions could, theoretically, affect every other player. You can read the histories of other players' endeavours if you can't actually be bothered to play yourself.

Role Playing Game Association
www.rpg.net
A seemingly unlimited number of fantasy resources are available here for the dedicated avoider of reality if you live in the British Isles or South Africa. Computer software generates characters for a number of games, automatic dice rolling can be done online, and there are links to dark corners – where the arcane art of putting capes on and running around with rubber swords in groups is published.

Wizards of the Coast
www.wizards.com
If the games Dungeons & Dragons, Magic: The Gathering, or Pokémon (the card game) mean anything to you, you'll know that Wizards of the Coast publishes them all, along with stacks of others. Each game has its own area, sometimes providing such things as (free) character sheets and attributes, and the latest must-have add-ons (not free).

Rules and information

Card games
www.pagat.com
If you can't remember what beats a straight flush in poker, or what happens when it's the banker's turn in pontoon, this is the place to seek help. It is an utterly comprehensive guide to card game rules and links to frequently asked questions.

Gambling e-magazine
www.gamemasteronline.com
Thoroughly digest the "Casino Survival Guide", where you can learn which games pose the least disadvantages and consult the online adviser to become clued up with the hot tips for playing many card games including video poker, craps, and blackjack. There is also a special report on Internet gambling using online casinos.

Gaming dictionary
www.gamedev.net/dict
This online dictionary is not just restricted to computer gaming terminology –

some of the terms are indeed generic to computers or the Internet, but the main thrust is to explain the repeated jargon that crops up on almost every gaming website. It's good news that this site exists because anyone who claims to know about trilinear filtering is either downright lying or just won't spare the time to explain it to you.

Scrabble
www.scrabble.com
Anything from the basics right up to "weird words" that you can use to get rid of those pesky letters is included on this site, along with hints and tips, history, competitions, and some winning ways from the world's top Scrabble players. A Chamber's Scrabble word checker is on hand to sort out disputes, and there is also a children's area for all you younger fans, with various other games with which to expand your minds.

Wargames Forum
www.wargames.co.uk
This is a terrifyingly comprehensive site, devoted to little metal and plastic models used in war games. You can find businesses that will paint them for you, discover new ranges of figures, and use the searchable index of the *Miniature Wargames* magazine. There's much more than just this, though. See the site for yourself.

— Toy histories and collectibles —

Arcade games archive
www.gamearchive.com
If you have a thing for the arcade games of old (ie from around 1976), then this enormous archive of what I can only call "stuff" will doubtless satisfy. The electric wiring for many different pinball machines is documented, pre-production sketches from famous arcade favourites are included here, and there are answers to technical questions that normal people just don't ask. Sound interesting? Then visit it yourself and find out more.

Fast food toy collectibles
www.fastfoodtoys.com
Aimed at those who collect the toys you get at fast food outlets, Aunt Linda obviously spends too much time at McDonald's, as 99 per cent of her collection comes from there. There are toys and memorabilia, although when it gets to staff pins it might be time to call someone ...

You can find a list of those useful two-letter words, in any language, at www.scrabble.com

For all toy enthusiasts
www.toy.co.uk
This site provides a service enabling toy collectors to find new things to fill their spare rooms with. Essentially the site contains some very handy links to toy museums, magazines, and books. A chat forum is available for collectors to haggle on, and a list of essential toys is provided for the astute purchaser. Still promised are online shopping, toy reviews, and worldwide contacts.

History of home video games
www.videogames.org/html
This site has a museum with a directory of video game sites categorized in an original way — by the year the games were released. And the dates go right back. For example, if you remember playing a tennis-style game back in 1975 you'll find that Atari Pong was the one. There are all sorts of interesting details about each video game available for your perusal.

Star Wars figures
www.rebelscum.com
The one-stop shop for *Star Wars* figure collectors, Rebelscum also looks closely at other action figures, Lego, and other collectors' collections. You can find out about custom figures, too, and view some film scenes re-enacted with these toys, possibly by people with far too much time on their hands.

Toy collecting
r2toyforce.net
If you collect action figures from television shows or films, this is the site for you. The $3^3/_4$-inch Archives have information on all products released from your favourite shows from *Airwolf* to *Zorro*, with helpful links to related sites. So if you need to complete your Simpsons collection or find out if there were ever a *Love Boat* action range, this is the place to start.

Toys 'R' Us
www.toysrus.co.uk
Avoid dragging mewling children around shops crowded with other people's brats by doing your shopping at this impressive online toy shop. There are also links to toy manufacturers so that you can check out the latest train sets or Barbie dolls. Strangely, you can buy mobile phones here, too (Bob the Builder ones, actually).

See also "Collections" in Hobbies, pages 152–4.

g — see also...

One of the very first "practical" uses of the Internet was to provide access to games, and this fine tradition continues today. There are online magazines such as *PC Gamer Online* (**www.pcgamer.com**), which provides news of the latest computer game titles. There is always plenty of opinion on the web, and *Game Over Online* (**www.game-over.net**) publishes alternative previews, reviews, and games' cheats. Some people prefer to play games on console systems such as Sega, PlayStation 2, and the sadly now defunct Dreamcast. If you are one of those individuals, then you should look to websites such as PlanetDreamcast (**www.planetdreamcast.com**) for information on the games still available. Games Domain (**www.gamesdomain.co.uk**) will appeal to those PC games players who want to know how to beat popular titles and find out what everyone else is buying. Similarly, GamerZone (**www.gamerzone.com**) will appeal to owners of PCs and consoles games, providing a forum to swap tips with other players. PC games are big business. If you get stuck, make sure that you get your money's worth by visiting the game's own website for hints, tips, and cheats. Here are a few suppliers and game sites to get you started ...

ActiVision (**www.activision.com**) is the home of many popular PC, Mac, and console games, including the Quake range of titles. The Stomping Grounds (**www.stomped.com**) covers all things Quake, including weird add-ons developed by other players, and the other tournament games, including Unreal.

Games

Eidos Interactive (**www.eidosinteractive.com**) is a leading creator of PC games providing forums, clubs, and demos. Epic Games (**www.epicgames.com**) is the place to go for the great Quake-pretender, Unreal, and Unreal Tournament – if you want to play other players online, go to GameSpy Arcade (**www.mplayer.com**), although those outside the United States might experience slow gaming. Visit id Software (**www.idsoftware.com**) to find the source of all today's 3D first person kill-'em-up games. Gamers.org (**www.gamers.org**) is holding the torch for the classic 3D game Doom, with extra levels to download and links to modern 3D games' sites. Try **www.tombraider.com** if you are just desperate to see the latest screen shots of Lara.

Windows manufacturer Microsoft also makes the Xbox and related games, the details of which may be found at **www.microsoft.com/games**, and includes **www.zone.msn.com**. It also gives some valuable information for its various consoles, such as Sidewinder, which are used with many PC games. NovaLogic (**www.novalogic.com**) is the place to find updates for a good many military simulation games, while Vivendi Universal Games (**www.vugames.com**) will also be of assistance should you own Homeworld, or any of its other groundbreaking efforts. Not all computer games use 3D graphics. FunBets (**www.funbets.com**) provides a range of share dealing games. On a more traditional note, the Domino Games site (**www.gamecabinet.com/rules/DominoGames.html**) provides all the dominos rules you can handle. Or did you ever love drawing with your Etch a Sketch (**www.etch-a-sketch.com**)? Alternatively, are you a loner who loves playing solitaire (**www.solitairegames.com**)?

The Internet is games heaven for those with the console. Game Pro is a must for the hardcore gamer, with tips for PlayStation, Nintendo, Xbox, and PC games. GameScanner (**gamescanner.com**) is also another very good site.

Playing games need not be a solitary affair. Family Game Night (**www.hasbro.com/familygamenight**), run by Hasbro, contains explanations of games and guides for popular family games such as Monopoly. You can find people to play Internet games with at Access Denied (**www.accessdenied.net**). Excite Games (**games.excite.com**) features online board, card, word, and arcade games. You can use the rules here for fun in the living room, too. Those in need of strategy, and possibly the odd Orc or two, will find plenty of websites to plunder. GameWorld Technologies (**www.gameworld.com**) features live role-playing games and other online adventures.

HEALTH

Whether you are looking after your family's health, would like to try some alternative therapies, or just want to keep fit, there is an abundance of help and advice waiting for you online. You'll find special diets, information about drugs, literature on sex education, and calculators that will help you to assess how healthy you really are. And because the Internet is more interactive than a leaflet from your GP's surgery, you can ask questions and research areas as much and as deeply as you want, until you feel much more in control of your own health.

Alternative therapies

Align your biorhythms
www.facade.com/biorhythm
Need to keep in tune with your energies? This online engine will plot the interactions of your physical, emotional, and intellectual biorhythms when you enter your birth details. Other parts of the site provide advice and guidance.

Alternative Medicine magazine
www.alternativemedicine.com
This regular online magazine is a digest of all things offbeat. Holistic practices can be found here alongside reflexology and nutrition therapies. For those willing to suspend their disbelief, this US magazine is well worth the subscription fee.

British Medical Acupuncture Society
www.medical-acupuncture.co.uk
This UK site aims to promote the ancient Chinese practice of acupuncture, but it is also up to the minute with the latest reviews of acupuncture-related software. As well as this it includes details of meetings and courses for practitioners. Downloadable PDF documents provide information and advice on the whole subject, and a search engine helps you to find and identify qualified practitioners.

Find advice on everything unconventional at www.alternativemedicine.com

in your area. Those interested in learning more about acupuncture for themselves can find details of courses listed here, too. A thoroughly useful site.

Homeopathy
www.homeopathyhome.com
Make this site your first port of call for queries about the world of homeopathy. Here you'll find frequently updated news on this popular branch of alternative medicine and details of forthcoming educational courses and seminars, together with bookshop links of various countries, enabling you to buy titles on the topic over the Internet. Online chat and message boards let you swap views and experience with like-minded users.

National Federation of Spiritual Healers
www.nfsh.org.uk
This UK body promotes healing by prayer or meditation. Its site provides a crash course in the practice and a service to find a willing healer in your area. It even extols the virtues of "distant healing" over the Internet.

Natural health info and shop
www.thinknatural.com
Find out what herbs and oils will help with insect bites, rashes, and menopause, as well as learning about homeopathy and natural bodycare. A shop is available

which sells vitamins, aromatherapy oils, and other items to keep you young and happy. If you need to alleviate depression and allergies, then look no further – those are just two of the areas that this site has items available to help you with. You can also select gifts for your friends and family.

UK directory of alternative therapy centres
www.synergy-health.co.uk
Aside from selling decidedly non-prescription remedies, Synergy provides a useful directory of complementary therapists in the United Kingdom. The regularly updated "Health News" provides some useful pointers towards alternative health, and the site's listings let you know what's going on in your area. A prescription drug database gives information on side effects and drugs that don't mix.

Beauty sites

All your questions answered
www.makeupdiva.com
This site is basically a straightforward question-and-answer session on all aspects of beauty. It covers health and beauty regimes for skin and hair, too. You can subscribe to the free "Ask Diva" weekly e-mail, but, if you can't find what you're looking for in the archive, fire off a question to the Diva yourself. A link to Heather Kleinman's Cosmetic Connection (**www.cosmeticconnection.com**) gives you access to more vital cosmetic and make-up info and reviews – go for it, girls!

Beauty consultancy for aesthetic surgery
www.wlbeauty.com
This painfully pink website, Wendy Lewis & Co, dishes out well-meaning beauty advice on cajoling back into shape those wrinkles, bags, and body parts that migrate as we grow older. Any questions? Ask the pleasantly named Beauty Junkie. And if that doesn't work, Wendy's got plenty of links to a surgeon who can, with consultations in London and New York ...

Health and wellbeing
www.beautyenquiries.com
Beauty Enquiries aims to skip the jargon and get you on the right track with your health, beauty, and wellbeing routines. You can e-mail its team of experts for advice or explore the list of UK salons available. A lengthy list of problems may make you feel somewhat worse than when you began. Let's hope the sensible advice does its job.

Create your perfect look
www.beautyandthedirt.co.uk
A fresh and funky site with fun animated icons for the social butterfly. Mimi, a busy make-up artist, dishes the dirt on the latest fashion and beauty products and spills the gossip and the lowdown on men and shopping. Share a martini with Mimi as you read her reviews of bars and eateries in London and New York, as she swans from party to party. Mmwah, Dahling!

Dental health

American Dental Association
www.ada.org
This site offers information and resources for patients and dental professionals alike. There are details about dental treatments and diseases, along with a guide to dental benefits and a directory that will help you to find a dentist in your area – if you live in the United States, of course.

British Dental Association
www.bda-dentistry.org.uk
The BDA's online presence is aimed both at practitioners and patients. The "Dentists" section offers support for professionals, while the "Public" section provides articles on aspects of dentistry for general readers. A handy directory also helps users to locate a dentist in their area.

A guide to dental healthcare
www.jnj.oralhealth.com
This site from healthcare firm Johnson & Johnson provides basic dental health and hygiene advice to kids via some colourful cartoon characters. The site provides an easy step-by-step guide on how to brush teeth. Interactive diagrams help parents and kids alike to learn a little dental terminology.

Disorders and illnesses

All about the heart
www.heartpoint.com
Everything you didn't know, and probably didn't want to, about the human heart and its frequently found conditions may be found here. There are health tips to

www.kidshealth.org is full of practical suggestions for bringing up your child

keep your ticker in top shape, nutritional guides – including lots of recipes – and an editorial page where professionals give their views on healthcare developments.

My Wavelength
www.mywavelength.com
If you are suffering from an illness or caring for someone with an illness, sometimes only a person who has experienced this can truly understand and empathize with what you have been going through. Now you can talk to those people worldwide. This service is and will always be free. People can chat to like-minded people about their hobbies, interests, plans, and aspirations. Anyone and everyone is welcome. It's a great idea.

Macmillan Cancer Relief
www.macmillan.org.uk
Macmillan nurses form part of the backbone of cancer care in the United Kingdom. The home pages of Macmillan Cancer Relief help to put patients in touch with the resources in their area and also provide online access to various self-help publications such as *The Cancer Guide*. There's worthwhile advice to sufferers on the various benefits they're entitled to, and details on how you can support the charity.

Marie Curie
www.mariecurie.org.uk
The excellent site of UK cancer care charity, the Marie Curie Foundation, is a superb source of information for sufferers, carers, and those wishing to make a

donation. This well-designed site hosts information on fund-raising events, Marie Curie campaigns, and news about care and treatments. The "Day in the Life" column written by a Marie Curie nurse is worth a special look.

Mental health issues
www.mentalhealth.com
This site draws together a range of resources on mental health issues. A list of conditions is available, with definitions for both North American and European physicians, and there is an excellent encyclopedia of the most popular psychiatric medications. It also outlines treatment plans and provides diagnostic tests.

Migraine Action Association
www.migraine.org.uk
The UK site of charity Migraine Action aims to increase awareness of this common but debilitating condition. Here, you'll find information on symptoms, as well as help and support contacts for sufferers. The site also features a brief discussion of treatments for migraines and lists the common migraine triggers such as stress, environmental factors, and certain foods. The site provides an online facility for subscribing to the organization and a list of clinics.

Schizophrenia
www.openthedoors.com
A friendly site, accessible in five European languages, that seeks to demystify this misunderstood disorder. There is information for professionals and for families with schizophrenics, as well as a place where personal stories can be submitted.

Family health

Kids Health
www.kidshealth.org
Created by the Nemours Foundation's Center for Children's Health Media, the award-winning KidsHealth provides families with accurate, up-to-date, and jargon-free health information that they can use. KidsHealth has been on the web since 1995. Enter as parents, kids, or teens, and discover sites specially catering to each in design and tone. Well worth a look, even before you have an ailment.

Family issues and advice
www.thefamilycorner.com
This online counselling site hands out some useful, practical advice on home and

parenting issues from household budgeting to divorce. Articles are sensitive and well pitched for the average reader – unusually for this type of site on the Internet, Family Corner (largely) avoids lapsing into psychobabble. Join the community boards and chat with other parents about childrens' issues.

For all parents-to-be
www.babyworld.co.uk
Babyworld provides tons of useful information for mothers- and fathers-to-be, with in-depth articles on pregnancy and child health. Even legal issues surrounding childcare are given a thorough airing. You can put any burning questions to professionals: there are midwives, doctors, and fertility experts on hand to put your mind at rest if need be. Registration is free and enables you to chat with others sharing the experience of parenthood. There's also an area for birth stories and baby diaries.

Grandparenting
www.cyberparent.com/gran
Leaving aside a bit of schmaltzy self-promotion on its introductory page, Grandparents' Web provides a sensible insight to the world of grandparenting. This site doesn't flinch from tackling thornier issues such as marital break-ups or discipline, and it offers excellent tips on making the most of the time spent looking after grandchildren.

Happy Families
www.happyfamilies.com
If your home life drives you nuts, why not stay sane by swapping anecdotes with like-minded types on the Internet? Happy Families is a site devoted to looking at the lighter side of family life, with users posting stories and advice. You can even swap stories about your pets if you really have an urge to do so. Other resources include light-hearted e-postcards, which you can send to friends and relatives to cherish or trash as they see fit.

Fitness

Aerobics
www.turnstep.com
Turnstep is a page of frequently asked questions containing information drawn from Usenet forums on aerobics. Recent changes include a complete overhaul of

the "pattern" search engine (that's the aerobics steps, to you and me), which now searches from a library of more than 12,000 moves. Beginners might like to start by making selections from the most recent 50 steps which can be found on the site's opening page.

All you need to know about yoga
www.yogasite.com
The Yoga Site takes a more hands-on approach to exercise. It offers instruction on postures, as well as links to other sites of yogic note that are to be found on the Internet. So if you're brave (or flexible) enough to attempt such specialities as the "cobra" or the "downward facing dog", then you'll find all you need to get started at this useful site.

American Heart Association magazine
www.justmove.org
Just Move is an upbeat online magazine from the American Heart Association. Judging by its youthful tone, its aim is to stamp out the risk of heart attack before it sets in. Practical advice abounds on getting out and about, and, above all, getting yourself fit. Well worth a peek for Internet-obsessed couch potatoes who need a bit of exercise!

Fun & Fitness
www.fun-and-fitness.com
This highly illustrated US site offers a user-friendly way for you to get fit. It is organized by zones, which each concentrate on muscle fitness and nutrition. Exercises are prescribed for each set of muscles, and these are presented in simple point-by-point text. The "Nutrition Zone" provides information on different food types, an explanation of metabolism, and can also recommend a personal diet and exercise combination for you. The "Fun Zone" has a quiz for you to see how well you've paid attention to the details given on the site. If you want a more traditional guide to improving fitness, then why not browse the "Fitness Bookshelf" to see what is available there.

Get fit the cool way
www.self.com
This is a suave website with fitness, nutrition, and weight loss advice. Practical articles (such as how to make the best of dining out), "body" calculators, and quizzes make this a more interactive site than many other sites of this ilk. You can also "Go for a Goal" – such as getting a six-pack. All the pages and categories are well illustrated and make this an excellent all-round health site. Well worth a visit if your aim is to get fit.

Great alternatives to dieting
www.ivillage.com
A good site for finding out more about health matters. There are various health centres to visit, an extensive library and resource centre, and a health calculator. Chat rooms deal with related topics, and there's even an online radio station to listen to while you browse. Packed with helpful tips and information. Waiting rooms were never this interesting.

Online health and fitness network
www.efit.com
Nutricise has a wealth of information for would-be exercise fanatics. The site boasts a massive quantity of superlative content, and special features examine topical health issues. Membership is free and entitles users to a free customized fitness programme.

The world of yoga
www.yoyoga.com
For those taking a (slightly) less active approach to fitness, the Yoyoga site promotes a holistic approach to getting in shape. Soothing words from celebrities, recipes for healthy eating, and some thought on the philosophy that lies behind this Eastern art are the order of the day here.

— Information and advice —

All you need to know about health
www.healthy.net
Arranged around a virtual "map" of health resources, this site covers all aspects of health, providing access to information and self-diagnosis tools, as well as general advice about how to keep yourself in tip-top condition. The style may be a bit fusty, but that's because it's aimed partially at professionals. In fact, the site provides access to Medline, the international medicine and pharmacy database.

ASH – Action on Smoking and Health
www.ash.org
ASH has been well known for badgering smokers into giving up for years. Its online presence provides more of the same, plus advice and support on combating those cravings of the evil weed. More interestingly, ASH lifts the lid on a few things that the tobacco industry has tried to keep quiet. Worth a look if you've been meaning to cut down a bit …

www.ivillage.com gives you new ideas about food and health

British Medical Journal
www.bmj.com
The electronic *British Medical Journal* features articles about the latest research and discoveries in the medical world from the paper version, as well as listings of jobs, courses, and careers. There is a searchable archive, a debating forum, and a letters page, too, and you can arrange for articles to be e-mailed straight to you hot off the press.

Drug abuse
www.trashed.co.uk
The Health Education Authority's stylish and hip site Trashed is all about substance abuse, with each drug's origins, their components and effects, and how the law deals with them. More streetwise types can search for drug information by typing street slang names for drugs into the site search engine.

First aid
www.parasolemt.com.au
Okay, so in a medical emergency you won't have time to log on to the Internet to find out what to do, but, if you spend a few minutes on this excellent website every week, then you'll be able to react more effectively if something nasty does happen. The subjects covered include how to deal with the traumas, as well as the first-aid training.

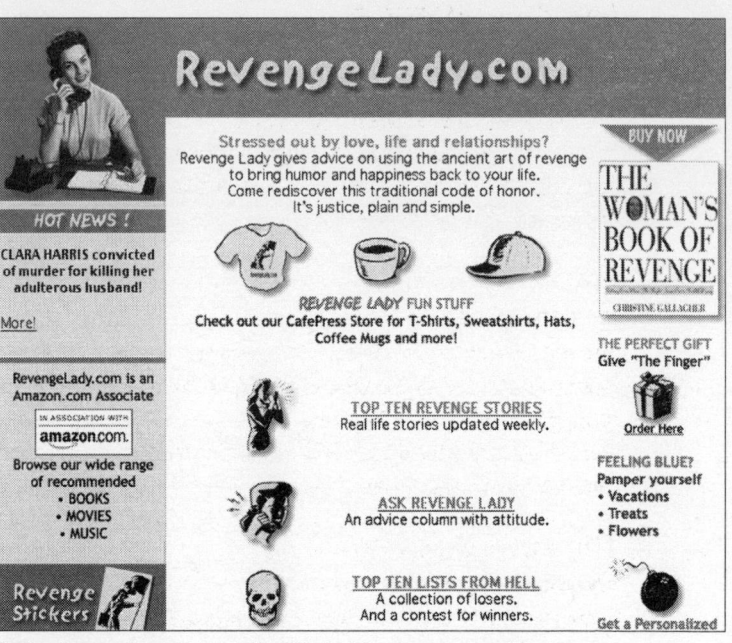

Feeling depressed about relationships? Seek advice at www.revengelady.com

Health advice for students
www.studenthealth.co.uk
It's no fun being ill when you're away at college. Click it better with this fun but informative site written by doctors and updated weekly. You may never have an excuse to miss a lecture again. Problem pages, advice leaflets, and warnings about carbon monoxide in student housing. Whatever you're reading, read this.

Healthcare issues
www.healthbond.com
US site HealthBond provides up-to-date information to businesses about policies and issues affecting healthcare, but it's also useful for patients to browse. It includes news on major political and legal stories in medicine, plus an interactive polling of users on important topics.

Information for all patients
www.patient.co.uk
Patient UK is a thorough primer on getting the best out of health services in Britain. This well-designed site includes a glossary of medical terms, information on and links to NHS services, health events, and details of patients' rights. A link to the Scoot business directory enables you to locate doctors in your area.

Live more healthily
www.adam.com
Learn how to live a healthier and therefore longer life with the advice from this site. You can ask the experts questions that you could never bring yourself to pose to your own GP, or just browse through the illustrated health encyclopedia and, of course, buy the goods on offer. Just make sure that you don't contract a good dose of paranoia while visiting the site ...

Lovelife advice
www.revengelady.com
Stressed out by life, love, and relationships? Let the slightly fierce-sounding Revenge Lady offer advice using the ancient art of revenge, which the site refers to as the "traditional code of honour". A somewhat tongue-in-cheek site for scorned lovers and the unlucky in love, it has games and quizzes, top ten lists, e-cards, and celebrity comeuppances.

The Love Calculator
www.lovecalculator.com
Sometimes you'd like to know if a relationship with someone could work out. Therefore Doctor Love himself designed this great machine for you. With the "Love Calculator", you can calculate the probability of a successful relationship between two people. Just type in your name and the name of your intended, and the likelihood of eternal happiness is calculated. So if you need to find out whether you and Britney or Robbie are perfect for each other, here's where dreams may come true. It's available for download, too, and there are links to other love-related sites. Thanks, Dr Love!

NHS Direct: health info and advice
www.nhsdirect.nhs.uk
Part of New Labour's strategy for cutting waiting lists, NHS Direct aims to get people out of GP's waiting rooms by providing basic diagnoses over the phone or online. Advice is given by trained nurses, and the topics covered are all basic ailments. There's also useful information on getting the best from NHS services.

Online Medical Dictionary
cancerweb.ncl.ac.uk/omd
Online cancer research body CancerWEB provides a patient-friendly glossary of medical terms, covering a broad sweep of disciplines. Words can be searched for alphabetically or by subject, and updates let users know about any recent entries and amendments. Word lists are long, though, so they may take time to download on your machine.

Private healthcare
www.privatehealth.co.uk
This site presents you with a a database of private healthcare resources in the United Kingdom online. There is guidance about using private care facilities and getting health insurance, as well as useful hospital and doctor finders. The site also features a database of nursing homes.

Terrence Higgins Trust
www.tht.org.uk
The Terrence Higgins Trust is one of the organizations at the forefront of AIDS awareness in the United Kingdom. Its online home provides advice to sufferers about treatments, legal issues, and other concerns, and it is aimed at gay and heterosexual people alike. The trust provides one-to-one support via its helpline number. You can also make a donation or even become a volunteer yourself.

Women's Health
www.bbc.co.uk/health/womens
This is part of the excellent BBC Online Health site aimed specifically at tackling female health issues. Easily digestible articles cover topics from osteoporosis to breast cancer, to the trials of cellulite and sexual health. You can "Ask the Doctor", with responses posted daily. The site even supplies links to pages on medically minded radio and TV programmes such as *Casualty* and *Horizon*.

Interactive sites

NOVA Online: Electric Heart
www.pbs.org/wgbh/nova/eheart
Find out all about the human heart, courtesy of this TV programme's website. There is an annotated, animated map of the organ, a list of "amazing" facts, and even a virtual operating theatre where you can perform a heart operation – if you don't mind downloading a few files first.

Visible Human Project
www.nlm.nih.gov/research/visible/visible_human.html
This is a groundbreaking project that involves slicing a male and female body into very thin slices (up to 1mm thick) for use in medical research. You can read about the project here and find links to related projects that have used the data, as well as learn to create your own interesting 3D images and movies using the images supplied by the project.

Nutrition

Ask the Dietitian
www.dietitian.com
This is a question-and-answer–driven site that covers all aspects of food, cooking, and nutrition. It also provides extensive material on eating disorders. The friendly, agony-aunt style enables Ask the Dietitian to tackle extremely thorny issues in a sensitive manner. The detailed articles are cross-referenced with hypertext links.

Cyberdieting
www.cyberdiet.com
If you are serious about going on a diet, then this site will answer all your questions and worries. There are categories on "Self Assessment", "Nutrition", and "Exercise and Fitness", and live chat forums where you can talk with others and receive answers to your questions from professionals.

Nutrition
www.mynutrition.co.uk
Beautifully designed and easy to navigate, you can find out everything to do with healthy food, eating, and supplements. Free consultation is available. The latest news and health library is supplied by Patrick Holford, a leading nutritionist.

Pharmaceuticals

Database of pharmaceuticals
www.rxlist.com
Here a database of currently prescribed pharmaceuticals allows users to access the official US government-approved patient information on any of the listed drugs, including prescription information and details of any known side effects. You can also check out the parent site, **www.healthcentral.com**.

Food and Drug Administration
www.fda.gov
This website is the home page of the US government's Food and Drug Administration, the regulatory body that approves drugs for prescription in the United States. It has an exhaustive database of pharmaceuticals and cosmetics, the latest news on medical drugs, and advice on buying drugs safely online.

Psychology

Psychology explored
www.psychology.com
This decidedly California-speaking online journal doesn't talk an awful lot of science – it's mostly aimed at punters wanting to improve their lives. There are plenty of online psychometric and personality tests here to scare yourself with and the chance to ask a therapist a couple of your burning questions. There is also a link to Amazon that enables the fraught to buy books that will sort them out. Or how about a gift certificate to give someone the gift of therapy? This is indeed a worthwhile place to call in ... but don't take it all too seriously.

The technology behind psychology
www.victoriapoint.com/catalyst.htm
This is an online journal examining psychology in the modern world – with specific reference to computers. Articles outline the good and bad in technology, covering topics from pathological Internet use to the benefits of using computers to analyse patient behaviour. The social effects of new technologies are discussed in some depth.

Sexual matters

Health awareness
www.intelihealth.com
This is a good-looking and informative general health site drawing resources from the Harvard Medical School, which is divided into "zones" for easy navigation. The site is particularly good on sexual health subjects, such as HIV and AIDS. Other "Featured Health Areas" include arthritis, diabetes, and pregnancy. There are useful links to other healthcare resources. The Flu-o-meter tells you which states are suffering the most.

Marie Stopes International
www.mariestopes.org.uk
Marie Stopes's pioneering birth control clinics provide advice and information to both men and women on issues from contraception and sterilization to abortion. Here you'll also find details of the location of local centres. There is no one-to-one online advice and a pregnancy calculator to sort out your dates.

catalyst.
on computers and psychology

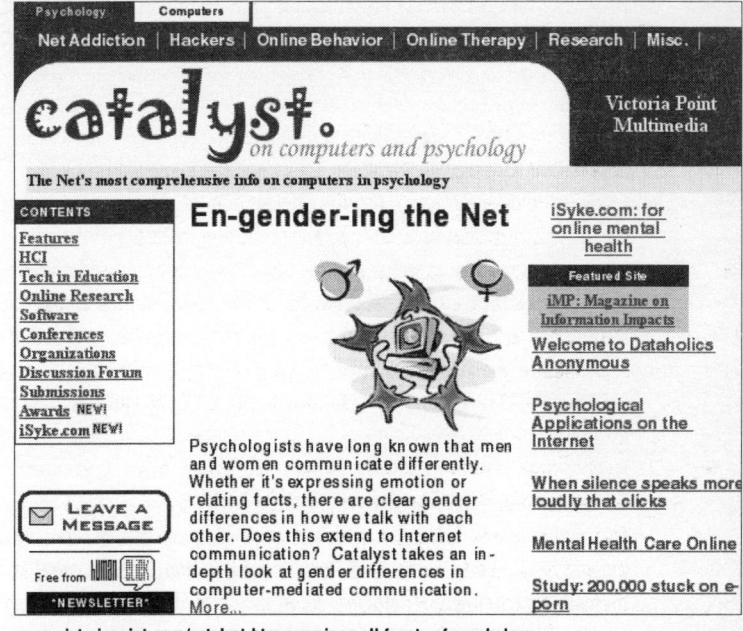

The Net's most comprehensive info on computers in psychology

En-gender-ing the Net

Psychologists have long known that men and women communicate differently. Whether it's expressing emotion or relating facts, there are clear gender differences in how we talk with each other. Does this extend to Internet communication? Catalyst takes an in-depth look at gender differences in computer-mediated communication. More...

www.victoriapoint.com/catalyst.htm examines all facets of psychology

Sexual freedom issues
www.glandscape.com

Stridently political — and mischievously titled — page arguing the case for sexual freedom. Covers homosexuality, pornography, celibacy, and disability, and other areas considered outside the sexual "mainstream". Topics are discussed seriously, but content can be explicit (cyberdildonic injuries, anyone?), so be warned!

Teenage health issues
www.iwannaknow.org

The web is an ideal medium for you to learn about issues such as sex that are too embarrassing to ask parents or friends about. Advice here from the American Social Health Association can seem uncompromisingly explicit, but it's necessarily so. Sound and reassuring.

Viagra
www.viagra.com

Viagra hit the headlines as a "miracle" cure for impotence, but this coverage was quickly followed by scare stories about the drug's less-wanted (and less-publicized) side effects. This site, created by drug manufacturer Pfizer, provides the company's official line — and addresses a number of the allegations.

— see also...

There is a huge number of sites on the Net with advice on staying fit and healthy. For starters, a trip to the online chemist run by Boots at www.wellbeing.com may be in order. Or you could consult the medical reference site at MedicineNet.com (www.medicinenet.com) for its advice and a store selling non-prescription medicines and beauty products. Hayfever sufferers may want to check pollen levels in their area at www.allergyinfo.com. Those undecided about parenting can get their facts straight at www.ippf.org, while couples considering help with fertility can find mutual support at www.fertilethoughts.net.

Of course, the happy arrival's only the first of your worries. As well as talking you through pregnancy, www.thebabiesplanet.com will help mums and dads through the early days after the birth, too, although you should try to ignore the terrible music on the home page! Dads even have their own channel on www.iparenting.com and www.fordads.com. Kids can find medical advice for themselves at www.brainpop.com, which has lots of movies to maintain their interest. But make sure that your mothers and fathers take good care of themselves, too: Home Doctor at www.web-internet-cafe.co.uk/doctor.htm should help you to do just that. Disorders and illness, unfortunately, befall many a person, and you will find excellent advice on the world wide web, including information on AIDS (www.hivpositive.com) and lesser ailments such as eczema (www.eczema.org), while www.mentalhealth.net has an extensive list of mental health professionals.

Some people say that if you look good, you'll feel good. And a quick trip to www.lorealparisusa.com should sort you out for health and beauty tips. Of course, if you're desperate (and rich) enough, www.cosmeticsurgery.org can advise on the latest in cosmetic surgery. More natural solutions to health issues can be pinpointed at www.accupuncture.com. For definitive guidance on alternative therapies, consult NOAH at www.noah-health.org.

One tragic fact of growing up in this current age is the risk of becoming involved with drugs, and www.homeoffice.gov.uk/atoz/drugs.htm will help to educate young adults and parents about the dangers.

Of course, you'd be better off never getting sick in the first place, and the web can help you nip those symptoms in the bud. Try health.discovery.com or www.cbull.com/health.htm for size. It pays to live well, too, and you can fight the flab at www.slimming-world.co.uk or www.shapeup.org. Men wanting to toughen up their torso can head to www.menshealth.co.uk for tips. Those who'd prefer to stay less paranoid about their physique should try www.bodypositive.com And for the follically challenged among us, visit www.regaine.co.uk for the latest in miracle treatments for hair.

But there's only so much you can do for yourself, and sometimes you'll need to call in the professionals. In the United Kingdom, that's the British Medical Association. You'll find its website at **web.bma.org.uk**. BUPA, Britain's largest private healthcare provider, can be found at **www.bupa.co.uk**. The latest information on nursing can be found at **www.nursing-standard.co.uk**. Help and advice on nursing in a crisis are on the web at **www.emergency-nurse.com**.

HOBBIES

No matter what your hobby or interest, someone else who shares your passion will have created a website dedicated to your favourite pastime. The most popular activities, including driving, crafts, and collecting, are admirably catered for online, more often by amateur than professional sites, while there are thousands of more esoteric sites out there. You can live vicariously through the experiences of other hobbyists, pick up hints and tips on how to spend your free time more efficiently, and even brighten up your computer with related pictures, icons, and screensavers. If your hobby is not listed among those here, then put your hobby into a search engine – you can almost guarantee that you will find a relevant site out there ...

Animals

All things aquatic
www.aqualink.com
If you keep, or would like to build and maintain, an aquarium, the information on this site could prove invaluable for you. AquaLink covers tropical fish from fresh water and marine environments, and its online store should be able to provide for all your specialist needs. An online disease diagnoser could help to save your fishies' lives at some point in the future.

Birding on the web
www.birder.com
Use this site to find out the best places to go bird watching, receive alerts when rare birds have been spotted all over the world, and browse the Nature Store for more than 3000 related titles, some possibly going cheep ... There are links to images, bird songs, and games, too. (For bird organizations see "The Natural World", pages 211–25.)

Find out about caring for your favourite pet animals at www.petsmart.com

Choosing and caring for your pet
www.petsmart.com
Pet Smart claims to offer a clear pawspective (ouch!) to help in the decision-making process of pet care, whether it's what kind of food to feed your kitten or what the best training techniques are for a stubborn pup. This large site is packed with useful information on the tiniest critter to looking after a horse. There are pet food calculators to make sure that they don't go hungry, or you can just submit a pic of your pooch for pet of the day.

The Complete Hamster Site
www.petwebsite.com/about_hamsters.html
Hamster fans can find out everything they need to know about looking after the different varieties of these fluffy rodents. There is a chat forum, lists of approved books and care products, and a few nice images of hamsters for you.

Pet accessories
www.groovypets.com
Now you can browse and find everything you could possibly be looking for. Whether you have pets yourself or are looking for that "Groovy" gift for someone who has one, no pet-owning home should go without these unusual, exclusive products. From aromatherapy products to luxurious beds and baskets, or maybe you can spoil them rotten with some, er, jewellery. I'm sure they're worth it …

152 Hobbies

Serious collectors can bid on items worldwide at www.icollector.com

UK Animal Rescuers
www.animalrescuers.co.uk
This small but handy site lists most of the animal charities and organizations you're likely to need if you have an animal in trouble. There are "Lost and Found" notices and links to animal rights activist groups, although there appears to be no political preaching on this site.

— Collections —

Clarice Cliff – Art Deco ceramics
www.claricecliff.co.uk
Collectors of Clarice Cliff pottery can use this site's services to get a valuation for insurance purposes, view available items in the classified ads, and offer their own pieces for sale. "The Guide to Shapes" should help you date your favourite pieces. Unfortunately, a silly design element makes this site slow and a touch irritating.

Collecting coins
www.pcgs.com
Calculate the value of your coin collection with the Professional Coin Grading Service. Discover the rarity of your coins and see how they compare to others. The

daily price guide keeps an eye on the markets, and a Submission Center allows you to let the PCGS experts to do their stuff. A look at the lingo would probably be helpful before you start.

Directory of dealers and retailers
www.collectiques.co.uk
If you are a collector, whether of barometers or Beanie Babies, Collectiques's large online directory of dealers and retailers should help you to acquire more stuff. You can also buy tomorrow's antiques from the site, such as a Noddy Toyland Car or a model of the Millennium Dome. The "Library", containing "The Hallmark Database" and articles on antique collecting, adds value to what is already an extremely useful website.

Internet Collector
www.icollector.com
Trust me when I say that every form of collectible item is available for auction at this site. The site acts as a portal to the world's auction houses and allows you to bid on any item you want. Subscribe to the "My Agent" service, which will search the auction houses for the items you want and send you the results by e-mail. The site is very easy to navigate and is a must-see if you are serious about collecting.

Pokémon cards
www.pokemon.com
The playground craze has naturally transferred online and includes all the information needed to trade Pokémon and Digimon cards successfully, including prices, strategy, the various cards, and news links. There are also areas for the next new crazes, Dragon Ball and Monster Rancher.

Scrapbook ideas
www.scrapbook.com
If your idea of fun on a wet weekend is to attend to your scrapbook, you might pick up a few handy tips from this site. You'll find good ideas, a huge community layout gallery, featured artists, poems, articles, and message boards. The Scrapbook.com Superstore will supply all your bits and pieces.

Stamp collecting
www.bl.uk/collections/philatelic
The British Library's website contains a rather sparse philatelic section, which has details of its stamp collections, speckled with a few close-up photos of old specimens. Researchers wanting to drop in will find the contact details handy, as well as details of the library's services, including photography and maps.

Stamp info and services
www.wardrop.co.uk
Stamp collectors will be over the moon when they see the wealth of information available here. There are details about philatelic software, including databases of stamp analysing programs and virtual albums. Wardrop's "Philately Online" will help you find a trading site, request an insurance quote for your collection, and seek out a local stamp club.

Toy soldier collections
www.williamking.com
Serious toy soldier collectors can subscribe to William King Military Miniatures to receive notification when new model sets are released or just to buy from the current stock. The online store deals with dollars and sterling, and all the items are illustrated and come with small background histories.

Crafts

For all woodworkers
www.woodprojects.com
Browse through Wood Projects's thousands of plans for inspiration. Once you have selected a plan, you will discover that some are free courtesy of the suppliers, while others can be bought straight off the page. References to practical books are sprinkled throughout, and the site's owner guarantees that the projects are linked to shops with the lowest prices.

Furniture and object design
www.house-of-design.nl
Find inspiration to design your own furniture and other bits and pieces for the house by viewing the work of other designers and using the links to categorized sites specializing in textiles, jewellery, and architecture. You can also view a catalogue of previous and current exhibitions.

Home Sewing Association
www.sewing.org
Containing free sewing projects, tips, and a comprehensive collection of online lessons, this site is ideal for all those that are wanting to design their own clothes or even if you are just hoping to take up a pair of trousers. A page dedicated to younger readers contains fun tasks such as groovy CD bags and computer wrist rests to make.

Hobbies 155

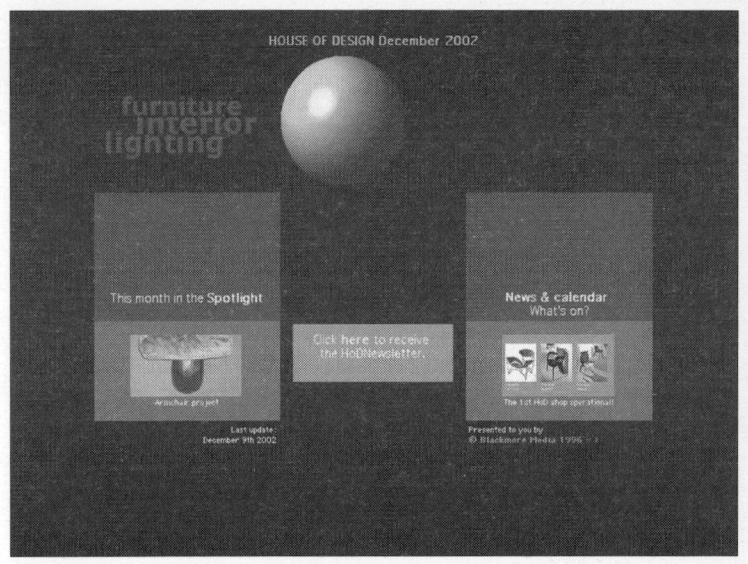

Everything you need to know to start designing your own furniture at www.house-of-design.nl.

Knitting compendium
www.woolworks.org
Providing information for those who like to knit, Wool Works has an archive of patterns including sweaters for adults, clothing for toddlers, and even dolls with accompanying accessories. There are photographs of garments that other readers have made, as well as advanced hints and tips on tricky and sometimes vexing subjects such as sock heel options.

The Lace Guild
www.laceguild.demon.co.uk
The Lace Guild's site will help you to find out when the next UK lace exhibitions are happening; locate suppliers of relevant books, courses, and, of course, lace; and browse through a limited number of articles from the newsletter. There is also a small introduction to the craft and a mail order service for buying some books containing patterns direct from them.

Make your own candles
www.candlecauldron.com
Don't spend a fortune buying candles when you can make your own for pennies. The Candle Cauldron gives advice on how to mix scents to make smelly candles, as well as providing a dictionary of candlemaking terms and a troubleshooting

www.ancestry.com allows genealogists to trace their, and other, families' history

guide. The measurement conversion guide and colour-mixing chart provided make this a handy reference site.

Electronic parts and kits

Electronic Rainbow
www.rainbowkits.com
This US site supplies various electronics kits for all manner of weird and wonderful projects, including gadgets to attach to your CB radio, digital thermometers, and even a box that can control your home's heating and lighting when you call it on the phone. Purchase your next gimmick from this site, and you'll be so involved putting it all together that your friends won't see you for days ...

Electronics for the advanced
www.chipcenter.com
You can use ChipCenter to locate electronics components and find exactly the right websites to help you with your own electronics projects. It's all pretty techie on this particular site, so don't expect to pick up the basics here. However, if you are already an electrical engineer and want more details about spectral analysis or IC design, then this is a great starting place for you.

Rocketry online
www.rocketryonline.com
This site is all about the kind of homemade rockets that hobbyists can invest thousands of pounds in. The "INFOcentral" area provides a detailed introduction to the scene, and there are links to the companies that sell mini altimeters, onboard computers, and engines. There are chat forums to discuss your experiences and news and reviews of events and products. A "Launch Calendar" gives you a month-by-month view of forthcoming rocketry events that are taking place around the world.

Genealogy

Cemetery records on the Internet
www.interment.net
This collection of largely US burial records has been made available on the Internet to aid genealogists in researching family histories. If you're having trouble tracking down a long-lost grave, this is the place for advice. If you've been researching and want to share your results, they would be happy to receive your findings and add them to the database.

Online genealogy
www.ancestry.com
Ancestry.com is a professional-looking site offering daily news, software reviews, and searchable databases all aimed at the busy genealogist. Message boards are provided, too, care of **www.familyhistory.com**, which is owned by Ancestry.com. Another related site, **www.myfamily.com**, offers a free website service to help "connect family members".

Motoring

American Automobile Association
www.aaa.com
Enter your US zip code to find out what the road conditions in your area are like, pick up a few holiday ideas (using AAA membership benefits to cut the cost), and read the monthly reports on the average prices of airfares, lodgings, and rental cars. You can also get a quote online for the company's auto insurance or apply for a car loan.

Automobile Association
www.theaa.co.uk
Apply for membership of this popular UK breakdown service, receive motor insurance quotes online, and access the Internet version of the company's restaurant, pub, and hotel guides. You can also plan your routes and find out where the cheapest fuel can be had.

Automobile buyer's guide
www.edmunds.com
Get the latest automobile prices (yes, it's a US site), and read reviews of all manner of gas guzzlers. There is plenty of useful consumer advice for those buying new and used cars, and the site has valuable know-how on eyeing up the past history of your intended purchase.

Autotrader
www.autotrader.co.uk
The online equivalent of the popular car magazine is the site to visit if you want to find a vehicle in the western world. Search for new or used cars by location, model, year, and, of course, price. Its six-step plan will give you advice on what to look for and what to watch out for.

British Motorcyclists Federation
www.bmf.co.uk
UK bikers can find out when rallies and other interesting events are taking place; read news stories tailored for road warriors; and take advantage of the library – which contains tips, law updates, and the lowdown on other biker issues. The advantages of membership to the federation are all listed, in order to entice you to sign up straight away.

Cars in the United Kingdom
www.carsource.co.uk
Don't be put off by the rather drab design – this is a brilliant place to visit if you're renewing your car insurance, want to price a second-hand car, or simply have some time to kill and just feel like browsing the car photo library. Car Source will even try to locate the car of your dreams for you, should you leave details of your desires. What nice people.

Institute of Advanced Motorists
www.iam.org.uk
If you'd like to improve your driving skills, whether you drive a car, an LGV, tow a caravan, or ride a motorcycle, then check out the official site of the Advanced

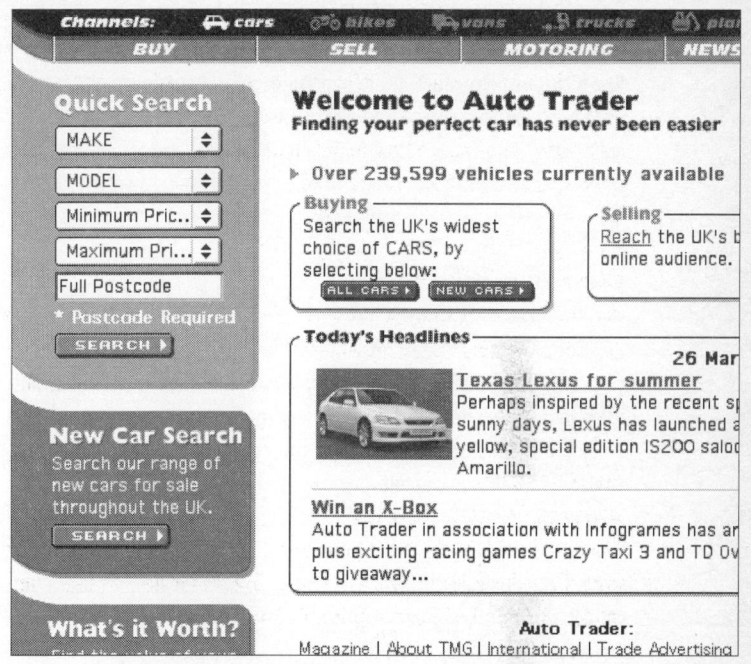

If you want an Aston Martin or an Austin Metro, new or used, then www.autotrader.co.uk is for you

Driving Test. You can also read about member benefits, cheaper car insurance, special services from the AA, and discounts from various companies.

Lorryspotting
www.lorryspotting.com
Do you find yourself checking out the liveries of lorries, hoping to spot a new Eddie Stobart vehicle? Lorry spotting must be a serious business because the incredibly in-depth search engine with more than 15,000 lorries is only available to members, and membership costs around £25 per year. A gallery of images is available to non-members, who can join in the chat with fellow lorry lovers ...

RAC Motoring Services
www.rac.co.uk
Receive live traffic news; read advice on buying, maintaining, and driving your car; and buy travel insurance, accessories, and maps online. The route planner covers the whole of Europe, and a "Hotel Finder" provides details of accommodation throughout the United Kingdom and Ireland. For a fee, the site will even run a check on any registration number you provide, to ensure that you aren't about to buy stolen goods.

Top Gear
www.topgear.beeb.com
The top-rated British TV show has its own site here, with all the advice you could need. Choose your make and model, and find out the lowdown from those in the know. There are tips on how to get the best deal and, of course, the staple of the show – the expert opinion on the test drives. Disagree with Mr Clarkson? You can give him a slap at **www.urban75.com/warp**.

What Car? Online
www.whatcar.co.uk
Locate new or used cars in Britain, sell your old one, and find out how much you've been ripped off doing both on this site. There is a large number of articles here that detail the road tests this magazine has put all new models through, including a child seat test, so that you can get an idea of what to look for when taking a test drive yourself.

Pot luck

Juggling Information Service
www.juggling.org
This excellent resource for jugglers has web versions of *Juggler's World*, instructions on how to juggle, and even details of juggling software that can help teach the techniques. There are movies of famous, old-time performers and a list of organizations to join.

Online kite magazine
www.kitelife.com
Kite flyers should come here to find out about international events, information on indoor kite flying, and photo galleries documenting kite expos. There are links to cool kite stores and useful book stores. A Kitelife CD-ROM is also available to help you out of any tangles.

Patenting advice
www.patentcafe.com
If your hobby has led you to create a fantastic invention, then this is the site for you. Aimed at inventors who want to create new devices then protect them from unethical companies, the advice here will take you through from the stage of "having an idea" right up to when you can apply for a patent and start earning profits from your invention.

Puppetry
www.sagecraft.com/puppetry
Whether you are interested in traditional shadow puppets, Pinocchio-style marionettes, or computer-animated figures, there will be something here for you. Features include indices of worldwide puppet theatres, information on festivals, and practical advice – including the use of smoke and how to write scripts.

Space

Alien-locating program
www.setiathome.ssl.berkeley.edu
Download the screensaver software from this site and help search for other life forms in our universe. The SETI@home project provides individual pieces of data from the Arecibo Radio Telescope to you, the supporter. Your software then analyses it and sends back the results. If your computer is involved in a discovery, you can be credited as a co-discoverer.

All things astronomical
www.stsci.edu/resources
Astroweb – a one-stop shop for astronomers – doesn't look flash, and the front page frankly looks intimidating, but underneath the harsh exterior lies extensive information on large telescopes, data centres, and scary-looking governmental sites that thankfully feature some very pretty pictures. Professional scientists and child prodigies will get the most from this site and the sites linked to it.

High-energy astronomy
imagine.gsfc.nasa.gov/docs/ask_astro/ask_an_astronomer.html
You might not want to know much about quasars right now, but there may be a time when you do, so remember that this site exists and return when you want to ask a question about high-energy astronomy. You can also browse through previously answered questions.

International Meteor Organization
www.imo.net
Start here if you are looking for information on meteors and meteorites. Showers are recorded, and "The Visual Meteor Database" contains more than 1,500,000 records of sightings, although its name belies the fact that it lacks graphics of any kind. You'll just have to take your own photos, with the aid of the information here. If busy, try the mirror site **www.amsmeteors.org/imo-mirror**.

—see also...

There is a huge array of sites offering advice and help on all sorts of activities. Model airplane enthusiasts are able to find out about Airfix models at **www.airfixcollector.co.uk** and buy plane kits, modelling tools, and spare parts from Hobby Hangar (**www.hobbyhangar.com**). If you'd actually like your model to take off, you can follow the advice at the many sites listed by the radio-controlled model web directory Tower Hobbies (**www.towerhobbies.com**). Killer model robot fans will enjoy the online presence of the British TV show *Robot Wars* (**www.robotwars.co.uk**).

Entertainers are catered for with such excellent sites as All Magic Guide (**www.allmagicguide.com**), providing links to conjuring sites, while the Center for Puppetry Arts (**www.puppet.org**) features a museum, links, and a gift shop. Lovers of ballroom dancing should try **www.ballroomdancers.com** to brush up on their steps.

Healthcare for your furry companions may be found at Pet Education (**www.peteducation.com**). Water-bound friends are catered for at such sites as Aquaria Central (**www.aquariacentral.com**), which describes how to stock and build a good tank. Look after your own birds with advice from Bird On! (**www.birdcare.com/birdon**), which contains an encyclopedia of bird care articles. The House Rabbit Society (**www.rabbit.org**) is aimed at those who want a tame rabbit to roam around the house, while the Royal Society for the Prevention of Cruelty to Animals (**www.rspca.org.uk**) makes sure that people look after their pets properly and provides helpful advice. If you can't have a real dog, then why not adopt a computerized web version at Virtual Puppy (**www.virtualpuppy.com**). You'll compete with other players to see who's the best overall owner (or **www.virtualkitty.com** if you're more of a virtual cat person). But if it all sounds too much like hard work, just sit back and let the virtual fish tank at **www.virtualfishtank.com** soothe you.

Collectors and arts and crafts fans should find Aunt Annie's Crafts (**www.auntannie.com**) an extremely useful resource of advice on making all sorts of things, from paper airplanes to cuddly animals. The Crafts Council Online (**www.craftscouncil.org.uk**) will help you to locate craft fairs, while Potters.org (**www.potters.org**) has discussion forums based around potting, glazing, and other ceramic technologies. If you prefer your plates readymade, try the Franklin Mint (**www.franklinmint.com**), purveyor of ceramic collectibles. It's possible you already have treasure stashed in your attic — check with Antique Talk (**www.antiquetalk.com**) to find out. Locate long-lost relatives and friends using the people search engine at WhoWhere? (**www.whowhere.lycos.com**) or **www.distantcousin.com**. The Internet

Address Finder (**www.iaf.net**) might also be able to find their e-mail address for you ...

There a large number of amateur photography sites at The Amateur Photography Ring (**www.gtdesigns.com/photoring**) while motorbike clothing, parts, services, and links can be found at MotoDirectory.com (**www.motodirectory.com**). Trainspotters should try The Historical Model Railway Society (**www.hmrs.org.uk**) for a history of the railway and the National Model Railroad Association (**www.cwrr.com/nmra**) for links to rail sites.

If your particular hobby hasn't been listed here, try one of the departments that are categorized at Liszt (**www.internethobbies.com**).

HOME AND LIFESTYLE

If your personal computer sits in drab surroundings in a half-empty room, then these are all sites that will help you decorate, furnish, and improve your surroundings and lifestyle. Whether you need plumbing advice or a comfy bed, want some antiques, or wonder whether a little feng shui will improve your wellbeing, then this list of sites should be able to help you. There are plenty of shops prepared to sell you the paint, nails, and other potential makings of a lovely abode, many with online calculators and guides to help you choose the colours of your walls or work out how much wallpaper or wood you'll need for your latest project. Here you can also discover the luxury of buying clothes from the comfort of your own home.

— Clothes and jewellery —

Accessorize
www.accessorize.co.uk
This UK high-street store has created a fun presence online, with a fresh approach to accessories for women. A style guide will tell you what's "in", while a cheeky "Make a Move" page e-mails a chat-up line movie to your unsuspecting intended. All in all, this is a successful creation of an online presence.

Freemans
www.freemans.co.uk
You can do all your clothes shopping online this season at Freemans of London. The site is broken down into four simple categories – women, men, kids, and sports. It offers a full searching facility, saving you valuable page-turning time. You

The distinctive style of this clothes' retailer continues online at www.gap.com

can fill in an online order form, or fill up your virtual trolley as you browse through the goodies on offer.

Gap
www.gap.com
This online presence follows the same style as the stylish offline branding. Choose men's or women's clothing on the home page, and browse the store at your convenience. The site also runs a great gift service. It has a store locator, too, should you not know where you to find their clothes and accessories locally.

Links of London
www.linksoflondon.com
This online jewellery store delivers to the United States, Canada, United Kingdom, and the rest of Europe. The distinctive products include photo frames, hip flasks, clocks, rings, cuff links, and other jewellery. Have them giftwrapped, or receive a gift recommendation by explaining who the present is for and your price range.

Online shopping mall
www.get-trolleyed.co.uk
This online shopping centre offers shop space to anyone who wants to rent it, so if you need to set up a secure shopping site yourself you can do so with the

166 Home and Lifestyle

Bargains galore are to be had for all types of goods at www.loot.com

minimum of technical skill. The rest of us can use it to do a spot of online shopping from the variety of shops that sell audio systems, jewellery, clothing, arts and crafts, and interiors and furniture.

Discounts, ads, and auctions

Bargains
www.bargains.com
A US site where you can get virtually anything you want by browsing through the many categories, from computers to gardening equipment. It also has its own auction house. Rather than list the actual items, the categories list various retailers who then justify why their site is so cheap. There are also links to sites with rebates or coupons. The light blue text sometimes makes it hard to read, but you can find some real bargains here.

Buying and selling
www.ioffer.com
iOffer is a trading community that allows you to buy and sell – just like you would in real life. Unlike other auction sites, you don't need to wait for days to buy something, only to find you've been outbid at the last minute. This offers interaction between buyer and seller through negotiation. You can buy outright, make an offer, or put in a counterbid. A refreshing change and potentially a lot more fun.

Electronic Yellow Pages
www.yell.com
Search for contact details of more than 1.7 million companies without wearing your fingers out. This online version of the *Yellow Pages* for both the United States and the United Kingdom also includes a dedicated travel section, a website for home buyers, and a shopping centre that lists sites conforming to its secure transaction specifications. It has a useful business section for both UK and international companies as well.

Exchange and Mart
www.exchangeandmart.co.uk
Find used cars, furniture, holidays, and business services in the online version of this classified ads paper. Garden tools and even properties for sale can also be found. You can place ads, too, take part in online auctions, and browse through all the weird and wonderful items that always crop up in these sorts of places, such as spy cameras and phone taps.

Internet auction
www.ebay.com
Take part in an Internet auction, buying and selling just about anything with people all over the world. There are localized versions of this site (**www.ebay.co.uk** for the United Kingdom), and the company offers to investigate should deals go wrong. You can view the track record of a seller's past, which may help you to avoid any crooks that may be lurking around.

LOOT
www.loot.com
The famous classified ads paper has been online for a long time and provides an easy way to place your own ads and to search for the things you want or need. Particularly handy is the property section, where you can specify areas and prices – essential for finding student accommodation. To get that vital one step ahead, the Early Bird can e-mail you warnings as soon as what you are after appears. (For other property sites see "Property and mortgages" in Money, pages 187–9.)

Online auctions
www.qxl.com
You can easily buy and sell things over the Internet using this online auction house. QXL will handle all the bidding for you to keep things simple. You just receive an e-mail when the auction has concluded, with the highest bidder's e-mail address – assuming that your reserve price has been reached, of course. You should also check out the special offers, where auctions often begin from only £1.

Senior discounts
www.seniordiscounts.com
This site strives to provide the most complete and accurate listing of all senior-related discounts for goods and services throughout the United States. From national chains to local stores, bargains and deals are hunted out. There's even a Senior Discounts Prescription Plan which promises to save up to 65 per cent on medicines. Sounds promising.

Furnishings

Advice on buying a bed
www.sleepcouncil.org.uk
Lumpy bed cramping your sleeping style? You need the online bed-buying advice that is only available at The Sleep Council. This site also has tips on how to improve the quality of what little sleep you may get (why not do the Bed MOT – yes, really!). It also provides some fascinating statistics on which nationalities buy the biggest beds (the Brits like to snuggle up close, apparently).

Crate and Barrel
www.crateandbarrel.com
This online version of the US store is packed full of classic products for virtually every room in your home. You can order the items of your choice online, or simply view the catalogue to find out what is on offer. The site will even send you birthday reminders if you give them important dates for loved ones. If you live in the United States, you can also find out where your nearest store is so that you can see the furnishings for real.

Fine English Furnishing Worldwide
www.clubchesterfield.co.uk
Plenty of fine crafted items of furniture here, from traditional leather sofas to modern pieces, fireplaces, tables, and desks. They also do a fine line in medieval armour and weapons so if you are in a hurry to kit out your castle this could be the place to start.

Getting smart about shopping
www.shopsmart.com
Whether you want to buy a refrigerator, stereo system, or some flowers to brighten up a room, the stores in the Shop Smart online mall have something to offer. The categories are clearly displayed on the home page and very easy to use. There are

Tempt yourself with the array of household goods on offer at www.habitat.net

editors' guides that review films and products, and special offers are flagged on the home page if you want to find some real bargains.

Goods for your home
www.cucinadirect.co.uk
You could almost completely stock your home with the goods on offer here. There are cooking equipment, electrical appliances, food, barbecues, and linen. If you need any inspiration, there are some clever recipes designed to get your mouth watering and your purse opening.

Habitat
www.habitat.net
Europeans looking to spruce their homes up in a thoroughly modern fashion should pay Habitat's online showroom a visit. You can browse through a catalogue of sofas, beds, and office furniture, although you'll have to contact your local store directly to actually buy anything. Its rival company, the slightly more expensive Heal's (**www.heals.co.uk**), does go one better by having online buying facilities.

The Internet antique shop
www.tias.com
This online shopping centre concentrates solely on antiques – and mainly the selling of them to you. As such, it is a good site for collectors (see "Collections" in Hobbies on pages 152–4 for further collectible sites). However, if you are

Selling antiques is just one of the features at www.tias.com

interested in flogging your heirlooms, the Internet Antique Shop can help there, too, with online auctions and classified advertising. You can search for the items for sale using an online database, by browsing through categories of objects, or by simply looking at the antique showcase.

Shopping for home and family
www.aboundonline.com
Abound is a helpful online store full of great ideas for the family and home, from toys and games to footwear and electrical items. With free delivery and no cost for returns, plus useful deals of the week, this could be what you were looking for. It's pretty easy on the eye, too.

Sound systems and sound advice
www.richersounds.com
The garish website of the hi-fi store allows you to order most of its catalogue items. Not content with selling you products, Richer Sounds spends considerable effort explaining hi-fi basics to all beginners, providing invaluable information such as how and where to mount your speakers. A "Tips" section provides a more in-depth look at ways to improve your aural experiences. Unfortunately, while you can see everything from the catalogue online, some items can only be bought in the store itself. A new Student Zone area has just been added.

Home improvement

Achieving the look you want in your home
www.hometime.com
Do you choose the colour of your walls before or after decorating the rest of a room? How do you achieve an authentic country/industrial look? If similar questions keep you awake at night, take note of the advice supplied by DesignViews. Simple to navigate, features include design projects, tips, useful books, and a guide to vintage style.

Better Homes and Gardens online
www.bhg.com
Whether you want to re-plan your garden or view an interactive tour of the house of the future, this site does it all in style. It also covers cookery, crafts, and health and fitness, with a special kids' section that provides, among other things, tooth-rotting recipes. It has a number of useful tools including "Plan-a-Party" and kids' etiquette and kitchen guides.

DIY
www.hometips.com
Need to sort out that squeaky floorboard? What about replacing that tile in the bathroom? Find sensible tips and advice on all the jobs you've been meaning to get round to. Now you have no excuse.

DIY Network
www.diynet.com
Get the job done right with this television and web network. It has thousands of projects from arts and crafts to decorating, car care, and gardening. So whether you want to do something constructive with the kids on a rainy day or sort your car brakes out, this is the place to start. Cool tools and workshops along with a chat room will put you on the right track.

Dulux
www.dulux.co.uk
This manufacturer of paint has a "Mouse Painter" on its excellent site, which lets you paint a virtual room in different colours so that you can get an idea of suitably pleasant schemes – do remember, though, that the web can only display 216 colours, so you will not be getting the whole picture. There are also expert decorating tips, a database of decorators on call, and a selection of articles from their *Inspire* newsletter.

Feng shui
www.feng-shui-shop.co.uk
Not the prettiest of sites, but if you want to know where to put your plant pots and what direction your sofa should point, then this is the site for you. You can buy anything feng shui–based, from candles to the eight-sided Pa Kua mirror to rid your home of its malignant "chi".

Greenfingers
www.greenfingers.co.uk
Anyone who who loves the great outdoors, or at least their own back garden, will be absolutely riveted to this site. There is an online superstore for you to purchase all your gardening goods and a magazine section full of tips and ideas, and you can also receive expert advice from the Professional Gardener's Guild. Another advice section, "Ask George", will tell you where there are beautiful gardens to visit and where to hunt for specialist plant growers near you, and it will also demystify gardening jargon for you.

Home and garden design programs
www.fasttrak.co.uk
Home to programs such as "Visual Home Professional", "3D Landscape Professional", and "3D Kitchen", this site can sell you software that may help you to design your garden or rearrange rooms – on the computer if not in reality. You can order online.

Homebase
www.homebase.co.uk
Seek inspiration for home makeovers from the people who can supply absolutely all the necessary accoutrements for change in both your home and garden. A sprinkling of tips, complete with a list of all the necessary ingredients, a "store locator", and an inspiring *Ideas Magazine* make this DIY/interior decor site definitely one to watch.

Home decor
www.interiorsforyou.com
If you are looking to do up your house and need a few helpful hints, this site is a good place to start. From decorating tips and step-by-step instructions to helpful products and the mysteries of feng shui explained, it is all here. With finishing touches and weblinks to other related areas all provided, you should have everything you need to crack on with the actual job. If you simply can't face the prospect of doing it all yourself, try **www.improveline.com** to find an expert contractor in your area.

Choose the perfect paint colours for your style of room at the interactive www.dulux.co.uk

Home improvement ideas and advice
www.homeideas.com
Upgrade your home with the help of the articles here. For example, not only can you find out how to wallpaper your abode, but also the online calculator will help you to work out exactly how much paper you'll need. There is even advice on how to reduce the static electricity-generating effect that your home can produce.

Ideas for your home and garden
www.homestore.com
Homestore aims to educate you in the ways of colour balance and how to set up your first home, and it will generally organize your life for you! There are sections on decorating, sewing, gardening, saving money, and buying a house, and, with step-by-step projects on subjects such as maintaining a garage door, you just can't go wrong.

Martha Stewart home improvements
www.marthastewart.com
One of the most popular US home improvements purveyors comes online here. Not only can you buy a range of products for every room in the house and every corner of the garden, but if you need inspiration or advice, this site will put your mind at rest as well. There are a selection of magazines available, including ones for weddings, babies, and holiday baking.

Lifestyle

Direct Marketing Association
www.the-dma.org
Find out what rights you have to prevent companies from selling your personal details to each other and also learn what benefits can be had from actually allowing it to happen. Half of this (slightly bland) site is only open to members, but there is still plenty of useful stuff for non-members to be found here, especially if you run a business yourself. There are also events listings for direct marketing professionals.

Fraud protection
www.paypal.com
Are you worried about buying and selling online, or have you been stung when a cheque has bounced? This site will relieve all your worries about online payments, as it ensures that buyers get what they pay for and also protects sellers against fraud. It is extremely useful if you are making international transactions.

How the media works
www.adbusters.org
A sometimes hard-hitting site that relies heavily on graphics to illustrate how the media works, often not to the good of the consumer. There are witty spoof adverts and articles on how advertising has, to some extent, become an important defining elements to our lives.

Safety hints and tips
www.safewithin.com
Covering all aspects of personal and domestic safety, Safe Within offers short snippets on things such as how to avoid hurting your back, prevent skidding a car on water, crime protection for the elderly, and how to shun hypothermia when out rambling. The information glosses the surface, and much will seem obvious to many, but it's nevertheless sound advice and, you never know, could even answer a question you didn't dare ask.

Stay safe online
www.staysafeonline.com
This web site is designed to give you the information needed to secure your home or small business computer. You'll find tips on how to safeguard your system, a self-guided cyber security test, educational materials, and other Internet resources. Security for kids is also heavily featured. For peace of mind when

www.adbusters.org will give you the truth about all those advertisements you watch every day

shopping, try www.tradingstandards.gov.uk/worcestershire/shopping.htm which offers sound advice for shopping safely on the web and what to do if you think you've been ripped off.

Which? online
www.which.net
This site holds the Internet magazine of the Consumers' Association. It provides unrivalled consumer legal advice, plus objective reviews of hundreds of products. The site includes more than 60,000 pages of content, and it is available for a free 30-day trial – after that, aside from the little tasters there are, the content is strictly for subscribers only.

Women's online magazine
www.femail.co.uk
Femail is a site aimed squarely at women and contains a mixture of advice, magazine-style articles, and message boards. There are articles on shopping, sex and relationships, and how to look and feel great. You can receive expert advice on subjects as diverse as nutrition through to analysing dreams. Sign up for the newsletter to be kept up to date on what is happening on the site.

— Upkeep

All about chimneys
www.chimneys.com
Whether you want to learn how to set a successful fireplace, check a chimney, or find out how it all works, then you are likely to find your answers at Chimneys.com. The sheer number of words, undiluted by diagrams, can be off-putting; however, true disciples of the chimney stack will find what they seek here.

Improve your home
www.improvenet.com
This is a home improvement site for those who find the thought of DIY just a little too much or have the money to spend to do without the aggro! Search here for a designer, contractor, or architect to make your dream home. You can find help on getting started and how to plan your project, or go to the Pro advice library to receive advice from the experts. You can also use the site to match remodelling professionals to your particular job.

Maintaining an old home
www.oldhouseweb.com
If you own, or want to own, an old house and intend to learn how to fix and maintain it, the Old House Web is a good starting place. There is a glossary of construction and housing terms, as well as an energy checklist (old houses can be real heat wasters), an introduction to new products, and gardening tips. All your questions about bouncy floors, fixing cracks in plaster walls, and insulation are dealt with, and there is also a bulletin board.

Tackling carpet stains
www.a2zcarpet.com
When little Harry sloshes blackcurrant juice all over your brand-new, authentic yak's wool rug, a2zcarpet is the place to turn to. An interactive stain removal page offers both general and very specific information to help shift tricky marks. The terrifying phenomenon known as "Rug Ripple" is also tackled, and all manner of other carpet conundrums are cracked.

The Tide Fabric Care Network
www.clothesline.com
Take care of your clothes and follow the laundry-oriented advice available from the manufacturers of Tide washing powder. The interactive "Stain Detective" works

out how to attack your stains (predictably with a large dose of Tide, in most cases), and those funny little symbols on clothes labels are finally explained.

Utilities

AT&T
www.att.com
Find out all about the services you did and didn't know that AT&T provided, including its cable TV services and Internet access. A handy account management section can give you an online statement, and you can also learn about wireless fraud and how to safeguard yourself against it. If your phone system at home is completely satisfactory, then there is also plenty of information on AT&T's services for your business.

British Telecommunications
www.bt.com
Visit this site to read in-depth information on BT's latest telephone services or just to check what the going call charges to various parts of the world are. There are also handy snippets on how to explore broadband options for your home or business, and there is a useful online directory enquiry service. Information on BT's extensive subsidiary Internet service provider can be found at its own site, **www.btopenworld.com**.

Cost-reducing power suppliers
www.powercheck.demon.co.uk
Not the most attractive of sites but utterly functional, PowerCheck's aim is to save your business money by suggesting alternative suppliers of electricity, telephone services, and gas. A quick and easy savings calculator for gas is supplied, just to prove you'd be better off using PowerCheck's brokering services. There are also potential savings to be made with water suppliers. Individuals can browse archives for reference.

Toilet repairs
www.toiletology.com/index.shtml
Almost everything you ever wanted to know about your toilets ... and some things you probably never knew you needed to know. If your toilet's on the blink, you may want to find a few pointers here before you shell out for an expensive plumber. From dire emergencies to preventative care, this online course will be sure to come in handy one day ...

—see also...

Get handy around the home, fixing it up and buying new accessories, by using the plethora of home-related websites that there are available. 411 Home Repair (**www.411homerepair.com**) provides help on maintaining your abode and choosing contractors to carry out important work. For large projects, you can make use of the building techniques detailed at Andy's "How To" Homebuilding (**www.andyshowto.com**). RoofHelp (**www.roofhelp.com**) has instructions on fixing roofs, although those with less ambition should maybe stick to designing bathrooms and kitchens – try Kitchen-Bath.com (**www.kitchen-bath.com**). Damp basement? You need MisterFixit (**www.misterfixit.com**), who will also help sort out problems with household appliances. The Natural Handyman (**www.naturalhandyman.com**) is a good, general home repair site, if slow to load, while The Plumber (**www.theplumber.com**) discusses plumbing problems and documents the history of plumbing since ancient times. For those emergency repairs, This to That (**www.thistothat.com**) will inform you which type of glue you'll need to fix any two materials together. Other mundane household items are available to buy online at Homefree (**www.homefree.co.uk**).

High-tech homemakers might find the advice on computerized home automation (à la Jetsons) and X-10 Ideas (**www.x10ideas.com**) to their liking, while TipzTime (**www.tipztime.com**) is handy for general household tips. The New Homemaker (**www.newhomemaker.com**) is aimed at those who have just purchased a home and has all sorts of information on parenting, decorating, managing money, and connecting with your community; however, for the less-than-perfect among us, the friendly and diverse discussion forums at That Home Site! (**www.thathomesite.com**) will be of comfort. If you want to get rid of the woodchip, then you can find some new wallpaper at **www.wallpaperstore.com**. For a good variety of home and lifestyle offerings, The Housewife Pages (**www.hausfrauenseite.de/index_eng.html**) provides a weird mixture of homely recipes, wedding gift ideas, and some possibly offensive jokes, while, almost as surreally, Wood Heat (**www.woodheat.org**) promotes the responsible use of wood as a home heating fuel. For details of UK trade fairs and exhibitions, check out the home and lifestyle section lists at **www.exhibitions.co.uk**.

Keen gardeners are amply provided for with such sites as the Backyard Gardener (**www.backyardgardener.com**), Burpee (**www.burpee.com**), and GardenWeb (**www.gardenweb.com**), which all offer an abundance of tips, seeds, and nutritional guides. If you'd rather see the fruits of someone else's horticultural labours, you could do worse than the Royal Botanical Gardens at Kew (**www.rbgkew.org.uk**), which contains details of festivals, as well as an online tour of the gardens. There are good gardening articles at Home and Garden Television (**www.hgtv.com**), which also includes items on food, lifestyle and crafts, decor, building, and "remodelling".

Shopping on the web can be therapeutic, especially with sites that can provide you with real bargains. QVCUK.com (**www.qvcuk.com**) is an enormous online store stocked with health and beauty goods, jewellery, electrical items, fashion, and almost everything else. The Marks and Spencer site (**www.marks-and-spencer.com**) is pleasant and replicates the store online excellently. US shoppers should try the Fashion Mall (**www.fashionmall.com**), where you can shop by "floor" or by brand name. Those with a big bonus to spend can visit the Conran Shop at **www.conran.co.uk**. Boxclever (**www.boxclever.co.uk**) can provide a whole range of items for renting, from DVD players to home theatre systems. To own your own television, video, or other home entertainment equipment, browse Web Electricals (**www.webelectricals.co.uk**) to find the best bargains.

MONEY

Banks, property, taxes, and other money matters – here wannabe stocks and shares dealers, homeowners, and other investors have access to the sort of free resources that they could only have dreamed of five or more years ago. There are guides for the uninitiated, online dealing services at competitive prices, and information that could save you or your business serious money. Online banking services are also available – offering control of your accounts directly from your computer – and you can peruse financial newspapers and share prices. You can also save days from your house-hunting schedule by viewing lists online. Job hunting through the web is also big business.

Internet banks

Abbey National
www.cahoot.co.uk
The Abbey National online bank that caused a storm when it launched with its low customer rates is, like most of the online banks, very pleasant to look at, but what of the content? It's not bad, giving you all the regular banking features, and it allows you to do your banking through your mobile phone. If the thought of making a will sends shivers down your spine, then at least you can do it online here in a simple and straightforward manner.

Barclays Bank
www.barclays.com
Barclays Bank was the first in the United Kingdom to provide its customers with the option of Internet banking, but it has not rested on its laurels. You can sign up for its Internet banking facility, apply for a bank account, subscribe to the free Internet access package, or trade stocks and shares using the Barclays Stockbrokers service – all online.

Abbey National has finally branched onto the web at www.cahoot.com with its own saving site

Egg
new.egg.com
People in the United Kingdom can apply for loans, a credit card, or insurance; or make a will and use its other financial services, too. There is a sports section where you can check up on the Egg team racing drivers or find out what it takes on the Drive Time page (a lot of money, actually). The online shop is another place to blow your savings.

First Direct
www.firstdirect.co.uk
Bank accounts, mortgages, credit cards – all the usual services that you'd expect from an online bank. Added incentives are a £25 golden hello when you open an account online and the promise that you will always speak to a real person when you call them up. There's free text message banking. What's more, if they make a mistake when opening your account, you'll get another £20. People with difficult names step right up ...

MasterCard
www.mastercard.com
Remind yourself of the services your credit card company offers you. A Zero Liability policy should enable you to shop with ultra-safety and convenience on the Internet. Cardholders can subscribe to a special mailing list and receive exclusive offers that might include restaurant deals, travel tickets, or beauty products. It's a bit slow loading, though.

www.monster.co.uk is one of the most comprehensive job-finding websites around

National Westminster
www.natwest.com
This site has a good, simple design and is full of services, including links for mobile banking and online share dealing. Lots of advice is given on travelling abroad (including, of course, the chance to use its currency converter and bureau de change), and small businesses have their own section. You can also access your bank account through Yahoo.

Smile: The Co-operative Bank
www.smile.co.uk
Sign up at the United Kingdom's first fully Internet-run bank to get a current, savings, or credit card account. As the bank runs completely online, you'll see your statements here as well as receiving them by e-mail. There is also a competitive rate of interest, as a bank without high-street branches has fewer overheads.

US online banks list
www.moneypage.com
Websites that consist almost entirely of links to other sites are generally bad news, but the Money Page's comprehensive selection is unusually good. There is a large

list of American online banks and investment-related links. The discussion forum doesn't see much discussion, but it's easier to use than many others around.

Visa International
www.visa.com
Find out what discounts and offers cardholders are entitled to. You can also find your nearest cash machine anywhere in the world, pick up tips for safe online shopping, and discover new ways to use your card, such as in public phones.

Jobs

Career magazine
www.careermag.com
The online presence of the job-hunting bible is full of features to help you find a better career. Upload your resume for employees to look over. You can post a photograph of yourself looking employable, search a database of Hot Jobs, and create your own website here.

Career management
www.future42.com
Dissatisfied with your current job? Thinking of a career change, or planning your retirement? This innovative site will take you through a questionnaire to evaluate your levels of satisfaction at work and offer solutions. It's Choice! software will also help you to identify your priorities and evaluate various jobs of your choosing, according to your needs. The Emotions@Work tool allows you to turn your negative feelings into positive ones. Refreshing and enlightening!

Headhunters
www.careerbuilder.com
Search by job type or industry for your perfect job – although it may not feel like it. There are more than 250,000 to choose from internationally. There is also an extensive resources section with interview assistance, information on new cities that you might want to work in, and links to the best training resources on the web. You can also make money through their affiliate programme.

Internet job search
www.monster.co.uk
If you've just had an argument with the boss and want to find a new job, use this site and do your research on company time. It includes special advice for

graduates, as well as specialized job markets such as healthcare. You can have help on your CV and advice on interview techniques, and you can also search through almost half a million jobs worldwide.

Search for jobs or potential employees
www.jobsearch.co.uk
Search for jobs at this recruitment site, and find contact details, job descriptions, and salary details online. You can also submit your CV to the site so that it can be accessed by employers. If you're an employer, this is a great place to vet potential employees. For a similar site in the United States, visit **hotjobs.yahoo.com**.

Money management

The Bank of England
www.bankofengland.co.uk
The central bank of the United Kingdom has historical and political interest, but its website also provides useful background information on issues such as the Euro and the bank's role in setting interest rates. A full archive of press releases is available, as is a mind-boggling statistics section.

BankSITE
www.banksite.com
A no-frills site containing a selection of interactive work sheets, BankSITE takes the pain out of making financial decisions. There is a "One Minute Loan Test" to assess how easy it will be for you to borrow money, and students will do well to follow the advice on financing an education and how to manage money after graduating from a degree course.

Blay's financial services
www.blays.co.uk
The established financial information service has opened some of its doors to the public via the web. Receive impartial advice on mortgages, savings, utilities, and business and personal banking. There is also an area to help students in particular. The information on savings and mortgages is updated daily, taking into account the fluctuating nature of these two areas.

Family money
www.bhg.com
Cost-cutting tips and practical advice for singles, partners, parents, and

homeowners – whether you're starting out or settled in. From raising kids to buget balancing, banking and planning for retirement or taking in reality checks on mortgages, insurance and maintenance. It's all here in this site from *Better Homes and Gardens*. Youthful innocence goodbye.

Financial information Net directory
www.find.co.uk
Locate financial services with this directory, which includes listings of investments, insurance, advice, mortgages, and other services. There are online calculators to work out what sort of mortgage, loan, or investments you can afford, or not.

Financial strategy centre
www.money.cnn.com
With advice and articles on almost all aspects of money management this site is hard to fault. It even has features on how to spot an Internet fraud, investing using the Internet, and the mistakes that you'll make – with useful tips on how to avoid them. Complete newcomers should check out the "Money101" section for a lowdown on the essentials.

The Financial Times
news.ft.com
The *Financial Times*'s offering is an utterly essential website for anyone with an interest in making money or the people who make it. The latest financial news and

The *Financial Times* website (news.ft.com) has all the financial advice that you will need

analysis are provided along with a truly gargantuan archive of articles that contains many free pieces, as well as some from other publications costing money. It is also a useful source of information on the international financial markets.

HM Treasury
www.hm-treasury.gov.uk
Catch up on the latest government budget details, press releases, and the Chancellor of the Exchequer's recent speeches at the seemingly unexciting but thorough official Treasury site. The undaunted will also find here in-depth information on ISAs and CATs, as well as ministerial biographies (perfect for those long, rainy days) and all you have ever wanted to know and a whole lot more besides about the United Kingdom's economic policy, including information on the budgets since 1994.

Money Extra
www.moneyextra.co.uk
If you are wanting to make your money go further, this excellent site, with lots of calculators and comparison tools, will more than adequately satisfy your financial curiosities. Compare Stocks and ISAs, mortgages, deposits, and travel insurance.

The Motley Fool UK
www.fool.co.uk
Despite a frivolous-sounding name, the "Fool" is one of the web's most respected financial sites and aims to offer sound financial advice, albeit served in a potentially humorous manner. Help can be found on investment strategies, personal finance, and other areas. Novices can learn about finance at the Fool School. This site is UK-based, so American investors should try **www.fool.com**.

Society of Financial Advisers
www.sofa.org
Whether you are an adviser yourself or want to receive online financial advice, you'll find interesting material here. Consumers can find online guides and an easy way to locate their nearest adviser – independent or otherwise. The advice even gives information on how to evaluate your adviser once you've found one.

Virgin Money
www.virginmoney.com
One of Richard Branson's many web fingers can be found on this money site. You can receive lots of advice here, of course, all leading towards telling you that the best company for your savings, ISAs etc is ... Virgin. There is a fun Flash-run section on shares should you want to browse around the site.

Financial advice is demystified at the essential www.fool.co.uk

Worth
www.worth.com
Access the online version of *Worth* magazine and learn about investing, pensions, and just about everything else related to money. The latest quotes on the Nasdaq, Dow Jones, and other indices are shown across the top of the site and refreshed frequently during trading hours. But most interesting, and unlike most financial sites, is its section on philanthropy and the best ways to give away your wealth – very refreshing.

Property and mortgages

Car loans
www.peoplefirst.com
If you live in the United Statesm then you can get leases and loans on new and used vehicles from this site. A focus on convenience, fast approval, a hassle-free loan experience, and, above all, exceptional customer service provides the foundation for a company that has grown tremendously since inception. Approval decisions are still made within 15 minutes, despite the fact that thousands of applications are processed daily.

Use www.upmystreet.com to find out all about your neighbourhood

Find a Property
www.findaproperty.com
Find a house or flat to rent or buy at this listings site. You can select local editions to restrict your searches to the most relevant areas and, although the main areas are London, Surrey, and a few other places in the Southeast England, there are versions for the whole of the rest of the United Kingdom and for Europe. You have to be quick, though, as the best properties are often snapped up quickly.

Guide to buying, selling, and renting
www.houseweb.co.uk
HouseWeb is an all-inclusive property site, containing a good set of guides on how to buy, sell, and move house; an updated list of average UK house prices based on different regions; and a formidable set of handy links. There are good sections on mortgages and insurance. The chat forum is unusually well populated and stocked with sensible advice.

How to sell your home
www.homegain.com
HomeGain.com offers an introduction service for house sellers and estate agents. It also provides thousands of articles and guides on diverse topics – from choosing an estate agent to readying your house before a sale. A home valuation tool may

help you to decide on your asking price. It also includes a list of its greatest success stories for all those doubting Thomases that there are among you.

International Real Estate Digest
www.ired.com
Covering 50 US states and 115 countries worldwide, this is the mother of all real estate directories. With a host of extensive links (50,000 at last count), IRED also publishes articles and news stories regularly. The site claims most of its visitors are real estate professionals, but there are some great articles for consumers, too.

Research your chosen area
www.upmystreet.com
This original site will let you chart UK national statistics such as the average flat price, A-level results, council tax, child care info, and truancy figures against those of the area you are considering moving to. Smug home owners just curious about their current area's status are advised to prepare themselves for a shock.

UK property database
www.homepages.co.uk
Homepages contains a large, searchable database of UK properties. Details of properties include photographs, a map, and local details including schools, crime statistics, removal firms, and train timetables. Leave your details and receive e-mail alerts when a property fitting your requirements comes on the market. Once you find the correct property, you can get advice on moving.

Virtual relocation
www.monstermoving.com
Find out what other US cities are like before you up sticks and move there. This website will automatically link you up with sites based on the area you plan to relocate to and can also find resources such as schools, businesses, and other services for you.

Stocks and shares

American Association of Individual Investors
www.aaii.com
Whether you want to know how to track your portfolio's performance or need advice on spending during retirement, this site has everything that you need. Many of the articles are for members only, but don't let that put you off visiting

the site. There is still plenty to read and the membership isn't expensive anyway. You can always take a free two-week trial first, just to make sure that the site has what you want.

Ample
www.iii.co.uk
This powerful investment site is suitable for absolutely anyone, from complete beginners with a desire to learn through to professionals who know everything but the latest pension fund performance figures. The free online portfolio makes tracking shares, whether they are real or imaginary, almost too easy. If you only visit one site in this whole section, then make sure that it this one. Thoroughly recommended.

Charles Schwab International
www.schwab-global.com
Claiming to be one of the world's largest online brokers, the Charles Schwab Corporation's website will deal in global funds and securities, and is suitable for traders, amateur or otherwise, in Asia, Canada, the Caribbean, Europe, Latin America, and the United States. A joint Schwab-Reuters service publishes 20-minute-old stock price quotes. The day's Dow Jones graph is always published on the home page, too.

TD Waterhouse
www.tdwaterhouse.co.uk
If you would like to take part in the current online stock trading frenzy, TD Waterhouse is a good place to start. See the latest company quotes and settle down to browse through the introductory investment guide.

E*Trade UK
uk.etrade.com
If you fancy making your fortune on the stock exchange from your desk, this is the place to visit. Account holders can participate in real-time trading in UK equities, with each transaction costing less than £15. A further £5 per month will authorize access to the share price information service, complete with quote and portfolio tools. US moneymakers will probably find that the sister site **www.etrade.com** is more useful.

Financial journals online
www.financial-freebies.com
Investing is a daunting prospect for many, made more so by the sheer numbers of specialist publications available. Try many of them for free, using this site. It will

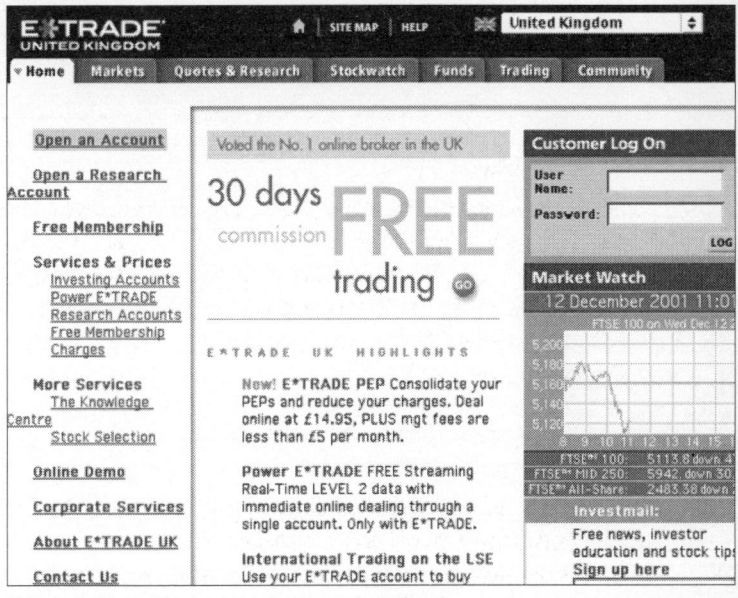

Make (or lose) a fortune from your desktop at uk.etrade.com

take requests for sample copies of some of the world's most popular and respected journals, including the *Wall Street Journal*, the *Investors Chronicle*, and the *Penny Share Guide*.

Internet trading
www.ameritrade.com
Why not trade shares online. Ameritrade offers top-notch trading tools, 24-hour client services, convenient account access, and a secure online trading experience. You can track all of your personal financial accounts in one place, manage your investment portfolios, and access a variety of financial planning tools and mortgage services. You can also monitor your checking and savings accounts and keep track of credit card balances.

An introduction to bonds
www.bondsonline.com
Learn all about the many different types of bonds there are, starting with the basics and progressing through the intricacies, courtesy of the "Bond Professor". A glossary of terms, lists of frequently asked questions (FAQs), and a "Question of the Week" make this site an instantly accessible resource. The latest headlines will keep experienced investors coming back time and time again to the Bonds Online website, too.

If stocks and shares are your thing, watch yours go up (and down) live at www.thestreet.com

ISP Shares
www.totalise.net

Totalise is one of many sites that offer you shares in the business in return for using its services. Positioning itself as a service provider, it gives you shares for using its e-mail and dial-up networking services. If you buy from one of its affiliates, then you will also receive cashback and the chance for more shares. Blue Carrots (www.bluecarrots.com) runs a similar scheme, although its is a more fun approach to the whole subject. It is worth registering here, however, as there is little to lose.

Latest investment news
www.thestreet.com

Boasting an impressive up-to-the-second news feed and market analysis, TheStreet.com is an attractive option for both new and advanced investors alike. The site also features an interesting range of articles, which comment on a whole range of current financial affairs. Some areas of the website, such as the "Basics" pages, are freely available, but you'll need to pay for a proper subscription before you will be able to access more than half of the pages that can be found on this site. Why don't you give the free trial a whirl first before committing yourself, to find out if the site is what you are after.

Learn about the world of Internet stockbroking
www.kiplinger.com
Learn the truth about Internet stock brokers, read how to pick stocks, and play with the large gallery of calculators to work out how much investment risk you can afford and what your current dividend yield is, and to compute an appropriate amount of life insurance.

Loyalty points
www.ipoints.co.uk
This is a loyalty website where you are rewarded for shopping at affiliates of this company. Shop online at various partners and you will be rewarded with ipoints, which in turn you can exchange for high-street or online vouchers to spend at various shops. Like most loyalty sites, though, you need to spend a lot first to gain any of the benefits.

NASD Regulation
www.nasdr.com
The guardian angel of investors, the National Association of Securities Dealers has a website containing help for those with complaints to make against brokers. It can also aid new investors in choosing a broker and advise what to do when telemarketing salespeople call.

Online investment guide
www.wisebuy.co.uk
Home of the excellent *AAA Investment Guide*, this site offers you the opportunity to read large chunks of this online book. Some of it is only available to subscribers, who pay around £30 for two years of unlimited access. The guide, which is aimed at UK investors, is also available on CD-ROM. There's even music to listen to while you read. It's pretty awful, though ...

Your money

Accounting for everyone
www.accountingweb.co.uk
Once you've registered with the site (for free), you will have access to a dedicated resource for accountants containing bluffers' guides, workshops, and industry news. The website is also relevant to non-accounting professionals, as it has a useful facility enabling you to locate an accountant, by location and speciality, from nearly 16,000 firms.

Financial advice
news.ft.com/yourmoney
The *Financial Times* newspaper has branched out and decided to offer impartial advice on your finances. As well as giving the latest financial news, it offers help on topics such as buying your first home or planning your retirement. There is an extensive section on ISAs and other ways to save your money. If you want advice from true professionals, then this site is worth bookmarking.

HM Customs & Excise
www.hmce.gov.uk
If you're not sure where you stand with VAT (Value Added Tax) payments when importing goods, perhaps paid for using the Internet, HM Customs & Excise can put you straight. The site also advises on buying cars in the EU and explains how to calculate VAT when bringing items into the United Kingdom from abroad.

Inland Revenue
www.inlandrevenue.gov.uk
Providing the official source of information on UK income tax and self-assessment, the government's Internet home of the tax man benefits from a simple design – for most articles you can choose a text or graphics version. Aimed at individuals, businesses, and tax professionals, the site has a list of frequently asked questions alongside electronic versions of Inland Revenue leaflets and other publications.

The Insurance Centre
www.theinsurancecentre.co.uk
Save time, energy, and hair when shopping around for cheap insurance by using the services of this site. Fill in your details in a simple online questionnaire, and it will provide quotes from a number of companies on motor, pet, house, travel, and healthcare cover. It's as easy as that – no frills, no nonsense.

Internet taxation
www.e-tax.org.uk
As people start to purchase items using the Internet, sometimes from abroad, the government has realized it may be missing a tax opportunity. This site discusses the issues and provides international links. The news is provided by an external service and is not strictly relevant to Internet taxation.

US Customs Service
www.customs.gov
More exciting than its UK counterpart, this site not only has information about import, export, and enforcement, but also has pictures of smugglers caught in the

Find out the rules and regulations for travel in and out of the US at www.customs.gov

act. The rules and regulations are outlined, and there is traveller information regarding mailing goods to the United States. It also provides all you need to know about taking your pets and medications, for example, in and out of the country.

— see also... —

Before you do anything in life, and especially before buying anything on the web, you will need a bank account – and there are many financial institutions out there to oblige you. Here are just a few of them: **www.lloydstsb.com**, **www.nationwide.co.uk**, and **www.wellsfargo.com**. Break out of that rut and find a new job using an online recruitment agency such as Manpower (**www.manpower.com**), Brook Street (**www.brookstreet.co.uk**), Reed (**www.reed.co.uk**), or Top Jobs on the Net (**www.topjobs.co.uk**). The *Guardian* is also well represented at **www.jobs.guardian.co.uk**.

Once your income is flowing, you can investigate other ways to save. The Cheapskate Monthly (**www.cheapskatemonthly.com**) offers advice about living on a budget, while Epinions (**www.epinions.com**) and FinPlanDotCom (**www.finplan.com**) provide online calculators to help you to plan your finances.

The Financial Pipeline (**www.finpipe.com**) has general financial advice, and Smart Money (**www.smartmoney.com.**) aims to help you take control of your finances. If you need one-on-one advice, then find an independent financial adviser at **www.find-an-ifa.co.uk** – very helpful when buying property. Property prices are pretty high in Southeast England, so it would be sensible to check out the current prices at **www.hot-property.co.uk**.

There is an immense amount of help for potential and experienced investors on the Internet. Investing Basics (**www.aaii.com/invbas**) is a good place to start, while more specialist advice, including taxation, is available at the Vanguard Group's website (**www.vanguard.com**). If you'd like to know more about the stock market before throwing away your money, try Ample at **www.iii.co.uk/shares**. As ever, Yahoo! has a magnificent section on finance (**finance.yahoo.com**). And you can find out about the place where US money is physically created at the US Bureau of Engraving and Printing (**www.bep.treas.gov**).

More investment and general money-handling advice, aimed at women, is available from iVillage Money (**www.ivillagemoneylife.com**), while glossaries of technical terms can be found at MoneyWords (**www.moneywords.com**) and the *Critical Trader Stock & Commodity Newsletter*'s Glossary of Trading Terms (**www.centrex.com/terms.html**). UK Share Net (**www.uksharenet.co.uk**) is a good general source of investment resources. If you're really getting your teeth into wheeling and dealing, try Turtle Trader (**www.turtletrader.com**), the Hedgehog (**www.hedge-hog.com**), and Sensible-Investor (**www.sensible-investor.com**) for some top tips. You can also get the lowdown on the movers and shakers at The Real Internet News Initiative (**www.rini.org**). If you want to try your hand at celebrity trading to earn a virtual mint, head for **www.bbc.com/celebdaq**. It's all the rage apparently.

Once you've put together a nest egg, you'll want to protect it. Try Investor Protection Trust (**www.investorprotection.org**) and the Federal Deposit Insurance Corporation (**www.fdic.gov**) for essential investment advice. Don't forget to keep your pension healthy – look up the Department for Work and Pensions (**www.dwp.gov.uk**) to find out what you need to do.

It makes sense to write a will, and Crash Course in Wills & Trusts (**www.mtpalermo.com**) will help. And if it all goes wrong? The Bankruptcy Lawfinder (**www.agin.com/lawfind**) might prove invaluable. Let's hope not.

MUSIC

Music is one area of the Internet that is growing at an exponential rate. The advent of MP3 has meant that never has so much music, in all its different forms, been available to so many across the world. Music of all forms is catered for – want to form a garage band? Or do you want to learn how to read music? You may just be desperate to find out where and when your favourite band is playing its next concert and want to buy a ticket, or even their latest CD as well. The Internet will do all this for you. Many companies that began by just selling CDs branched out into selling videos, games etc, so these sites are listed within "Entertainment" on pages 96–9. However, the section below also includes special Internet radio stations, as well as all your favourite music magazines that are now online.

Concert information

Gigs USA: previews, news, and tickets
www.ticketmaster.com
The world's largest online ticketing resource boasts tickets for more than 350,000 US-based events a year. Find out what gigs are coming up in your area, and check out the associated merchandise available. Read up on your favourite acts, and find out about other events, too, such as sports fixtures, art exhibitions, music shows, or family days out.

Pollstar: the concert hotwire
www.pollstar.com
Find out where your favourite musicians are playing, all over the world, and check out the band gossip. There are a few online concerts listed, too, if you don't mind connecting to the Internet for a couple of hours to listen to low-quality sounds.

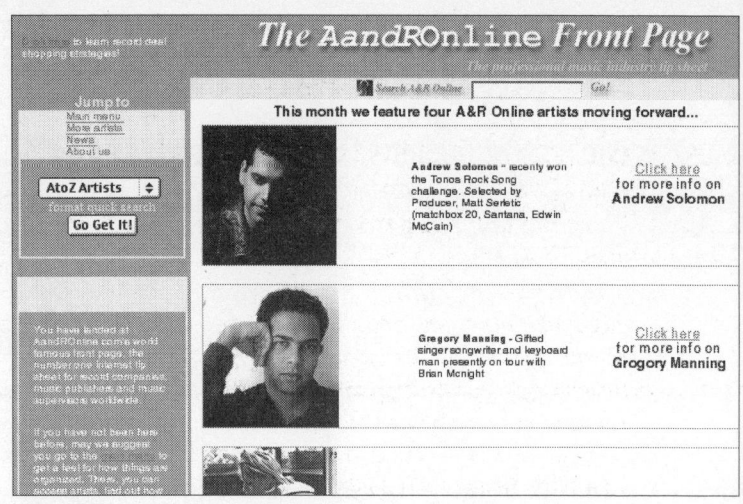

www.aandronline.com gives budding musicians the chance to get their music noticed

What's on in the UK
uk.ents24.com
Find out what's on where with this event listings. It covers live music, clubs, theatre, and comedy, and you can even have updates beamed straight to your mobile phone. The latest tour dates are always listed. There is a good mixture of famous, tribute, and unsigned bands here, and each entry is accompanied by a small map to help you to find the venue.

For musicians

A&R Online
www.aandronline.com
The place to get yourself noticed by the professionals who will (you hope) get you noticed. Submit your music to be showcased, and learn how to copyright your songs online. Artists are showcased each month, with long promotional sheets and the chance to listen to their work in MP3, Real Audio. Pass your comments on these artists on to others in the discussion forums.

Get Signed
www.getsigned.com
If you're hoping to make it big in the world of music, then here is a plethora of insider information to get you started. Find out about all the record labels and

what they look for in an artist, how to book your own tour, and reasons why your demo could be rejected. Sister site **www.garageband.com** gives you the chance to listen to what other bands are doing, too.

Hints and tips for budding stars
www.lyricalline.com
If your idea of a good time is to write angst-ridden songs about your teenage years, or you feel you are a budding rock and roller, then the Lyrical Line Songwriting Resource has plenty of advice to offer, even including a rhyming dictionary! There are articles on objectively judging your material and opportunities to post your lyrics and audio on the site for constructive criticism. Unfortunately, most of those who do the latter haven't read the former, I'll wager. See also **www.iwritethesongs.com** for the Songwriters' Radio Show.

Locate sheet music
www.sheetmusicplus.com
If you have trouble locating sheet music for the pieces you need, try this excellent, searchable site. You'll have to order and pay for the manuscripts, of course, but the size of the stock and the search engine makes this much more convenient than using your local library or music shop.. Modern pop music is available, as well as classical works, animated e-cards and musical equipment.

Music industry database
www.1212.com
The site states that it is the largest database of music industry-related web information in more than 50 countries. Find information about session musicians and legal services, buy and sell used equipment, and even locate security bodyguards at this huge site.

Resource centre for music makers
www.harmony-central.com
If you want to make music using computers, guitars, basses, or synthesizers, then this is a great resource. There are articles on buying equipment, touring, and building and maintaining your instruments. Product news sits alongside the articles and, although the stories are largely copies of press releases, they'll appeal to music shop addicts.

Shareware for musicians
www.hitsquad.com
This is the top place to find shareware for musicians, and it also acts as a gateway to a range of other musical sites, including ones with books, sheet music, advice

on getting your band signed, and guitar tablature. There are music-making tutorials and discussion forums so that you can benefit from other people's expertise, opinions, and criticism.

Teach yourself to compose
www.musicarrangers.com
This site sets itself a serious target: to teach you how to orchestrate, write, compose, create film scores, and so on. The course for beginners is ideal for GCSE-level studies, although it does become more advanced. The "Instruments" section is strong, too, providing a guide to all of the standard instruments in an orchestra.

Magazines

Mix Magazine Online
www.mixonline.com
Mix Magazine Online is a recording magazine aimed at pro and semi-pro DJs and producers. Unusually, this online version of a paper magazine actually provides exclusive material, rather than using the archives of previously published articles.

New Musical Express
www.nme.com
The online version of this opinionated music mag is an improvement on the physical thing. Check out the news, as well as gig and album reviews from recent years, and find out who's on tour, where and when. There are charts of all different types of music, and you can buy gig tickets online. The video index allows you to watch video promos and interviews of your favourite stars. There's now a radio station, and you can have ticket alerts texted to your phone.

Q Magazine
www.q4music.com
This popular music magazine's online version contains huge numbers of music reviews — more than 20,000 in fact — and a virtual mixing studio where you can arrange your own music. If you like what you read here, then you can always follow the advice and buy the recommended CDs through its shopping facility.

Rolling Stone
www.rollingstone.com
This music magazine has created a quite brilliant website that not only has all the usual news, reviews, and competitions, but also contains a massive artist archive.

www.mp3.com is just one site where you can download your favourite music from the web

Each band or performer has a dedicated page with an introduction, other articles, biographies, discographies, discussion forums, and links to places where you can read more and buy the music. Watch promos on the video section, too.

Top of the Pops
www.bbc.co.uk/totp
The Top of the Pops site has all you need to keep you abreast of the current top 40 and beyond. You can check out the charts and new releases, and browse the TOTP magazine. Buy CDs and other products online, or just check out Will's favourite albums or test your Gareth knowledge. Rock on, mate!

MP3

Download music
www.mp3.com
Find out everything you need to know about MP3s and also download them. You download sound files in a digital format (MP3) containing the tunes of thousands of artists worldwide. You will be able to access some really different, and sometimes good, music from largely unsigned bands. You can also order CDs that contain both normal and MP3 format songs. You can discover what software exists to play the songs that are available on the Internet, and learn how to transfer your

An essential guide to classical music sites at www.classicalmusic.co.uk

MP3s onto CDs. There are more than 150,000 sites listed here, so it's a good place to start. For fans of digital video and Flash animation, head for www.mp4.com where a wealth of downloads is just waiting for you.

Lycos MP3 search
music.lycos.com/downloads
Quite simply, this is the world's biggest MP3 directory, with more than half a million files online. You can search files by genre or by the biggest artists. It has its own features with official downloads and the chance to see web chats with the biggest stars. It also offers you videos to view. The site has its own good but rather garish media player available for download, too.

MP3Board
www.mp3board.com
Certainly not pretty but still very effective, with this site you can search not just over the Internet, but also through ftp sites (see the Glossary on pages 307–9 for an explanation of these if you are starting to glaze over) for your favourite tracks. The gnutella search system is good for finding tracks as well. If you cannot be bothered to do a specific search for something, then why not just browse through the various categories that are available here? You are sure to be tempted by something. Beware, once you start ...

After Napster
www.afternapster.com
The site that probably gained the most column inches in the past couple of years is alas no more. With some artists and music companies up in arms over its open attitude of sharing music, it came to a swift end. The basic premise was that you downloaded the special software and shared all the music on your hard drive with hundreds of thousands of people around the world. It's ghost lives on, however, in a wealth of sites springing up to take its place. Find out more here.

Musicals and classical music

BBC music magazine
www.bbcworldwide.com/magazines/music
Highly respected, mostly classical, music magazine in its online form, and, being under the Beeb banner, it gives you the chance to purchase recommended items. Find out about local concert listings by region or search the large review database.

Classical composers archive
voyager.physics.unlv.edu/webpages2
Find out the names, nationalities, and periods of classical composers using this basic but comprehensive database. You can also search by birth date to find out which geniuses share your birthday and discover important dates in their lives.

Directory of classical music sites
www.classicalmusic.co.uk
This site contains a directory of other classical music sites, with categories including bassoonists, CD-ROMs, early music, and live webcasts. If you "Join the Upper Circle", the site will e-mail you with the latest concerts in your area. The online shop provides classical music CDs, videos, and books, while a set of mailing lists aims to keep musicians in touch.

Everything you need to know about musicals
www.musicals101.com
This outstanding effort is a one-man project documenting musical theatre and film. It is, indeed, everything you need to know about musicals. There are mini-histories of the different eras, lowdowns on the composers and directors, and even some modern reviews. The author is clearly devoted to his subject, and much of the site is his subjective opinion. Still, it is a very well written site and worth visiting if you are at all interested in musicals.

Global Music Network
www.gmn.com
A site to suit lovers of classical and/or jazz music. Watch webcasts or read reviews of the latest classical or jazz CDs. The two areas are separated completely, so no annoying scrolling. And there are the obligatory Real Audio clips, too.

Musical Theatre in Europe
www.eur.com
Musical Theatre in Europe is a great way to find out where your nearest opera house is, although the inconsistent spelling of theatres is rather irritating. Each entry is accompanied by an exterior photo and includes details of the theatre's repertoire. You can also use the site to find out where and when your favourite "artistes" are appearing.

The world of classical music
www.classical.net
This site includes handy advice on how to pursue your interest in listening to classical music, reviews of a mind-numbingly large number of CDs organized by composer, and a fantastic selection of links to help you to find concerts, as well as information on composers and orchestras.

Popular music

The Beatles
www.thebeatles.com
This official Flash-based website for the Fab Four was launched at the same time as the record-breaking *Greatest Hits* album in 2000. A long time coming, it is still impressive, mainly because it gives web access to video and audio clips seldom available due to Apple's strict vetting of all Beatles material. The site currently focuses on the 27 singles, but each is meticulously accompanied by biographical and recording information, chart positions, audio, and video. So if you want to see the Beatles performing "Get Back" on the roof of Apple Studios, then come here.

CD database
www.gracenote.com
This database holds the titles and track names for every CD you can think of and hundreds of thousands more. If you play CDs using your computer, you can use this database to update your software so that when you insert a CD it displays the artist's name, which album it is, and what tracks are playing. It also has a list of

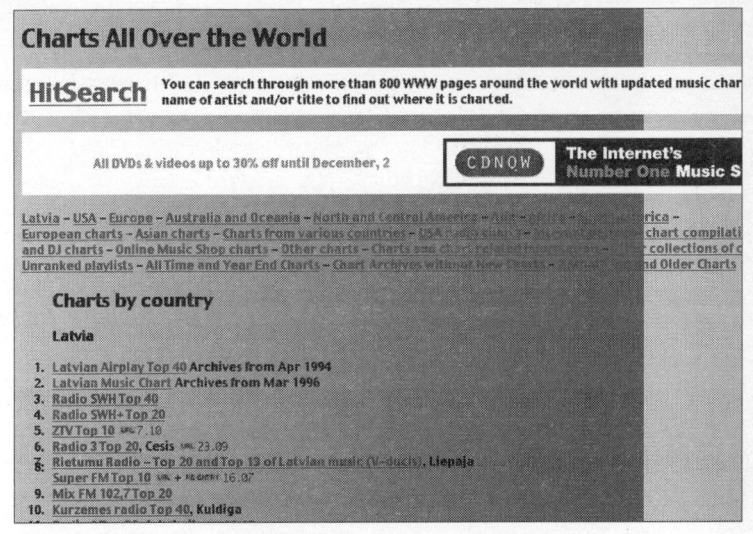

Access music charts from around the word through www.lanet.lv/misc/charts

charts, featured CD players/samplers, and advice on how to build your own computer media player. Indispensable.

Chart lists worldwide
www.lanet.lv/misc/charts
If your interest in chart music isn't limited to the buying habits of those in the United States or United Kingdom, check out this comprehensive list of links to music charts all over the world. Okay, so the site's design is basic to say the least, but you won't find a link to Latvia's Rietumu Radio Top 13 on the same page as Malta's Top 10 Albums anywhere else!

Country music
www.countrymusic.about.com
Garth and Emmylou are waiting for you here at this extensive site. Every thing you need is here, from album reviews, videos, and MP3s to fan clubs and festival guides. There are even lyrics and chord charts should you be inspired to join in.

Gossip and news from the music world
www.artistdirect.com
Home of the official online channels operated and maintained on behalf of a myriad of superstar acts; UBL **www.ubl.com**, an award-winning, all-inclusive music portal and search engine with a database of more than 500,000 artists and millions of links; iMusic (**www.imusic.com**), the premier online music community

site with message boards; and the ARTISTdirect Superstore, a full-service online shopping mall that features exclusive artist merchandise and other collectibles, limited-edition CDs, and an advance concert ticket window.

The Insider's Guide to Music
www.dotmusic.com
Get the latest chart music news here, with full-length interviews with the stars, the latest charts, a number of band microsites, a special dance music section, some audio clips of latest hits, and in-depth articles on highlighted bands that include discographies and discussion forums.

Jazz
www.allaboutjazz.com
Everything you want to know about jazz is here. There are articles, news, reviews, videos, interviews, and even a jazz humour section (yes, jazz lovers are not all serious musos). With such a diverse musical genre, you can choose your favourite style of jazz and search the site in that manner – find news and reviews on contemporary or ambient space jazz, whichever takes your fancy. The "Jazz Uncorked" section even recommends a good vintage to go with your listening. Niiice.

MTV Online
www.mtv.com
Packed with up-to-the-minute information and special music features, the popular music channel's website is a formidable construction. There are profiles of cult shows on the channel and "The Vault", where you can find old news stories, video clips, and reviews stored by band name. Catch up with the Osbournes, visit the celebrity auctions, or play fantasy music tycoon.

Rare records and CDs
www.netsounds.com
It ain't pretty, but it sure is thorough ... UK record shops from all over send a database of their stock to this site to create a huge central database, from which you can search for virtually every record or CD released, however rare. The search engine can be a little inconsistent, but the site is a must for any music buyer.

Sonic Net
www.sonicnet.com
Now part of VH1.com, every form of music is catered for here from rock to jazz, and classical to country. You can even add your favourite artists to the home page for quick access and find discographies, biographies, reviews, news, audio, videos, and concert listings. The site also has its own radio station, Radio VH1.

The latest official UK singles and albums charts can be found at www.dotmusic.com

Up-to-the-minute singles reviews
www.ukmix.net
UK Mix is a handy little site, giving honest-sounding reviews of the week's singles. It will also find websites dedicated to your favourite artist and provide a weekly news feed, as well as links to lyrics and multimedia. The features on the bands du jour are a little lightweight, and the whole set-up is based around the charts, but unless you're into a truly alternative scene it'll do the job admirably.

Rare Record Price Guides
www.drury335.freeserve.co.uk/price-guide.htm
Do you have some old vinyl mouldering away in the attic? Before you take a trip to the record exchange, check its worth at this handy site. You never know, that old Laughing Gnome 7 inch from your gran could bring you £50.

Radio

Connecting yourself to Internet radio
www.radio-locator.com
RadioSpy is the home of a top piece of free PC software that you can use to find and connect to thousands of Internet radio stations. It can help you to locate

Listen to millions of songs broadcast on more than 120 channels at www.spinner.com

small, fast channels suitable for Internet users with modems or even help you host your own webcast. The program will scan radio stations' play lists for your favourite bands, so you shouldn't be disappointed.

Online radio stations
www.spinner.com
Spinner is the first and largest Internet music service, broadcasting more than 22 million songs each week to listeners all over the world. With 375,000-plus in rotation on more than 150 music channels, Spinner spans an extraordinarily diverse range of styles. The free Spinner Plus downloadable music player offers reliable, high-quality audio while providing links to a vast array of artist info and purchase options. Radio@netscape is a new player offering local radio, sports, and news. All in all, indispensable!

Radio broadcasting resource
www.radioearth.com
This resource for professional radio broadcasters has advice on preparing a show as well as a host of wacky, potentially amusing (or irritating) links that could provide show material. Think more Howard Stern than David Dimbleby, and you

won't be far off. There is a jobs page, too, which might be what you need if you follow all of Radioearth's advice ...

— see also...

You can learn all you need about the calming influence of music at the site of the American Music Therapy Association (**www.musictherapy.org**) and about possibly less relaxing music at A Brief History of Banned Music in the United States (**ericnuzum.com/banned**).

Guitar players wishing to learn music by their favourite artist should visit the Online Guitar Archive at **www.olga.net**. Professional guitar information is available at Sound on Sound (**www.sospubs.co.uk**). Buying your gear should be done at **www.digibid.com**. If you fancy trying out a bit of music-making using your computer, try Cakewalk's site (**www.cakewalk.com**) for details of its popular software. Synthesizer lovers should head to **www.synthzone.com**, and all music makers should love **www.museumofmakingmusic.org** and **www.pc-music.com**. Evolution (**www.evolution-uk.com**) will sell you both software and synth-style keyboards, while those at a level approaching professional should try Sonic Foundry (**www.sonicfoundry.com**) for its ACID music and Sound Forge range of programs. Try the Sonic Spot (**www.sonicspot.com**) for music software reviews, news, and discussion forums.

Saturday night performers should read the gloriously tacky *Karaoke Scene Online* (**www.karaokescene.com**) for details of equipment, events, and club listings, while **www.karaoke.com** has a searchable catalogue of tapes that you can order. More cultured music lovers will find themselves tempted to buy CDs of *42nd Street* and other theatre hits at **www.dresscircle.co.uk**.

Visit Creative Music (**www.creativemusic.com/features/dictionary.html**) for an online dictionary of musical terms and the Library of Congress Recorded Sound Reference Center (**lcweb.loc.gov/rr/record**) for its collections of recorded sound from American history. View images of CD album covers at MegaSearch (**mega-search.net**), although if you are deliberately obscure with your search then you'll hit a brick wall. You can buy film and TV music from links provided by SoundtrackNet (**www.soundtrack.net**).

Fans of British country music will enjoy the site at **countrymusic.org.uk**, while those into fishnet stockings, and other paraphernalia will be satisfied with The Official UK Rocky Horror Fan Club (**www.timewarp.org.uk**). More genteel listeners and players will appreciate a visit to the National Association of Youth Orchestras (**www.nayo.org.uk**) for a list of concerts, details of exchange visits, and music festivals. The austere Royal College of Music site (**www.rcm.ac.uk**)

gives access to the college's library catalogue and information on The Early Printed and Manuscript Music Project.

Impress your friends after taking notes at Operas and Composers: A Pronunciation Guide (**patriciagray.net/operahtmls/works.html**). It contains audio instructions on how to say names such as "Aïda". Many sites dedicated to deceased composers exist – you could try **www.jsbach.org** for starters. For a hobby where talking, let alone pronunciation, is actually irrelevant, visit Bellringing on the Net (**www.easytorecall.com/bellringing.htm**), the monthly journal for church bell ringers.

Begin your search for a good Internet radio station at Radio MOI (**www.radiomoi.com**), which provides streaming sounds from a customizable site. Tune into Asian music, plus news and other channels, at Radio of India (**www.radioofindia.com**).

There are thousands of sites for popular groups, so here, sigh, are just a few of them – ABBA (**www.abbasite.com**), Robbie (**www.robbiewilliams.com**), Radiohead (**www.radiohead.com**), REM (**www.remhq.com**), Will Young (**www.popidolwilliam.co.uk**) and Gareth (**www.garethgates.uk.com**). The URL is often pretty obvious. Maybe you'd like to be up there yourself. Put yourself forward for stardom at **www.itv.com/popidol**. Good luck.

Many good-quality music portals also abound, such as Click Music (**www.clickmusic.com**) and All Music Guide (**www.allmusic.com**). Perhaps you are feeling a little nostalgic for a particular decade. If so, the 1960s (**www.summeroflove.org/sixties.music.html**), the 1970s (**www.glam-rock.de**), and the 1980s (**www.inthe80s.com**) are well catered for. Get all the lyrics you could care for at **www.lyricsworld.com**. Of the hundreds of MP3 sites that are available, **www.audiofind.com** and **www.emp3finder.com** are worth a look, while Music Choice (**www.crunch.co.uk**) will suit the more left-field music lover.

THE NATURAL WORLD

We often forget that before we began surfing through cyberspace there was already a huge world around us with plenty to recommend it. And sure enough, online there is an almost endless supply of information about zoos, ecology centres, and a host of museums and organizations to prove it. While there are some highly academic sites, there are more than enough others willing to enlighten children and most adults. The Internet also makes it easier than ever to do your part to protect wildlife or the planet itself, and you will find some of the most important conservation organizations listed within this section.

Conservation groups

British Mycological Society
www.britmycolsoc.org.uk
Interested in fungi? Come to this site to gather information on how to pick wild mushrooms, and view the society's schedule of events. Cost-priced publications are available from the contacts provided. Best of all, there is a very large list of specialized fungi sites. It's just a shame that the design is so rudimentary.

British Trust for Conservation Volunteers
www.btcv.org
Why not give Ibiza a miss this year, and break your fingernails building stone walls in the Pennines? You can choose from a wide variety of international working holidays on this site and book them online. There is also an online shop and a discussion forum where you can contact the organization and pose questions.

Countryside management & nature conservation
www.naturenet.net
Those interested in conservation, particularly in the United Kingdom, can use this site to find out where the country's protected areas are, what the countryside law

entails, and how to work out if you're allowed to cross a farmer's field while you are out on a Sunday walk. For your more specific questions, just "Ask the Ranger".

Ecology and biodiversity
conbio.net/vl
Find out all about various animals and their habitats. This virtual library has links to a broad range of related sites – it is a good starting place to find detailed information. There is also an endangered species list, including an extinct category, and a section on pollution.

English Nature
www.english-nature.org.uk
Responsible for looking after England's wild plants and animals, this official government-funded organization has a website containing its press releases, a database of walks and other events, and lists of the publications and maps available to buy online. You can download files with information on areas of special interest, although you'll need a GIS (Geographic Information System) to read them.

Friends of the Earth
www.foe.co.uk
Read about the local, national, and international campaigns run and supported by this organization. There are press releases available online, as well as articles on GM foods, the World Trade Organization, airport expansion, and other contentious issues. There is even help on buying "green" energy for your home and ways for you to become involved.

National Trust
www.nationaltrust.org.uk
Working to save the most important sites in Britain, manmade or otherwise, this informative site has a list of events, education pages, and much, much more. The list of places to visit includes various National Trust buildings, as well as areas of incredible natural beauty.

Royal Society for the Protection of Birds
www.rspb.org.uk
Learn all about the issues surrounding nature reserves and wildlife protection, and find out what you can do to help the cause. The latest news stories are published online, as are details of special events and holidays for young bird enthusiasts out there. You can also watch the fascinating live webcams that have been placed in special places throughout Britain.

Find out what the World Wildlife Fund is doing at the moment at www.panda.org

US Fish and Wildlife Service
www.fws.gov
Catch up on conservation issues, read about endangered species, and learn how to become a volunteer. If you need a permit for importing or exporting plants and animals, or for hunting and fishing, you can fill in online application forms.

World Society for the Protection of Animals
www.wspa.org.uk
This website highlights its endeavours to make life better for animals. There are details of its campaigns against the fur trade, bullfighting and other cruel sports, and any other ways in which animals are abused. There are also news stories on actions and successes, as well as some background information on WSPA and animal rescue projects. Join the organization here, or simply make a donation.

World Wildlife Fund
www.panda.org
Read the weekly news reports about the state of our environment and the animals that live in it, discover what the WWF is doing about it all, and find out how you can help. A catalogue of publications is available online, as are competitions, quizzes, and free resources for teachers. The UK version is at **www.wwf.org.uk**.

Follow the Terra satellite from your desktop at www.earthobservatory.nasa.gov

Geography and environment

Debunking eco-scare stories
www.ecotrop.org
Get an alternative view of the state of our ecology. The author of this site, who is a professor of biogeography, has some controversial views on topics such as global warming and GM crops. There's a scary world population clock that increases in front of you, and there are essays about why the media are purposely misleading about green issues.

Earth Observatory
www.earthobservatory.nasa.gov
Follow the progress of the Terra satellite, which is watching over our planet, taking measurements of our land, ocean, and atmosphere, from this site. You can customize and generate animations of ozone depletion over a number of years, and choose other sets of data to create visuals for an idea of what is happening on a global scale. You can also access the reference library on all things environmental that is available here or ask a scientist if things are still a bit foggy.

Eco-news
www.e-guana.com
For the latest in high-tech eco-news, you'll find e-guana's site is hard to beat. The site provides access to a plethora of web resources for those wanting to become active about the environment, and it also has plenty of insights for the armchair eco-warrior.

Environment Agency of England and Wales
www.environment-agency.gov.uk
Learn more about this public body, which is responsible for regulating the environment in England and Wales. There is some very specialized news, and there are also articles on important issues. If you want to know what's going on in your backyard, a special section is devoted to informing you. There are also articles about how your household affects the environment and suggestions on how you can reduce the negative effects.

The Farmers' Almanac
www.farmersalmanac.com
Not just for farmers, this almanac claims to know which are the best days of the month to bake, make jam and jellies, cut hair, and mow the grass in order to increase growth. It also offers US weather forecasts for up to two months ahead and boasts a special astronomy section, with a calendar of full moons and other information. Many of the site's other subjects, such as astronomy, are catered for by external links to US naval and other reliable sites.

Farming news
www.worldfarming.com
You'll need to register (for free) to enter this convergence of a number of agricultural magazines. On the site there are news stories, categorized into different farming areas, as well as general topics that affect farming countrywide. There is also a "Farming Forum" that enables readers to discuss issues and an agricultural archive.

Friends of the World
www.friendsoftheworld.com
A portal to other environmental organizations, Friends of the World is dedicated to helping consumers and businesses make more environmentally friendly decisions in their day-to-day lives. There is information on deforestation, environmental degradation, population growth, and much more. With its many relevant articles and information on eco-friendly products and ideas, this is a very worthwhile place to visit.

Greenpeace
www.greenpeace.org
Keep in touch with what this environmentally interested group is up to, and read news stories about the issues that will affect all of us and the events that Greenpeace have organized. Typical subjects covered include toxic waste, nuclear fuel, whaling, genetic modification of crops, tanker spills, and deforestation. There is also information on how to join.

Hubble Space Telescope
www.hubblesite.org
Your chance to see what the Hubble is looking at in outer space, this site also allows you to look at far away galaxies in awe-inspiring detail. All pictures are clickable to look at in further detail and come with detailed yet concise – and relatively simple – explanations.

The Hurricane Hunters
www.hurricanehunters.com
Fancy seeing what the inside of a hurricane looks like? Well, now you can with the images recorded by the scientists who fly into some very serious storms and take snaps. You can take a virtual "Cyberflight", which involves seeing the planning that goes into each flight, taking a peek inside the plane, and reading an account of flying into particular storms.

National Geographic
www.nationalgeographic.com
Read featured articles, view eye-catching photographs, and see what your part of the world looks like using the satellite-imaged maps available on this site. Its interactive features are marvellous, including the chance to see how truly deep the wreck of the USS *Yorktown*, which sank at the Battle of Midway, is, and you can also read the survivors' stories in the forum. There is also a calendar of National Geographic events in the United States, with information on how to apply for tickets. Younger researchers are catered for very well here, as there are interactive stories, the opportunity to create a cartoon, an online quiz, and fun ideas of experiments and recipes for you to try at home.

Oceanography database
www.mth.uea.ac.uk/ocean/vl
Students of the sea should find all sorts of useful and sometimes interesting sites listed at this directory. The links are organized by geographical location and by subject, so, if you want to find out about wave vectors or the depth of the ocean, this is the place to come.

www.nationalgeographic.com is an impressive website to match the revered magazine

The Old Farmer's Almanac
www.almanac.com
Find tidal times, learn how to predict the weather using a pig's spleen (yes, really), and, oddly enough, scan a selection of recipes. There are also tips for beginners in the garden and life expectancy tables for household appliances. An active discussion forum completes this mixture of slightly off-the-wall articles.

Planet Ark
www.planetark.org
There is all the environmental news you can handle here, thanks to a partnership with Reuters. Read today's news, and view the latest pictures of environment stories. There are also details on how to recycle, an Internet radio broadcast ("Pulse of the Planet"), and a searchable archive of news stories. You can sign up to receive the environmental news headlines via e-mail each weekday for free, and there is downloadable environmental software in both Mac and PC formats.

Rainforest Action Network
www.ran.org
If you feel strongly about the destruction of the rainforests and the indigenous

tribes that live in them, then visit this site. A "Kids' Action" team exists here to enlist youngsters before things get worse.

Sierra Club
www.sierraclub.com
This group acts as an environmental conscience and aims to protect and preserve the environment for future generations. Based in the United States, it considers the problem of pollution on a global scale and suggests ways to live in sympathy with nature. Articles and letters from the *Sierra* magazine are there for you to read.

Tsunami
www.ess.washington.edu/tsunami
This site features advice on how to recognize the non-visual signs of an incoming wave and what to do about it, facts about how tsunamis are formed and behave, and a link to the West Coast & Alaska Tsunami Warning Center (**wcatwc.gov**).

Volcano World
www.volcanoworld.org
Find out all about volcanoes. There are news of recent eruptions and images and movie clips of the fiery mountains all over this world and some other ones, too. There is also a kids' section, with pictures painted by children and stories explaining the origins of volcanoes.

Windows to the Universe
www.windows.ucar.edu
Find out about our planet, the way it works, and how it relates to other planets in our solar system. You can view images of asteroids "in the wild" and compare the Earth's surface with Mars'. There are also always very recent images of the Sun, using different wavelengths, and other "space weather" pictures.

— Learn about nature —

All about orchids
www.orchids.org
Pick up some useful hints and tips on cultivating orchids, and have a look at some pretty pictures, too. There is information here on where to buy plants, how to cultivate them, useful addresses, and news of orchid shows. There are even anecdotes and stories with an orchid flavour and an orchid delivery service for birthdays and anniversaries.

See how www.sierraclub.com aims to protect and preserve the environment

Alligators and crocodiles
www.crocodilian.com
Anything you'll ever want to know about the history and conservation of alligators and crocodiles can be found at this site, along with some excellent pictures, too. There is information on all the species, including those which are endangered, and you can even listen to crocodile distress calls and mating bellows. Should you feel the need to seek out further information, then there are links provided, along with some extra on-site articles, including a serious care guide to keeping crocs!

Amphibian embryology tutorial
worms.zoology.wisc.edu/frogs/index.html
University students of amphibian life can use this tutorial to find out more about our slippery little friends. There are embedded movie files, and a thorough glossary is provided. If the words "gastrulation" and "neurulation" mean anything to you, then this is the site for you.

Artificial life
www.agentland.com/resources/6artificial_life/worlds
A good selection of links to sites dealing with Alife (the computer synthesis of life systems). Make a primordial soup and watch life forms evolve in Gene Pool, or get excited about Poisson-random mutations in the Avida computer program. In the "Electronic Meeting Place", a virtual robot interacts with human visitors in a virtual reality environment. All very futuristic, I'm sure. It's life, Jim, but not as we know it yet.

All you want to know about the natural world can be found at the excellent www.discovery.com

Centre for Alternative Technology
www.cat.org.uk
View some sample publications from this educational charity, the aim of which is to balance the relationship between people, nature, and technology. If you are interested in the possibilities of alternative technology, then look no further. For example, you can buy instructions on how to erect a windmill in your garden and, at the same time, cock a snoot at the nuclear power everyone else in your street is benefiting from.

Children's butterfly site
www.mesc.usgs.gov/butterfly/butterfly.html
Browse through the photo gallery containing colour images of common butterflies from all over the world. The author has gone for a wide choice, rather than a fully comprehensive selection of species. There are black-and-white illustrations describing the life cycles of butterflies and moths, which can be printed out and then coloured in.

Cyberpet
www.cyberpet.com
Everything that you might want to know about cats and dogs is available here. Get past the jokey home page and dodgy Mission Impossible music, and revel in

the feline and canine information at hand. Chat with others about your pet, smirk at the breeders' showcase, and browse the list of pet rescue groups.

Discovery Channel online
www.discovery.com
This is one of the most fun and entertaining sites on the web. All you might need to know about animals is available at this vast site, not to mention information on dinosaurs, space, and the weather – basically anything that can be discovered is looked at in detail here. Much of the content is child-friendly, and the young ones can learn through videos, pictures, and other forms of interactive teaching. There is just too much to go into detail about, but a good example is the "Yucky Worm" area – choose the Flash-based version for an extra yucky experience.

The froggy page
www.frogsonice.com
This simple but excellent frog-based page is a mixture of fun stuff and links to more serious, science-based pages and sites. Frogs on Ice provides sounds, pictures, and stories of frogs. There are songs (including Kermit's "Bein' Green"); famous stories such as those from Brothers Grimm; and linked sites, which have dissection tutorials, pictures of deformed frogs, and advice on keeping pet frogs.

Hummingbirds
www.hummingbirds.net
If you want to watch, feed, or study these little birds, this site hopes to provide you with enough handy information to help. There is a page identifying different species, a list of ways to attract hummers to your garden, and migration maps. A photo gallery is useful for those of us without a garden packed with exotic wildlife, and a nice hummingbird follows your cursor as you flit across the page. Ahh.

The Life of Birds
www.pbs.org/lifeofbirds
Sir David Attenborough's TV programme of the same name is documented here, along with a background to how it was made and a lot of information from the actual broadcasts. Bird behaviour, evolution, record-breaking species, and even audio clips of bird songs are all covered, and, as if that weren't enough, there is a healthy library of links to other bird-related sites.

Virtual travel
www.armchair-travel.com
Travel to exciting parts of the world without leaving your chair. Explore the Taj Mahal, the Houses of Parliament or St Paul's Cathedral in comfort. Coming soon

are promised tours of the Valley of the Kings, the Golden Temple, Berlin, and Kew Gardens. Panoramic photography adds to the overall stunning effect.

Virtual game reserve
www.africam.com
Claiming to be the world's first virtual game reserve, AfriCam offers nearly live photos from different parts of real reserves. The game drive cameras are mounted on Land Rovers, which are driven around the bush looking for interesting photo subjects, such as an elephant or lion, which are posted here. You can also receive the latest Eco news, and live webcams provide just one of the ways in which you can discover the wonders of African wildlife.

Wildlife preservation for children
www.thewildones.org
This multinational site is aimed at teaching children about wildlife preservation, and there are articles about individual species of animals at risk. Many entries include a sound file, so you can hear what a jaguar or aye-aye lemur sounds like. Some schools have published the findings of their projects on the site, and children can contribute their artwork of animals and habitat, too.

Museums, zoos, and parks

American Museum of Natural History
www.amnh.org
Experience an online tour of the butterfly exhibition, see a massive giant squid, and learn about extinction and biodiversity. Likely to appeal largely to the younger visitor, this New York museum's site is a must for up-and-coming naturalists everywhere. Grown-ups who still crave education will be interested in the lectures and talks available.

London Zoo
www.weboflife.co.uk
Web of Life is a unique new kind of exhibit at London Zoo, combining the best of museum-style information with live animals, telling the fascinating story of the conservation of biological diversity. This site tells you all about it. There's a species game to play, and you can find out what's happening at the zoo. Help name a baby anteater or read a keeper's diary. There are details of daily events, educational activities, and ways for you to become involved through membership or creature adoption.

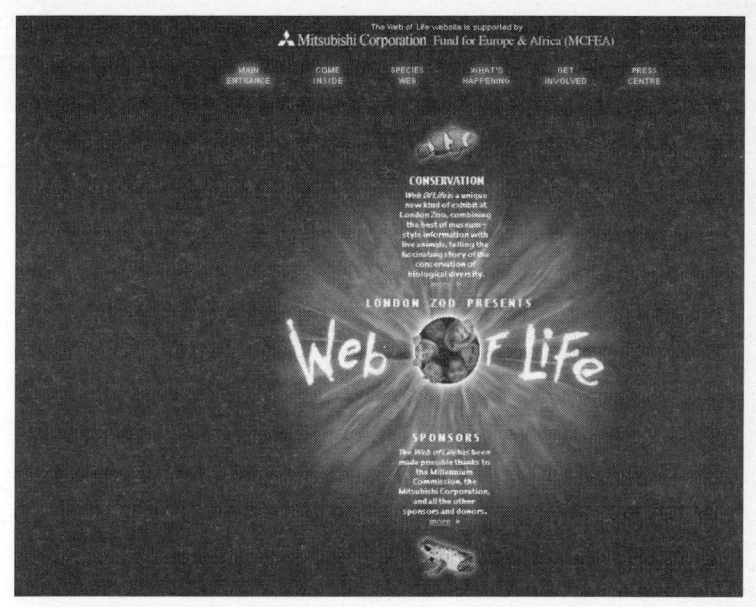

Find out about the exhibitions at the National History Museum by visiting www.nhm.ac.uk

The Eden Project
www.edenproject.com
Find out all about the stunning Eden Project from this comprehensive site. There's info on how to get there and details of the contents of the extraordinary biomes that house the thousands of plant species that thrive there. There's a virtual tour, too, that promises to allow you to take it all in in 3D. The greatest grow on Earth!

The Natural History Museum (UK)
www.nhm.ac.uk
Go straight to the "Galleries" to see a guide to the museum, stunning 360-degree panoramic photos, and details of the temporary exhibitions. There is a woodlouse survey that you can help with. The excellent "Interactive" section will bring explorations and scientific events to life. A "virtual reality fossil experiment" is just one of the other fascinating things available.

Natural History online magazine
www.amnh.org/naturalhistory
This promising effort from the American Museum of Natural History provides a selection of articles from the print version of its own magazine. You may find it a bit wordy and low on illustrations for a casual browse, but it is probably useful for the truly keen.

New England Aquarium
www.neaq.org
This US aquarium has a very worthwhile virtual tour that allows you to visit the exhibits almost as if you were actually there. With the online tour, you are guaranteed to see the sneaky octopuses, sea otters, and other shy undersea dwellers. When you've exhausted this, you can also browse through the monthly electronic newsletters.

San Diego Zoo
www.sandiegozoo.org
This well-designed site will take you on a cyber-safari around the world-famous San Diego Zoo. You can learn about the pandas and other endangered wildlife, read about the zoo's part in animal conservation, and download video clips of the keepers in action.

SeaWorld
www.seaworld.org
Another San Diego attraction, SeaWorld has a website with an online database which has answers to frequently asked questions about animals and articles on aquarium keeping, endangered species, and career advice. Send your questions in by e-mail. There is a range of teachers' guides available. There is also a "Penguin Cam", showing live coverage of the park's flightless residents.

The Smithsonian Institution
www.si.edu
From folklife to film, postal history to palaeontology (dinosaurs), the Smithsonian Institution has it all. View photos of the animals at the National Zoo, bones and butterflies at the National Museum of Natural History, and discover the truth about giant squid. The breadth of quality information here is astonishing.

— see also...

Read about conservation schemes, discover the burning issues surrounding our planet, and help if you possibly can using the information from such sites as the African Wildlife Foundation (**www.awf.org**) and the Born Free Foundation (**www.bornfree.org.uk**), which are concerned with saving elephants, wolves, and other endangered species. The world's rarest mammals are documented at **www.animalinfo.org**. The International Wildlife Coalition (**iwc.org**) protects general wildlife and highlights problems on its news pages. The National Botanical

Institute – South Africa (**www.nbi.ac.za**) is concerned with South African conservation, and the South African White Shark Research Institute (**www.whiteshark.co.za**) is, as you'd expect, interested in saving big, scary fish.

The threat to the world's dwindling gorilla population is highlighted at **www.gorillaaid.org**, while the UNEP World Conservation Monitoring Centre (**www.unep-wcmc.org**) takes an interest in the entire business of saving the world. Closer to home – if you live in the United Kingdom, that is – is the Game Conservancy Trust (**www.gct.org.uk**), while the National Biodiversity Network (**www.nbn.org.uk**) is concerned with conserving Britain's general natural heritage. Many miles away, the British Antarctic Survey (**www.antarctica.ac.uk**) is keeping an eye on the state of the Earth and penguins (apparently there is a rumour they fall over when watching low-flying aircraft).

You can learn about unknown species, including the Loch Ness Monster, at Cryptozoology (**www.ncf.carleton.ca/~bz050/HomePage.cryptoz.html**), as well as more feasible mysteries such as the beast of Bodmin Moor. Enquiring minds can find easy explanations of germs and what they do at the Microbe Zoo (**commtechlab.msu.edu/sites/dlc-me/zoo**). Back in the land of the furry, the Mammal Society (**www.abdn.ac.uk/mammal**) provides free fact sheets on British mammals, as well as the regrettable road kill surveys. Read about animals from Antarctica, as well as accessing geological information, at Glacier (**www.glacier.rice.edu**), and receive news and information about wildlife in the Shetland Isles at Shetland Wildlife (**www.wildlife.shetland.co.uk**). Those with an interest in birds from far-off places should try the Oriental Bird Club (**www.orientalbirdclub.org**), which covers birds from an area spanning India, Mongolia, and Japan.

Find out about government help for farmers, GM foods, and beef issues at the National Farmers' Union (**www.nfu.org.uk**). Details of the next Royal Horticultural Society London Flower Show can be found at the Royal Horticultural Society's website (**www.rhs.org.uk**). The National Park Service (**www.nps.gov**) is home to information on US parks, and it also contains links to cultural history pages. After all that, you can relax to the sounds of nature at Naturesongs.com (**www.naturesongs.com**), where you are able to listen to free recordings of, among other things, songs of birds, killer whales, and, er, skunks. Horse and pony lovers will find **www.equiworld.net** and **www.haynet.net** both invaluable resources.

NEWS

The immediacy of the Internet makes it an ideal way to broadcast and receive news, which can be downloaded to your desktop in a matter of seconds. What is more, most of this information is free, and many sites allow you to customize the news to suit your particular interest, be it the latest political news or the gossip on your favourite soap opera. But the beauty of the web is the scope of news that is available – interested in what Chinese or Russians read? You can find that out, too. Whatever slant you want on the news, there are TV networks, tabloid newspapers, and revolutionary parties all waiting out there to give it to you.

— Financial and business news —

American city business journals
www.bizjournals.com
Keep up with all that's happening in the American city market with distilled headlines from bizjournal.com's large list of newspapers. Expert business tips will be interesting to anyone starting or running a small business, news can be filtered through each particular area of industry, and there are tips on managing personal finance and networking opportunities.

Bloomberg News
www.bloomberg.com
This leading financial news site has investment advice, market and industry analysis, and insights from top Wall Street experts. Including a regularly updated market snapshot, this is a useful site for those managing a financial portfolio.

Citywire: news to make investors money
www.citywire.co.uk
The huge amount of daily financial news that is available on this site is accompanied by research reports and news on funds such as investment trusts,

One of the world's leading business authorities goes online at www.forbes.com

unit trusts, ISAs, and PEPs. An insider section will also help you to keep tabs on what all the big boys are up to out there, investment-wise, that is.

Dow Jones
www.dowjones.com
This is an excellent resource for news on business and markets. Categories are organized by industry area. There is an extremely useful area on how to set up your business – the various tools include how to organize your office, a list of company profiles, and how to manage a payroll.

Forbes magazine
www.forbes.com
The online presence of the business magazine is a flashy affair where you can find out about the world's richest people and the best places for single fun if you're rich enough. The normal business categories are also there, and you can track your portfolio. The thought of the day may inspire you, too.

New Statesman
www.newstatesman.co.uk
The *New Statesman* remains the essential read for bright thinkers everywhere. It has since introduced a subscriber-only service and an exact electronic edition of the magazine available to download hot-off-the-press anywhere in the world.

Financial news is up to the minute at *The Wall Street Journal* – online.wsj.com

Reuters Group Plc
www.reuters.com
Financial news, stock quotes, and all the top news stories are available from this focussed and well-established site. You can choose your main area of interest or go straight to the different story categories.

The Wall Street Journal
online.wsj.com
This site is not free ($79), so be prepared to take a quick tour and perhaps sign up for the free two-week trial. Or you can try the "Daily Edition", which will keep you up to date with business news, but you'll have to live without the full content of the site which includes free career advice, job listings, and business for sale.

See also "The Financial Times" in Money, page 185.

— Have we got news for you —

Expat World
www.expatworld.net
Moved away from your country of origin? You'll need Expat World, the news source

that aims to break through bureaucracy and make your life easier. The site claims that frequent travellers will benefit, too. There are a few free issues available to download (in Adobe Acrobat format) and a two-month free trial, but you'll have to shell out if you want to subscribe properly.

Home and Away: news for British expats
www.homeandaway.com
No, this site has nothing to do with the Aussie soap opera of the same name. Rather, it is aimed at British expatriates that are desperately wanting to catch up with goings-on in the United Kingdom. The site provides links to major newspapers, TV, and radio sites, as well as having more light-hearted nostalgia and gossip pages, too. This is truly a celebration of English, Irish, Scottish, and Welshness on the Internet, so you don't need to be an expat to enjoy it.

The Onion: spoof news
www.theonion.com
Hilarious or utterly offensive, this website takes a sideways view of the media, presenting spoof stories that are sometimes uncomfortably too close to the real thing. Language isn't so much of a problem, but the site is intended for over 18s, and so it should be.

Private Eye
www.private-eye.co.uk
The website of the satirical rag of the same name carries articles from otherwise unavailable back issues, as well as the latest front cover, an animation of the Yobs, and other favourites. You can submit your own small ad online (if you have a credit/debit card) and also follow links to a strange mixture of useful and very silly websites. Worth a look.

Reviews of UK media
www.anorak.co.uk
Daily reviews of the performances of UK newspapers and other media. The results are caustic, often funny, and sometimes in poor taste. At its best when it's slagging off newspapers rather than soap actresses. There is a pretty respectable set of links to press websites, while the caption competition may pass a few idle minutes.

Virtual newsroom
www.assignmenteditor.com
Assignment Editor provides lots of links – and that's all. But they are such a well-chosen selection that this site is an essential for any self-respecting researcher, journalist, or student. The main emphasis is on newspapers, with journals from all

over the world, local US papers, and a few Internet ones, but you can also find maps, telephone and fax listings, and a list of government directories.

News on demand

Directory of news sites
www.thepaperboy.com
If you have a very specific idea of the sort of news you want, then try this advanced web directory. "The Paperboy" will find newspapers and non-newspaper news from sources all over the world for you. The main international headlines are detailed, and there are links to online radio stations. A special UK section (**www.thepaperboy.co.uk**) lets you overload on current events. A headline metasearch has just been added.

Personalized news to your desktop
www.infogate.com
Receive news headlines, weather reports, and sports results up on your computer's desktop without even bothering to visit a website. This site provides a ticker program that sits on your screen feeding you the sort of information that you want to see (Yahoo! Messenger from **www.yahoo.com** does the same sort of thing). Other features help to organize your Internet passwords and fill in those annoying registration forms needed to access so many web pages these days.

Search engine for news sites
www.www.journaliststoolbox.com
The Journalist's Toolbox features more than 18,000 websites helpful to the media and anyone else doing research. Use the pulldown menu or search engine to locate information from a variety of beats and news industry-related topics. Using resources from The American Press Institute, this is a useful and informative site.

Up-to-date information
www.ananova.com
This is a rather different news site, where the latest info is disseminated through an animated character by the name of Ana Nova (hence the site's name). You can have stories fed straight to your e-mail address every day for no charge. This site can also provide up-to-the-minute news direct to your website or Orange phone (for a cost).

Help the homeless online by paying to read the articles at www.bigissue.com

Papers and magazines

The Big Issue
www.bigissue.com
Campaigning for the rights and welfare of homeless people, the paper is distributed on the streets by the people it aims to help, and it is now global. Don't expect to read the contents of these papers for free here – that's against the point of the project – but there are features that should help you part with your cash.

Electronic Telegraph
www.telegraph.co.uk
The original and arguably best online newspaper in the United Kingdom presents all the day's main stories, while a complete archive of previous issues can be searched. There are dozens of subsections, a bit like the Sunday version, to delve into.

Evening Standard
www.thisislondon.co.uk
The online branch of the London *Evening Standard* is an excellent news service. As an evening paper offline, it means that the articles are very up to date – it is good for finding out what is going on, as well as finding jobs and homes.

Gay Times
www.gaytimes.co.uk
This well-known gay news and features magazine is well represented on the web with a decent selection of extracts from the main publication, along with a handy shop selling books, videos, and CDs. There are also chat forums and links to other sites, plus a gay guide to the United Kingdom and the rest of the world and a useful section on relevant laws.

Guardian Unlimited
www.guardian.co.uk
The content of both *The Guardian* and its Sunday equivalent can be found live at this excellent site. There are headlines, breaking news stories, and special reports to be read here. The site also includes columns and short links to useful items, such as weather reports, TV listings, and information on events in the United Kingdom (unsurprisingly, each one of them is sponsored by the paper). There are many sister sites, too, equally as good, among them **books.guardian.co.uk** and **football.guardian.co.uk**.

The Independent
www.independent.co.uk
This newspaper's website was originally one of the online pioneers, but was desperately in need of a redesign, which it has recently had. The site offers news UK, world, digital, business, and people centred. Regular newspapery sections devoted to sport, columnists, and commentators abound, but you can also find careers advice and information about business schools. Entertainment and arts are also well covered, as you would expect.

International Herald Tribune
www.iht.com
"The World's Daily Newspaper" brings stories from all over together into one handy location. Features and special reports often seem a long time in coming, but news is published daily – you'll just have to subscribe to the real thing if you want instant access to it all.

The Irish Times
www.ireland.com
You can read the special features, find out what entertainment events are going on in Dublin, and get all the sports news, too. Obviously, politics is high on the agenda, but so are festivals. International news generally makes the headlines here. Have the main headlines from here e-mailed straight to your inbox if the size of the site worries you.

Jane's
janes.com

Jane's provides news on defence, transport, and law enforcement. In the defence section, you can find out about who's attacking whom, what's "in" this season, and which planes have crashed during manoeuvres. You'll get more detail here about military stories than any national newspaper can provide. Its "Regional News" section allows you to look at the latest happenings in areas across the globe.

Juiced
www.juiced.co.uk

The *Electronic Telegraph* (see page 231) has produced this online magazine, which is aimed at student readers. It features fashion, sport, and reviews of music, computer games, and films. There are puzzles, cartoons, and an opportunity to write in with your views. There are always plenty of competitions to keep you interested, too.

The Mirror
www.mirror.co.uk

Catch the latest headlines, receive advice from Miriam Stoppard, and find out what Jonathan Ross liked at the cinema. You won't find a full set of stories online, so you'll only be really happy with this site if you're interested in the sport section, which is the single largest area covered. The paper's other site is found at **www.sundaymirror.co.uk**.

The Moscow Times
www.moscowtimes.ru

This English-language newspaper publishes news based around Moscow and Russia in general. You can (try to) get to grips with the Russian stock market, discover what films and other entertainments are available, and browse the usually empty classified ads section. The majority of the international news relates to Russia in one way or another.

The Muslim News
www.muslimnews.co.uk

Providing news for Muslims in the United Kingdom, this site claims to be objective and independent of country or political party. There is a large archive of past issues and a mailing list for those who want to receive the site's press releases.

National Enquirer
www.nationalenquirer.com

Don't expect deep analysis of the Irish peace process here. You're more likely to

The Sun may not be high-brow, but there is still high entertainment value at www.thesun.co.uk

find details of Hollywood stars going into analysis or getting out of marriages, as well as stories you almost cannot believe are true. You can trace specific gossip back over a large period of time by entering a star's name into the search engine.

New Scientist
www.newscientist.com
You can read a fair chunk of features and news stories from the paper version of this technology and science-based magazine. There are also sections exclusively available on the web, so even current subscribers will find something new. In fact, some printed stories actually refer the reader to this site for further information.

New York Times
www.nytimes.com
Find full reports from this US paper, neatly sorted into arts, business, international, and so on. You can find out what happened "On This Day" in various years and even view a copy of the paper's front page from a featured year. A useful "Learning Network" section is aimed at teachers, parents, and students.

The Scotsman
www.scotsman.com
The stories that can be found here include Scottish issues and events, as well as the usual general UK and international coverage. A property section will prove

handy to those who fancy buying or renting north of the border. There's a web camera, providing 20-minute views of Edinburgh's top attractions, and a weather report for different regions.

South China Morning Post
www.scmp.com
The Internet edition of Hong Kong's English-language newspaper features news from all over the world, but concentrates on local and mainland China news. A searchable archive of stories is available, but you'll have to pay for the privilege of reading the results. There are links to other *SCMP* sites, including dedicated technology and horseracing papers.

The Sun
www.thesun.co.uk
The newspaper scorned but read by millions now has its own up-to-date website, featuring the day's headlines, as well as gossip, cartoons, and today's weather. The most comprehensive part of the site contains a database of page-three girl images, of course. Its Sunday equivalent, the *News of the World*, is found at **www.newsoftheworld.co.uk**.

Time magazine
www.time.com
Probably the world's most famous magazine has a remarkable online presence, with excellent resources and up-to-date information. Special features include "Person of the Year" and the *Time* 100 most important people of the century, and you can also look at its magazine photos. There are different versions for each continent, making this a truly global site.

The Times
www.timesonline.co.uk
Find news stories from one of the United Kingdom's most respected newspapers online. The site can actually be temperamental at times, but if you persevere you'll find daily news, obituaries, and all the usual business, weather, and highly opinionated stories that you'd expect from this paper.

USA Today
www.usatoday.com
Receive a summary of the stories available in the print edition, or view stories that have been listed in simple groups. There are the much-parodied "USA Snapshots" – a look at the statistics that shape our lives – as well as in-depth political and financial articles.

The Washington Post
www.washingtonpost.com
You can find a full range of US news stories here, including a section devoted to coverage in the morning paper. There is also work from a large staff of columnists and a searchable archive of stories, which could be a helpful homework resource.

The Week
www.theweek.co.uk
Why read all of the newspapers every day when you can find the week's news condensed into one, easily digestible magazine? Not only do you get the stories explained in plain English, but you can also see how different newspapers view the same events. Essential reading for anyone with an interest in the media.

Radio

BBC Radio 4
www.bbc.co.uk/radio4
Browse the programming schedule, try the daily quiz broadcast, and listen to the radio station online. Special features and favourites, such as "The Archers" and "Woman's Hour", make this a site worthy of your attention. Many of the site's apparent offerings are served from the BBC's main site.

VTuner
www.vtuner.com
VTuner is an easy way to find and listen to radio and TV broadcasts over the Internet. It lists thousands of stations from more than 100 different countries around the globe. You need to download the software (not free) and you're off.

Voice of America
www.voa.gov
International, regional, and US news is broadcast from this radio station in 52 languages. You can find which frequency you should use to tune in to, and just one click will call up an Internet broadcast in English. Written news stories are updated on the site every five minutes.

World Radio Network
new.wrn.org
Listen to a variety of audio news reports in different languages from various countries on this site. There are live broadcasts from WRN's own service, as well

All the technological news that you could possibly need can be found at www.wired.com

as many different links to other sources. The site also includes programmes for those that are interested in the arts, sports, music, and science rather than news.

Technology news

New Media Zero
www.nma.co.uk
Probably the leading UK Internet magazine caters for those interested in online advertising, marketing, and publishing. Find out about the Top 100 media agencies. An editorial feature called "Today's Comment" is updated daily, while articles from the magazine are reproduced online. There is also a large job section.

News on everything technological
www.wired.com
Aimed at people who use technology in their work or view it as a serious hobby. Wired runs news stories on anything from mobile phones to the Hubble telescope.

News for Internet businesses
www.thestandard.com
Business news for Internet-based companies is available here. You can register to get access to its informative daily newsletter for all the latest industry information.

There are excellent in-depth articles to browse through as well. US web workers should have a look at the Business 2.0 site (**www.business2.com**), although, in this integrated world, many stories overlap.

The world of high technology
www.ntk.net
Weird, retro design aside, this site provides a weekly view on high-tech news complete with snide comments and sceptical outlook. There are links to some very rude but occasionally funny sites, so keep an eye on the kids — who probably won't get most of the "jokes" anyway.

CNN
www.cnn.com/tech
CNN.com is among the world's leaders in online news and information delivery. It features the latest multimedia technologies, from live video streaming and audio packages to searchable archives of news features and background information. The technology site is full of the latest gizmo reviews and news stories. Covering everything from business tech to games and features on cyberbegging and the next big things, it also has links to fortune.com so that you can find out who the new technology is making rich. There are videos to watch too, but you have to be a subscriber to enjoy them. Still, this is a very useful site so may well be worth the investment.

TV

ABC News
www.abcnews.go.com
Displaying mainly US news, the straightforward layout makes this an easy new site to get to grips with — there are lots of live newsfeeds and audio and visual media to satiate your news demands. Other non-news features are also built into this site, including a shopping guide and a chat room.

BBC News
news.bbc.co.uk
This top site from a news source respected the world over provides an excellent service. Watch video footage, listen to reports, and follow links to build up an overview of world situations. The world service is available in many languages at **www.bbc.co.uk/worldservice**.

CBS
www.cbs.com
This well-designed site lets you know what's coming up on CBS in the coming week. There are pages dedicated to TV shows such as *David Letterman* and *CSI*. For those who like to be "in the know", there's also some gossip from behind the scenes of the top shows and exclusive interviews with top CBS stars.

CNN
www.cnn.com
There's something for everyone at this news site cum Internet portal. There is more US than "World" news, as you might expect, but other handy areas include "Technology" (see previous page), "Health", "Entertainment", and "Politics" (US). UK readers may find that they get a better Internet performance by visiting the European site that can be found at **europe.cnn.com**.

FOX News
www.foxnews.com
You can access a good mixture of current affairs news stories from this TV network's site. Special reports are included, and there are weather maps covering the whole world that are updated at least twice a day, too. You can also create your own newscast by compiling separate reports into a single video stream. This is a very clever site …

ITN
www.itn.co.uk
This independent news site offers some useful features. Find out how the news is brought to you and the teams of people involved. An archive of stories going back one year can be searched. It's also home to Channel4 News and Five News, too.

Microsoft and NBC
www.msnbc.com
This website is a combination of Microsoft and the NBC news network. It covers international and US-specific news, with lots of audio and video, or you can type in your ZIP code for local sports, election returns, and weather. The site also provides links to the US regional news affiliates, so that you can see what's going on in your own backyard, too.

News Now
www.newsnow.co.uk
Updated every five minutes, this site condenses news stories from multiple sources, including the BBC, CNN, and MTV, categorizing them into appropriate

sections. US and UK news stories are denoted by little flags, so that you can easily restrict your view to a national one. The most popular stories are listed to enable you to hone your search even further.

Sky News
www.sky.com/news
There is plenty of UK news here, as well as coverage of what is going on in the rest of the world. Stories are categorized into sections, making the site easier to navigate than a paper journal. There are plenty of video clips to view a radio station and webcams.

Teletext
www.teletext.co.uk
Carrying the same concise news stories as its equivalent TV service, Teletext's website is faster and less frustrating to use. You won't find detailed analysis here, just pithy headlines and the odd quote – ideal for those with limited time or small attention spans.

See also "TV, Radio, and Ads" in Entertainment pages 102–4.

Weather

The Met Office
www.meto.gov.uk
Receive weather reports from the UK's official Meteorological Office, and learn about the automatic weather stations – you can even have forecasts delivered to your mobile phone. A severe weather warning service is invaluable, and the tropical cyclone forecasting section is particularly good, as it includes links to advisories all over the world.

Weather reports for the active
www.intellicast.com
If you are planning to take a trip in the great outdoors, you'd be very wise to check the weather reports. Intellicast is aimed at just such adventurers, providing information on where the best places to play golf are, specialized forecasts for sailors, and regionalized entries for US national parks and other popular recreation areas. The current weather chart for the United States is regularly updated on the home page.

— see also... —

Almost all newspapers, broadsheets, and tabloids are now online, whether you want to look at the *Racing Post* (**www.racingpost.co.uk**) or the *Daily Star* (**www.dailystar.co.uk**). The UK radio station Independent Radio News (**www.irn.co.uk**) provides audio national and international news bulletins, while anyone looking for international news from internal sources should check out such sites as the *Times of India* (**www.timesofindia.com**), China Online (**www.chinaonline.com**), and the Canadian Sympatico (**www.ab.sympatico.ca**). For out-of-this-world news of events in space, try SpaceDaily (**www.spacer.com**). There is more high-tech news at SciTech Daily Review (**www.scitechdaily.com**) and Silicon.com (**www.silicon.com**), which also features web-based TV broadcasts. Use the customizable news ticker at News Index (**www.newsindex.com**) to have the latest headlines piped straight to your desktop. InfoBeat Inc (**www.infobeat.com**) will provide free news via e-mail, while O_2 (**www.o2.co.uk**) will go one better and beam stories directly to your mobile phone. See yourself as a hack? Join other journalists in the Fleet Street Forum (**www.fleetstreet.org.uk**). For local news with a satirical twist, you can't do better than the wonderful Framley Examiner (**www.framleyexaminer.com**).

If you only want the day's news summarized in one place, try Info Junkie (**www.infojunkie.com**), which provides links to the most important stories. The Omnivore (**way.net/omnivore**) brings in news from all over the world. Yahoo! News (**dailynews.yahoo.com**) keeps the headlines in an easily accessible place – should you use its search engine, too. If you're fed up with the gloom and doom of most news reports, read the Good News Network (**www.goodnewsnetwork.org**) for news with a positive spin.

The Children's Express (**www.childrens-express.org**) is a news agency and website run by under-18s, while the Drudge Report site (**www.drudgereport.com**) is a sometimes scurrilous gossip/news column frequently only suitable for older readers. Old favourite CBBC Newsround from the BBC is to found at **www.bbc.co.uk/cbbcnews**. Underworld gossip can be found at Intelligence Online (**www.intelligenceonline.com**); this is where the security services pick up their specialist news. Media, business, and financial news can be found at PR Newswire (**www.prnewswire.com**), *The Economist's* electronic version (**www.economist.com**) provides world political and business coverage, and Media UK (**www.mediauk.com**) carries a directory of UK television, newspapers, and other media sites. It also includes a downloadable TV guide that stays up to date using the Internet.

REFERENCE

This section deals with the sort of subjects you might delve through your 40-book set of encyclopedias for. Luckily, it is much easier to discover reference information on the Internet, with museums, encyclopedias, and libraries happy to share their resources with the general public. Whether you want to see the relics of a distant museum or need advice on complex legal issues, there are thousands of sites out there to help you with your specific tasks.

Any questions?

Ask an Expert
www.askanexpert.com
This site does exactly as it says, and you can challenge the experts with particularly difficult questions. There is an expert of the month to answer your queries. You can browse by categories to ask the correct expert, too.

Find out how to do just about anything
www.ehow.com
The answers to all those awkward questions (which direction do you shave in, how can busy people eat breakfast, which PR firm is right for my business?) are all contained within this site. The terminally disorganized may wish to use the personal reminder service, which sends you an e-mail on the appropriate date that you need to be reminded of something important, such as a family birthday.

How things get done
www.soyouwanna.com
A fast and easy way to find out how to do a variety of real-world activities. So You Wanna is a comprehensive source of step-by-step solutions on how to do things. Whether it's finding out how to be a model, pay off your student loans, get a pet ferret, or even get a sex change. There are full explanations and also mini wannas for those with less time.

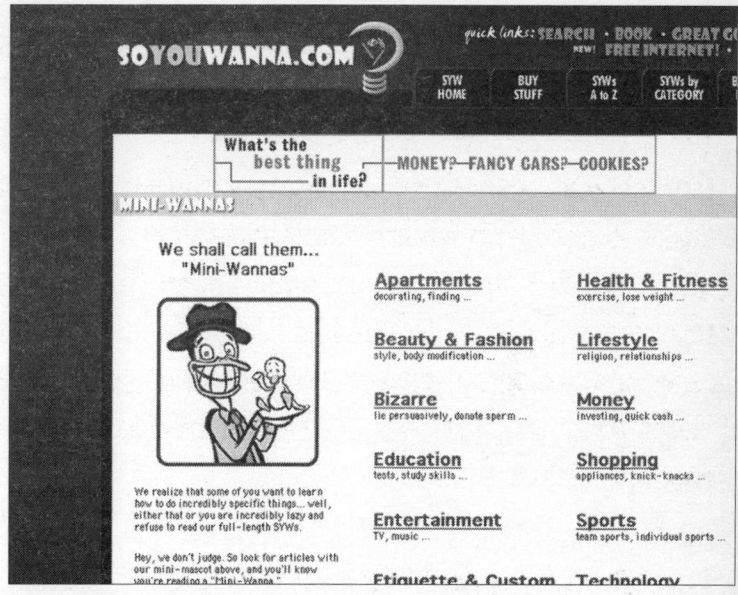

At www.soyouwanna.com you can find out how to do just about anything...

Internet FAQ Consortium
www.faqs.org
If you use the Internet regularly, you may have discovered a special type of free discussion forum called newsgroups, or "Usenet". Despite the rather basic look, you'll find it a useful information source. Each group has a set of rules and regulations, as well as lists of answers to particular questions that are asked so frequently that it's easier to document them than have to answer them continually. Try here first, before annoying other subscribers.

Scoot
www.scoot.co.uk
Search for businesses or services in any part of the United Kingdom and find the ones that are nearest to you. A "Business Finder" lets you run a search to track down, say, a plumber in Leeds, while the cinema guide has phone numbers, addresses, and programme guides, as well as the ability to send you e-mails with updates for your local cinema.

How far is it?
www.indi.com/distance
This service uses data from the US Census and a supplementary list of cities around the world to find the latitude and longitude of two places, and then

An online dictionary, encyclopedia, and almanac combined can be found at www.factmonster.com

calculates the distance between them (as the crow flies). It also provides a map showing the two places, using the Xerox PARC Map Server. Jolly useful when the kids are crying, "Are we there yet?"

Bits and pieces

Friends Reunited
www.friendsreunited.co.uk
Ever wondered what your old school and college chums are up to now? With more than eight million people already registered and drawing from a database of 40,000 UK primary and secondary schools, colleges and universities, Friends Reunited gets you back in touch. An annual membership fee is required. There are now 500,000 workplaces on the system if you feel inclined to look up that old boss ...

The place for pictures
www.ditto.com
Whether you want pictures to print out, for your computer screen, or to jazz up your website, Ditto is a good place to find them. Search for images of pop stars, animals, or even 1980s home computers. The pictures are provided by other websites, and a link is provided, so, if you are searching for an image of a certain model of car, you will probably find a page devoted to it.

Dictionaries/encyclopedias

Acronym Finder
www.acronymfinder.com
As this site's name aptly suggests, the Acronym Finder contains meanings for thousands of abbreviations, many of which IMHO (In My Honest Opinion, for the less knowledgeable among you) will have you ROTFL (Rolling on the Floor Laughing). Some descriptions, such as that for SNAFU (Simultaneous Navy Army Foul Up), have been sanitized to protect the sensitive. You can also discover what is allegedly the world's longest acronym.

All your questions answered
www.factmonster.com
This online dictionary, encyclopedia, and almanac provides a quick way to look up general facts and figures. Fact Monster is a big, colourful site with sections on serious topics such as world news, world history, major disasters and accidents, and war. However, "Fun Facts" tells kids all they want to know about heroes from Greek mythology, fairies, and dragons, and even lists the top bestselling books ever. The content is biased towards US events, though, so the site will appeal most to US browsers.

Dictionaries combined
www.onelook.com
If you just want to know the meaning of a word and can't be bothered trawling through all of the online dictionaries available (and we've listed just a few here), then try this site. It submits the word you are interested in to, at the time of writing, 848 different dictionaries.

A dictionary of visual art
www.artlex.com
Aimed at artists, students, and teachers, this encyclopedia for arty types contains the meanings of a multitude of technical terms and abbreviations. If you don't know your earth colours from your passe-partout, then give ArtLex a try. A respectable number of links to other sites adds to the site's usefulness.

Encarta online
encarta.msn.com
Microsoft's answer to an all-encompassing encyclopedia and dictionary, the online version of Encarta has 42,000 cut-down articles and a world atlas. The Deluxe edition is also available for a seven-day free trial. The search engine allows you to

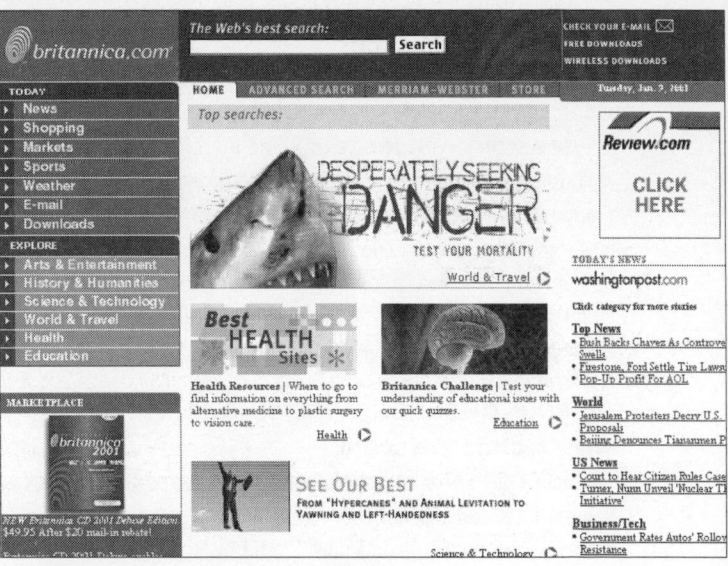

The ultimate encyclopedia is online at www.britannica.com

ask a question, and it will endeavour to take you to the answer. A reference and educational section will prove useful for those with sticky homework problems.

Encyclopedia Americana
www.go.grolier.com/go-ol/static/features/eafeatrs.htm
An online version of the extensive *Encyclopedia Americana* offers 45,000 articles covering all academic fields and curriculum topics, a searchable database of newsworthy current events from the *Americana Journal* and *Wall Street Almanac*, and over 4500 photos and images. You can sign up for a free trial here.

Encyclopaedia Britannica
www.britannica.com
The ultimate encyclopedia is online here. You can search more than 70,000 articles, a combination of articles and rated websites, or just the entire Internet. The latest news is also provided to keep things nice and current. It's no longer free, unfortunately – you do have to subscribe.

Encyclopedia
www.encyclopedia.com
There is a ridiculously large amount of information about anything and everything in the site that calls itself "the Internet's premier free encyclopedia". You can browse the articles by clicking on the appropriate letter.

Encyclopedia of Greek Mythology
www.mythweb.com
Mythweb is a site devoted to the heroes, gods, and monsters of Greek mythology. Everything you need to know, whether you are grappling with homework or preparing a lesson plan, can be found here. The Encylopedia of Greek Mythology is very extensive – there are illustrated stories and links to contests, learning products, and much more.

Getty Thesaurus of Geographic Names
www.getty.edu/research/tools/vocabulary/tgn
Research the names of different places in the world using this site. You can find out what your home town was called in the "olden days" and discover how many other cities exist in the world with the same name. You can then view the district, county, country, and continent in which the place you have searched for exists. It is also a good place to find out exactly how some tricky place names are spelt.

A glossary of literary terms
www.uky.edu/AS/Classics/rhetoric.html
This essential resource for English literature students is free, helping those on a grant to save their money for more righteous, liquid pursuits. Find out the difference between alliteration and assonance, parody and pulp fiction, and get an iron-clad definition of irony. The searchable database makes it easy to cross-link terms and write killer essays.

Grappling with grammar
www.edufind.com/english/grammar
Maybe you've forgotten what an adverb is, or perhaps you're unsure if the cat that belongs to Mr Jones is Mr Joneses, Jones's or Jones'. Whatever you need to know about English grammar, all of the usual terms and definitions we were supposed to learn at school but which have somehow managed to evade us completely are published here. Save yourself embarrassment, and check it out before the kids ask you any awkward homework questions.

Help with words
www.dictionary.reference.com
Featuring its own dictionary and thesaurus, this site also has crosswords and other word games, and it will even translate web pages written in foreign languages so that you don't have to. If you have a question about words and grammar, then you may well find the answer you need in the FAQ section. The links to writing style sites should be read by all students and, sadly, it has to be said, a fair number of journalists.

Search for the meanings of difficult words at www.yourdictionary.com

Online dictionary, word games, and bookstore
www.m-w.com
This is possibly one of the most popular online dictionaries – it is certainly one of the most linked-to. Merriam-Webster offers much more than just a boring word-search facility – there are "cool" words of the day, online word games, and a sort of online store where you can buy reference CD-ROMs and books via a real online store.

The Rap Dictionary
www.rapdict.org
If someone asks if you are "dissing" them or wonders if your "homey" is a "Willy" and you're not sure whether to take offence, don't worry. Check what they mean using this site's explanation of terms and you might avoid a "cap" in "yo ass".

A web of online dictionaries
www.yourdictionary.com
Choose from a vast selection of foreign-language dictionaries, thesauri, and specialized English dictionaries. The latter includes dedicated references to diverse

subjects including astronomy, politics, and music. If you have trouble with pronunciation or grammar, there are sites to help. You may be interested to see the 100 most misspelled and mispronounced words.

World Book online
www.worldbookonline.com
Visit the online version of this respected print encyclopedia, which is fortified and kept up to date by information from newspapers and magazines. It has an annual subscription rate of around $50, but you can try it out free for 30 days first.

The World Factbook
www.cia.gov/cia/publications/factbook
Although run by the CIA, you won't find the answers to any *X-Files*-style conspiracies here – just lots of information about different countries, their populations, and their economies. An essential resource for students with homework projects and adults who ought to know where Cambodia is but have forgotten. Clear maps are available, along with details of border disputes.

Legal issues

The Court Service
www.courtservice.gov.uk
If you are interested in what's happening in the UK courts, then this is the place to come to get the information from the right honourable horse's mouth. Many cases we read about in the papers are presented here, and it is interesting, if you have the time, to see what the papers choose to report on – or to ignore.

Desktop Lawyer
www.desktoplawyer.co.uk
Buy pre-prepared legal documents from this site for a great deal less than you'd pay in a solicitor's office. You can receive legal support over the phone and online legal advice for beginners. The latest legal developments are published as mini news stories. A top services list gives you a quick link to the most popular documents, which, unsurprisingly, are dominated by wills and divorces.

Divorce advice
www.divorcenet.com
If you are in the unfortunate situation where you are about to go through a divorce, then you can find advice here at this US site. You can search by state

for professional resources, while the "On The Couch" section has a question-and-answer session with a professional. Share your comments and thoughts with others in the divorce chat room.

Dumb Laws
www.dumblaws.com
This site is great fun to browse to find out what silly laws have been made in various countries, such as the right to marry your horse etc. Search by the engine or by categories, and find out that it is legal to drive down a one-way street the wrong way in Alabama if you have a lantern attached to the front of your car. Or why in Texas you cannot shoot a buffalo from the second storey of a hotel.

Law advice
www.findlaw.com
An easy way to search the web for law advice. Advice for legal professionals, students, and businesses on virtually everything that you can think of. You can find a local lawyer and get the latest legal news, too.

Law for All
www.nolo.com
The site for self-help on law matters with advice on all issues from wills and retirement to debt and bankruptcy. You can also buy all the legal advice you want from its online bookstore. Its tools include a legal encyclopedia and a house affordability calculator.

National Fraud Information Center
www.fraud.org
The National Consumers League in the United States has been advising consumers on the dangers of Internet fraud since 1992. There is also information on telemarketing fraud and fraud against the elderly. Although much of the consumer legal information is US-specific, the site is still an informative place to gen up on the technology issues behind Internet fraud.

Museums

The British Museum
www.thebritishmuseum.ac.uk
You can read about the exhibits in the museum through its world map, and make the most of your visit by planning your expedition. The Ancient Egypt section is

www.thebritishmuseum.ac.uk offers a great way to plan your visit effectively

especially good. You can view some of the highlights online, including the recently covered "Great Court", but you'll need to turn off the computer and actually go out to experience the museum properly.

Imperial War Museum
www.iwm.org.uk
Spanning the history of conflict from World War I to the present day, this museum occasionally puts selected exhibitions online, although you are guaranteed to always be able to get detailed information about each of the showcases. There is a notable espionage section, which young secret agents should be briefed on. Information is supplied on HMS *Belfast*, the Cabinet War Rooms, and Duxford – which is where the museum's aircraft are exhibited.

London's Transport Museum
www.ltmuseum.co.uk
Find details of the famous London's Transport Museum, and plan your next visit there. You'll find online exhibition previews and videos to download, visiting details, and learning services.

Museum of Science
www.mos.org
The online exhibitions from this museum have included designing your own robot, the secrets of ageing and a virtual fish tank Unlike some museums' efforts, here you can read full, non-patronizing, and educational texts accompanied by clear

The Museum of Science will provide all the scientific material you need at www.mos.org

diagrams. Relevant links to scientific sites, often government ones, make this a very useful place to visit.

Museum of Science and Industry
www.msichicago.org
Plan your visit to the museum, and find out about the latest exhibitions, both permanent and temporary. You can also preview forthcoming shows at the Omnimax theatre, a five-storey domed screen featuring films of places such as Everest and the Amazon.

National Art Library, Victoria and Albert Museum
www.nal.vam.ac.uk
Access the library's online catalogue, which contains a large chunk of the two million items held at the Victoria and Albert Museum. This is the backbone of the library's online services, so don't expect to see lots of flashy graphics.

National Maritime Museum
www.nmm.ac.uk
This museum is concerned will all things nautical, and it houses many painting, chart, and book collections. You can find out about Lord Admiral Nelson and the prime meridian, and search the frequently asked questions and library catalogues

online. You can also find help in planning your physical visit to the museum, and there is a reasonable resource for maritime links on the web here, too.

The Tech Museum of Innovation
www.thetech.org
Home of the "Robot Zoo", where robot versions of animals are used to explain how the real things work. There's an online earthquake exhibit, links to resources for teachers, and design challenges.

UK museums and galleries
www.24hourmuseum.org.uk
Designed to make finding worthwhile UK museums, art galleries, and heritage attractions easier, this site only lists those it considers worthy. Follow the "Trails" to learn more about the sites in your local area. An excellent online presence, it announces new exhibitions and contains news on such subjects as the Stonehenge bypass and online exhibitions.

See also "Museums, zoos, and parks" in The Natural World, pages 222–4.

Myths and conspiracies

Conspiracy theories
www.cruzio.com/~blackops
Those wanting to find the stories behind the headlines may want to pop in on Black-Ops for a different perspective. This directory of conspiracy theories on the Internet makes for interesting reading. But make sure that you don't fear going to bed at night as a result.

Greek mythology
www.thanasis.com/myth.htm
This website provides a humorous take on Greek myth and legend. Stories are presented by cartoon smoothie "Myth Man" and come complete with homework wizards. An archive of myths can be viewed. Packed with info – if you can separate the "fact" from the slightly odd editorial comment …

Independent Urban Dwellers
www.geocities.com/Heartland/Ranch/1216/index.html
Paranoia lies at the heart of city life for some Americans. Take this site, for instance. Some might call it wacko, but there's no doubting the sincerity of the

Plan your revolution with other anarchists at www.worldrevolution.org.uk

Sanders family's commitment to surviving the catastrophe they expect around every neighbourhood corner. Self-sufficient power, provisions, home-schooling and an essay or two on the encroaching power of the US government are the order of the day. Just see for yourself.

Urban Legends Archive
www.urbanlegends.com
Myth-making didn't stop in the Middle Ages. Some types are still at it. Take the story about the family that didn't know they'd been burgled until they developed their camera film, for instance. In any case, this site provides the most comprehensive collection of shaggy dog stories on the Internet. They're true - every one of 'em.

The World Revolution
www.worldrevolution.org.uk
With instant access to millions of minds, the web is a perfect home for anarchists and activists. This site's title gives you no small clue as to what it's all about. Conspiracy theories abound here – and there's plenty of optimistic talk about bringing the established order down. All this is accompanied by some pretty fancy design, too. This site is guerrilla warfare with a touch of glamour. And if you want to get involved, then there are plenty of e-mail contacts you can try out. Make sure you that know what you are letting yourself in for first, though ...

see also...

English scholars, especially poverty-stricken students, will be delighted to discover the wealth of reference works free on the web. The Quotation Center (**cybernation.com/victory/quotations**) will help you to look up those elusive famous quotes, while Thesaurus.com (**thesaurus.reference.com**) provides a handy online thesaurus dictionary. If you're more interested in graphic symbols than words, try the encyclopedia of symbols at **www.symbols.com**.

There are many online libraries and museums, including the impressive Internet Public Library (**www.ipl.org**) and the Online Computer Library Center (**www.oclc.org**), which explains all about the Dewey Decimal System. There is a directory of library and reference sites at Library Spot (**www.libraryspot.com**), and other good reference resources can be found at Refdesk (**www.refdesk.com**) and iTools (**www.itools.com/research-it**). The Internet Law Library (**www.lawguru.com/ilawlib**) provides easy access to details of US law, while free legal tips on the same subject can be found at Free Advice (**www.freeadvice.com**).

Macabre past disasters may be found documented at the Living Almanac of Disasters (**www.disasterium.com**), and you can try Time Zones for PCs (**www.globalmetric.com**) to discover the time in any country. Look up the Nobel e-Museum (**www.nobel.se**) for a history of the famous awards scheme, while potential winners of the science award should acquaint themselves with the Periodic Table of the Elements (**pearl1.lanl.gov/periodic**).

SOCIETY, POLITICS, AND RELIGION

As much as the Internet has to offer in entertainment, it also includes some informative sites on a huge variety of social issues. Charities, political parties, and religious groups all rely on the Internet to spread their messages and, as a result, have a wealth of information that they want you to have access to. So if your religious beliefs don't correspond with what's going on in your local church, you should be able to find like-minded people on the Internet to share your views and discuss the meaning of life. Similarly, if you have an axe to grind on social issues, or just want to know more about the machinations of government, then check out the varied sites listed in this section.

Charities

Amnesty International UK
www.amnesty.org.uk
Amnesty's award-winning website is easy to navigate and is packed with research and campaign information on the charity's work promoting human rights worldwide. Internet users can join AI online, as well as take a peek at its monthly magazine. Heart-rending reading.

Help the Aged
www.helptheaged.org.uk
UK charity Help the Aged provides resources for Internet-savvy senior citizens and their carers. There are also links to information on Help the Aged's 24-hour SeniorLink helpline. "Infopoint" is full of useful advice, including how to keep out the cold in winter. And if the text is too small, there is a tool to make it bigger.

Society, Politics, and Religion

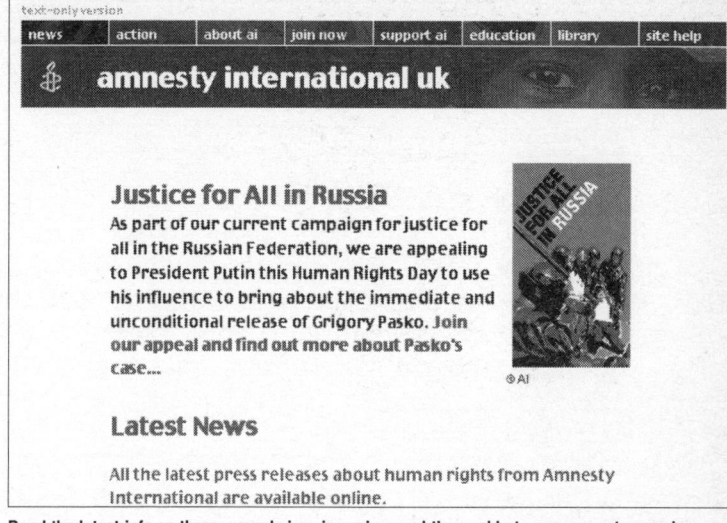

Read the latest info on those wrongly imprisoned around the world at www.amnesty.org.uk

International Committee of the Red Cross
www.icrc.org
Find out about this organization that "aims to protect the lives of victims of war and internal violence", discover the issues it is most concerned about, and get clued up on international humanitarian law. There is a history of the Red Cross, a photo library showing scenes from conflicts around the world, and links to related sites – including the United Nations and non-governmental organizations.

The Samaritans
www.samaritans.org.uk
Everyone's heard of the crisis-counselling Samaritans service, but did you know the organization provides help on the web, too? You can get replies by e-mail and the site includes a great many downloadable help sheets on specific problem areas, which might just provide the support you're looking for.

National culture

British Council
www.britcoun.org
This is the web organ of the cultural organization aimed at spreading the gospel according to Britannia. This site provides links and information on learning

English, plus courses that are available both in the United Kingdom and abroad, as well as giving an online showcase to UK business, science, and arts interests throughout the country. The site is a worthwhile stop-off for those in need of a dose of unquestioning patriotism.

Mad monarchs
www.xs4all.nl/~kvenjb/madmon.htm
Just what we all suspected, they've always been loopy. A site dedicated to celebrating the mad lives of royalty throughout history. There are the Crazy Caesars of Rome, the Raving Royals of Great Britain, the foolish Fursts of Germany, and the Kinky Kings of Spain. And that's just for starters! Nabodnimous of Babylon (+539 BC) ate grass and imagined he was a goat. Not much change there then.

The Royal Family
www.royal.gov.uk
The British Royal Family was hardly the first to get itself on the web, but its burgeoning website is certainly one of the most impressive. It's packed with family trees, royal history, and details of the current line-up's engagements. It also features fairly schmaltzy tributes to Diana, Princess of Wales, and the Queen Mother.

— Political parties and issues —

Conservative Party
www.conservatives.com
The official site of the British Conservative Party is an all-singing, all-dancing site featuring the latest leader, Iain Duncan Smith. It provides complete listings of MPs, MEPs, and shadow cabinet, together with topical news and views. It also allows users to join the party while online.

Conspiracy theories
www.conspire.com
There have always been conspiracy theories, and this site covers some — naturally, the most famous ones, such as the death of JFK, have their own category. From UFOs to terrorist activities, there is very little the site does not cover.

Current affairs: aiming for a better world
www.oneworld.net
The superb One World site takes a look at current affairs from a humanitarian perspective. At the site, you'll find detailed coverage of many stories that receive

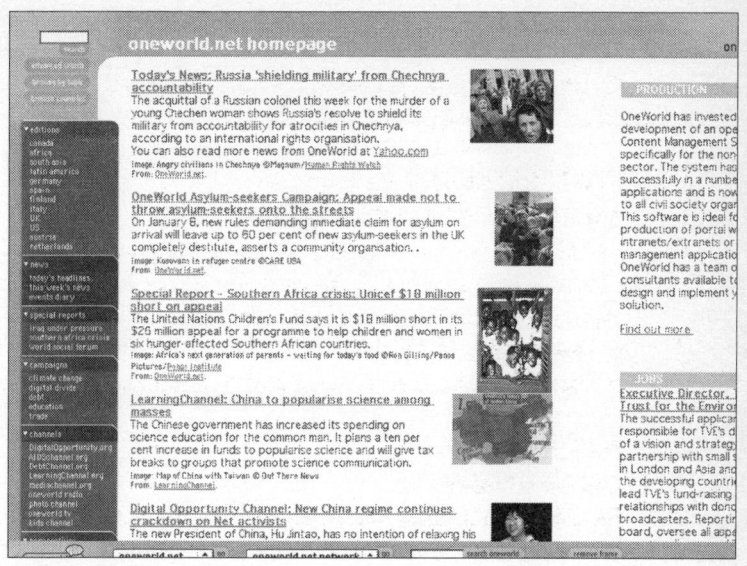

Read current affairs from a humanitarian perspective at www.oneworld.net

little or no mention in the UK media. The site also hosts a think-tank area. This is truly a set of pages that demonstrates the Internet at its caring best. The site is available in most European languages.

Democratic Party
www.democrats.org
Updated daily, the official US Democratic Party website has the latest party political news, including the usual spin-doctored press releases and campaign news. There is a voter outreach section to try to enlist more supporters. The party history is given, and there are links to local branches of the Democratic tree.

European Parliament
www.europarl.eu.int
The multilingual European Parliament site gives the official line on life in the European Parliament. With the heavy text content here, it's not quite riveting reading, but is still a useful insight into those goings-on in Strasbourg and The Hague. Europarl provides detailed information on European legislation and outlines procedures by which ordinary citizens can access European resources.

House of Commons
www.parliament.uk
The Houses of Parliament website is the authoritative site on the political

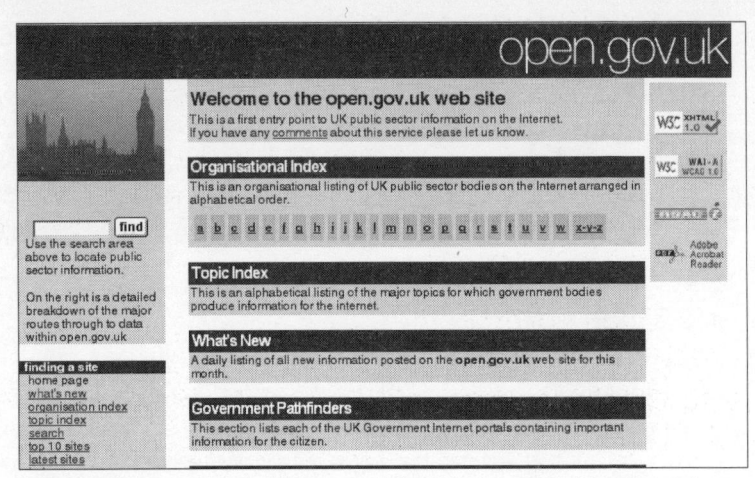

Curious about New Labour's open government? All the info you need is at www.open.gov.uk

institutions of the United Kingdom. Its massive archive from the parliamentary record Hansard is unbeatable. Plenty of information can also be gained here about the people and procedures of the Houses. You will also be able to read details of current and timetabled legislation.

Labour Party
www.labour.org.uk
This is the British Labour Party's official home site. It includes up-to-date governmental news from the party's perspective (such as the budget or the Queen's speech), together with facilities for joining the party, but it doesn't have a list of MPs. You can find out about all their policies here, though.

Liberal Democrats
www.libdems.org.uk
This is the most thoughtful of the three major British parties' sites. It provides a detailed history of the party and outlines some of the personalities of the Liberal Democrats. News stories are updated regularly, and an archive has speeches from the party's conference.

Local Government Association
www.lga.gov.uk
This umbrella body for local government bodies in the United Kingdom provides up-to-date news from Westminster and elsewhere, but it is mostly of interest to politicos. What is useful, though, is its database of local authority sites on the web – just the thing for tracking down the elusive URL of your council's site.

No. 10 Downing Street
www.number-10.gov.uk
This official site of the Prime Minister's residence is both stylish and informative. A "virtual tour" outlines the development of both office and house, and lists previous incumbents (with potted biographies of the most recent). There is the opportunity to have your say in the forums and the chance to view broadcasts of the incumbent PM. News available in the "UK Today" section of the site takes on a decidedly partisan slant.

Open government
www.open.gov.uk
New Labour's professed desire for open government gets an outing on the web in the form of this directory of government services. This database tells you who does what and how to complain if they're not doing it to your liking.

Party finances
www.opensecrets.org
Ever wondered how those US political campaigns became so glitzy? Well, this site will tell you where the money for these campaigns comes from. Find out which companies contributed the most funds to the presidential race and more recent elections. Find out about the congressional races, and read political profiles, too.

Red Pepper
www.redpepper.org.uk
Trendy journal *Red Pepper*'s website is the place to go for up-to-the-minute political analysis with a left-wing slant. While its web presence doesn't reproduce the entire contents of current printed editions, a formidable archive of news and features can be trawled for something of interest. The site also curiously includes a "Recipes" section – mostly using peppers …

Republican Party
www.rnc.org
Popularly known as "The Grand Old Party", the US Republican Party's site includes political stories with a predictably large portion of bias. This is the party's official site and so it includes campaign updates, candidate news, and also has a section for the "online activist", if you wish to make a donation or register to vote.

Slate
slate.msn.com
Slate magazine, the political pundits' corner of Microsoft's MSN network, has some worthy but interesting views on global affairs. Much of the content scratches

the underbelly of US politics and may not make much sense to UK readers. That said, the invitation to "Join the Fray" in frenzied e-mail discussions of, among other topics, McDonald's vs the environment, may prove all too tempting.

United Nations
www.un.org
This is the official home page of the world's leading political organization. The site provides information about current UN policy and activities across the globe, from peace and security to human rights and humanitarian affairs, together with text and audio excerpts from debates in the Assembly and Security Council. This site is vast, so make the "Site Index" your first point of call to pinpoint the information you're after. The "CyberSchool Bus" section is a good reference point for teachers.

The Green Party
www.greenparty.org.uk
For news on green activities and policies, the official Green Party of England and Wales site is the place to start. Campaign information and speeches are featured, reports and publications are available, and you can make donations, join up, or find a job while you browse.

The White House
www.whitehouse.gov
This official site is dedicated to the best-known residence on Pennsylvania Avenue, Washington DC. There's little in the way of current politics here, but the site has plenty of content about the seat of US government. The "Virtual Library" has an archive of White House documents, but sadly only those that have been publicly released. A beautiful line drawing illustrates the development of the House, and a presidential history shows the motley collection of the White House's previous tenants. The "Kids Only" section contains pictures of the Bush family's pet dogs and cat, Spotty, Barney, and India, and Ofelia the longhorn cow.

Religious sites

Buddhism
www.modernbuddhism.com
All you need to know about Buddhism is here. Ponder concepts of happiness and explore the questions of life after death. Advice on meditation techniques is offered, and lists of books are suggested for your journey. For Buddhists on the go, a three-minute meditation is provided.

Catholic Online
www.catholic.org
This Catholic Internet provider's website is a must for Catholics who want to keep in touch. News is provided courtesy of the "Catholic Communications Network", and a collaboration with Amazon brings you a massive range of books and videos. The "Saint Search" engine is particularly fine, pinpointing information about holy types on the Internet. Recent additions include Catholic Singles, a shopping section where you can buy your rosary beads and other goodies, and movie reviews with all the unsavoury stuff highlighted.

The Church of England
www.cofe.anglican.org
This is the official website of the United Kingdom's established faith. Information sections provide write-ups on the history of the church, together with its articles of faith, and a manifesto of the church's views on a range of social issues – its social campaigning stance can make interesting reading. It also tells you how to become more involved with the church. If you want to find out where Anglicanism is at in the 21st century, check this site out.

Church of Scientology
www.scientology.org.uk
Back in the 1970s, thousands followed in the wake John Travolta's *Saturday Night Fever* moves. Oddly, fewer seem as keen to ape the actor's conversion to Scientology. However, if you want to hear the official line on the religion founded by sci-fi writer L Ron Hubbard, here it is from the horse's mouth. A handy "Global Locator" tells you where you can find your local organization in the United Kingdom.

Pagan Federation Online
www.paganfed.demon.co.uk
The British Pagan Federation provides contact between like-minded seekers of the "Old Ways". This online home gives would-be nature-worshippers information on how to contact their nearest branch in Britain and Europe, and provides links to pages offering more specific information on practices, with links to shamanism, seasonal festivals, and other magic and folklore sites.

Religious tolerance
www.religioustolerance.org
If you are more interested in finding out more about new religions around the world, then this is the place to look. The site covers new religious movements, including most cults, and describes their ethical systems. Examining every viewpoint, this site definitely promotes religious tolerance.

Sikhism
www.sikhs.org
This user-friendly site is a worthwhile introduction to the Sikh religion, providing both information for believers and an introduction for general readers. The site is stylishly illustrated and easy to navigate. Coverage is a little academic, but still comprehensive – the section on Sikh history is particularly worth taking a look at.

Society for Promoting Christian Knowledge
www.spck.org.uk
The Society for Promoting Christian Knowledge (SPCK) has been doing just that since 1698 – in fact, it's the oldest Anglican missionary organization there is. Here they are, in 21st-century mode, evangelizing on the web. This site provides information about the society's aims and its history, plus a directory of the UK bookshops through which SPCK's Christian message is channelled. It also has a new site with assembly material for primary schools at **www.assemblies.org.uk**.

Statistics on religions
www.adherents.com
This religious resource provides statistical information for researchers on the distribution and demographic breakdown of followers for more than 4200 world religions, churches, faith groups, and tribes. Results come complete with links to original sources and can be viewed via alphabetical or geographical indices. The site also features a basic keyword search facility.

Virtual Jerusalem
www.virtualjerusalem.com
Bringing Jewish life right up to date, the living pages of Virtual Jerusalem handle, among others, such quirky topics as body piercings and tattoos versus Jewish theology. Well worth a look, this site takes a wry and progressive look at Judaism.

Social issues

Be more racially aware
www.britkid.org
This good-looking site for kids and young adults is aimed at tackling racism. It's headed up by an interactive game that highlights issues to make children more aware of racism – even if they don't actually live in an ethnically mixed environment. The site also carries information in a much weightier vein, with topics linked to parent and teacher resources: an invaluable teaching aid.

www.britkid.org is for British children, telling them about race, racism, and other social issues

Britain's security services
www.five.org.uk
Secret dossier styling gives these web pages a very hush-hush feel, but in fact the information that is contained within them is far from explosive – shame. This site provides the lowdown primarily on MI5 and MI6, together with some links to quite helpful articles in the British press – although they are all written from a slightly paranoid slant.

CIA
www.cia.gov
Like it or loathe it, there's every chance the Central Intelligence Agency is watching you. This website gives its users just a glimpse at the operations of one of the world's most pervasive organizations, together with providing a good dollop of jingoistic propaganda from them, too. There are links to the CIA's website for kids, too. No, really.

Citizens Advice Bureau Advice Guide
www.adviceguide.org.uk
While this is no substitute for popping into a CAB advice centre on your high street, the Citizens Advice Bureau's Advice Guide site does provide basic advice on a range of issues and may save a few pounds down at the solicitor's. A subject, keyword, or alphabetical search can be used to turn up the information that you require. Articles are cross-referenced and checked regularly for accuracy. There are separate sections for Scotland, Wales, and NorthernIreland.

Disability and technology
www.abilitynet.org.uk
A one-stop shop for need assessment, technical expertise, and support, AbilityNet also supplies adapted computer equipment for people with a wide range of disabilities. There are lists of services, factsheets, and links to suppliers here and also, currently, a rather alarming picture of Boris Johnson.

The Metropolitan Police Service
www.met.police.uk
In the wake of the Stephen Lawrence inquiry, the Met has been trying to get up to speed. The news section of its Internet presence is marked by the same desire to brush up on PR, while the "Crimestoppers" section gives details on how to help your local community in its fight against crime. There's also a rogues' gallery of wanted offenders and the chance to sign up for the life in blue online.

— see also...

Religion was an early starter, and few faiths are as primordial as the Druids. They're still alive and kicking today, of course. Visit their woodland grove in cyberspace at **www.druidorder.demon.co.uk**. More bearded shenanigans are available at **www.shamanism.co.uk**. Alternatively, make a quick pilgrimage to visit the Pope at the Vatican (**www.vatican.va**). For a cooler religious experience, young Jews should visit the trendy Generation J site (**www.generationj.com**). Westerners wanting to know about Islam could do worse than visit Islamic City (**www.islamiccity.org**), which describes the fundamental tenets of Islam in layman (or heathen?) terms. Worldwide news with an Islamic spin can be found at Muslim News (**www.muslimnews.co.uk**).

Some like their religion exclusive. You'll find a rundown of some of the world's freakiest cults at **www.mayhem.net/Crime/cults1.html**. Those people seeking to avoid the attentions of the Moonies and others should definitely check out **www.cultsoncampus.com**. The testimonies of ex-cult members at **www.ex-cult.org** make harrowing reading.

Politics has its share of oddities, too. Those on the fringes of UK political life also have a presence on the web: where else could you find communist daily *The Morning Star* (**www.poptel.org.uk/morning-star**) cheek-by-jowl with Class War (**www.geocities.com/CapitolHill/9482**) and the Natural Law Party (**www.natural-law-party.org.uk**)? The last, amusingly, trumpets itself as "the only party with effective and proven solutions". The more rational left-wing intellectual Noam Chomsky has his own archive (**www.zmag.org/chomsky**), mostly focussing on

Society, Politics, and Religion 267

his scathing views of US foreign policy. Read FBI documents released as part of the Freedom of Information Act (**www.fbi.gov**) or get into the real machinations of US politics at the US House of Representatives (**www.house.gov**) and the US Senate (**www.senate.gov**). At the other extreme, we have an anarchist site (**www.spunk.org**) that ironically is rather easy to navigate.

If you want a more mainstream take on current affairs, *UKPOL Magazine* (**www.ukpol.co.uk**) provides over 2500 political links. Seek out the annals of the Hansard Society (**www.hansard-society.org.uk**) if you fancy becoming involved yourself. That sort of community spirit is exactly what **www.kidsthinklink.com** is trying to propagate in future generations across the globe. The Office for National Statistics (**www.statistics.gov.uk**) can tell you about the state of British society, while **www.citizen.org.uk** aims to make the Brits better members of society. Behave yourself, and you may avoid a visit from **www.police.uk**. Be bad, and there's no escaping **www.interpol.com**.

But caring and sharing is what it's all about, really. And that takes work. Another worthwhile charity site is **www.justgiving.com**. Those in need of a little extra support with their loved ones will find it at **relationshipweb.com/odat**, while disabled users can find love at **www.dawn-disabled-dating.com/dearwendy.htm**, an Internet dating agency. At the other end of the scale, The Divorce Survival Guide (**www.divorcesurvivalguide.com**) may help with problems on the home front.

SPORT

If you have interests in something more physical than tapping away on a keyboard, then the Internet will more than satiate your demands for sporting activity. There are thousands of sports sites, both professional and personal, that will cater to your thirst for information, statistics, or buying sporting equipment. There are plenty of archives and sites that will bring you live audio coverage or feed you the latest scores, as well as places where you can learn how to play better yourself. Extreme sporters will not be disappointed either, as there is every hair-raising form of madness imaginable on the web, too.

Athletics

British Athletics
www.british-athletics.co.uk
There's an extensive directory of athletics clubs around the United Kingdom and a diary of all forthcoming events. All major domestic results are listed and there are links to other sites for further information. Whether it is cross-country, track and field, or coaching you are interested in, this site will put you in touch with the right organizations.

International Association of Athletics Federation
www.iaaf.org
Essential reading for any serious athlete or athletics fan, this official site publishes all the latest news, results, any number of forums, and photos of awards and other events. There are training tips, too, that are aimed at newcomers and appraised by the site's editor.

Online resource for runners
www.coolrunning.com
Refine your training, discover new ways to motivate yourself when you just cannot

Get grid-iron statistics galore at the informative American football site, www.nafl.org

be bothered to leave the house, and know when those aches and pains mean that you should "give it a rest". There are also running logs for your stats and discussion forums.

Ball sports

American football
www.nafl.org
The official site of the North American Football League. Get all the latest news on teams and sponsors, check statistics and records, or post your views (and argue with others) on the message board. Air your opinions of recent games in the chat room, or just peruse photos and press releases. Merchandise ranging from league products to sports goods and even CDs and music is available.

Baseball Links
www.baseball-links.com
Claiming to publish the web's most comprehensive collection of baseball links, this site will provide supporters with a route to the sites of their favourite teams and players. It will also provide you with a full set of results for their games. All the official sites are highlighted, which is a good thing because there are plenty of non-professional efforts listed, too. Other areas here include collectibles, software, and coaching sites, as well as the chance to have your say on the "Baseball Soapbox".

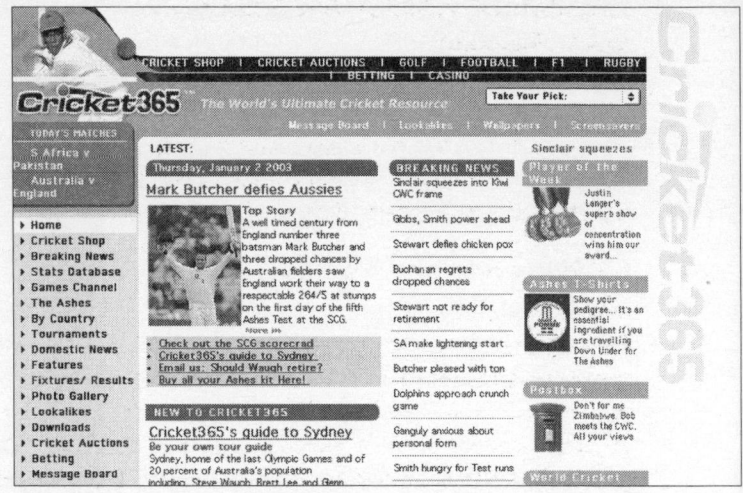

WG Grace would be proud of the information and statistics available at www.cricket365.com

Basketball worldwide
www.telebasket.com

A database of more than 19,000 players and coaches, and daily basketball news postings are just two of the features of this globally encompassing basketball site. Sadly, the involved way that the site has been designed means that it takes a while to get to where you want to. Die-hard basketballers will find perseverance worthwhile, though.

British Tenpin Bowling Association
www.btba.org.uk

All you need to know about tenpin bowling in the United Kingdom, including membership information, news and events, rules, and a guide to your nearest bowling centre or local association. There are lists of instructors and courses available, as well as details of leagues and tournaments. News of the Team England and Senior Team England is also readily to hand.

Cricket online
www.cricket365.com

Part of the excellent 365 network, all the cricket information that you could ever want can be found here. Follow the live scorecards. There are player profiles, both home and abroad, and the latest information on county cricket. All the statistics you could ever want are a few clicks away, too. Other sites on the network, with a similar look and feel, include **www.football365.com** (see opposite) and **www.planet-rugby.com** (see page 272).

English Ice Hockey Association
www.eiha.co.uk
This is not the flashiest of websites, but if you are one of the increasing number of ice hockey players, or are just a fan of the sport, it will allow you to catch up on the results of recent games and consult a glossary of terms. The EIHA site is also part of a web ring, which means that it is linked to many other, similar sites. Start here, and you'll certainly find something you like.

ESPN: world sports news
www.espn.com
ESPN is packed with information about sport of all kinds. This largely news-based website mainly covers the United States, although a fair few overseas events are also included. However, the linked UK site www.soccernet.com will appeal more to British football fans. That site has a similar design, but it deals almost exclusively with European matches, transfers, and other European football issues. At ESPN, you can also check out all the latest fixtures and the player profiles and fantasy leagues.

International Australian Football Confederation
www.iafc.org.au
Listing the countries involved, teams, and rules of the game, this site charts the game's history and publishes updates from teams all over the world. News is provided – but for really up-to-the-minute stuff you'll want to check out www.oztips.com.

International Federation of Netball Associations
www.netball.org
Read the rules, scan the headlines, and make sure that you know about future events. There are plenty of links to netball-related sites all over the world here, as well as an archive of World Netball Championship results for fans to mull over. You'll find the IFNA newsletter 'Shooting for Success' is available in PDF format to download, too.

Live soccer results
www.football365.com
Follow the latest results, live, from the comfort of your desk, and read walk-through descriptions of the matches. Newsflashes can be made to appear in a small box on your screen so that you can stay informed the entire time that you are working. This excellent site features all the results, a guide to radio and television coverage, and the league tables. You can also submit your views and questions to the site.

National Basketball Association
www.nba.com
This site has all that you might want from the world of basketball – players and game stats, the latest news, interviews, and when all the big games are taking place. It does also have a section on the global basketball world for those that live outside the United States.

National Wheelchair Basketball Association
www.nwba.org
Find out all about how the National Wheelchair Basketball Association started, what the rules are, and where your nearest (US) team is. You can also subscribe to an e-mail mailing list to keep completely up to date with the development of divisional information. There is also a good set of links to various other sites for disabled sports men and women.

Pool and billiards instructions
www.poolschool.com
The College of Cueing Arts and Sciences (really) offers tutorials to those living in Dallas, Texas. The rest of us can pick up tips for our pool game from its online video clips or by simply reading the basic advice on techniques such as how to hold the cue and the thinking behind the Bridge. The links section directs you to more lessons and online rule books. There are also tasty tricks to watch and learn. If you didn't misspend your youth first time around, now's the time to do it.

Rugby
www.planet-rugby.com
Providing information to rugby union fans, this site has the latest news on all the international teams and their players, a fantasy rugby spread betting game, world rankings, and features on the players who have shaped the sport throughout the game's international history. Professionals give their views on the state of the game. Upcoming fixtures are given with the time and place to ensure that you don't miss kick-off. The site's content is similar to **www.sportonair.com**.

When Saturday Comes
www.onetouchfootball.com
This is the online version of the independent football magazine *When Saturday Comes*, and all the same features are available here. For example, it is home to "The Half Decent Pub Guide", which is a database of drinking establishments that are suitable for soccer fans the world over. Each pub is rated and assigned an in-depth description, which includes whether or not there are "intrusive music/fights/entertainers" to spoil the game.

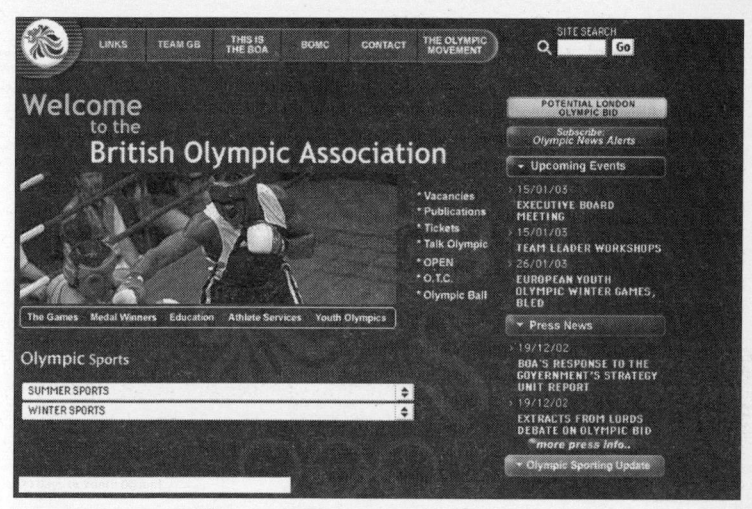

News of past and present Olympics, including current issues, can be found www.olympics.org.uk

Big sporting events

British Olympic Association
www.olympics.org.uk
Find out about the history of the Olympics, and read about the latest issues, including unsporting drug abuse, women's issues, and politics. You can read the occasional interview with a medallist, but if you are looking for really in-depth information you might well find that you would actually be better off with **www98.pair.com/msmonaco/Almanac**.

Commonwealth Games 2006
www.melbourne2006.com.au
The 2006 games will be held in Melbourne, Australia, and this site aims to fill us in with details of the latest developments, including the games village, actual games venues, the programmes, and information on how to become involved as a volunteer. It's a bit of a way off, but starting to shape up.

Olympic Almanac
www98.pair.com/msmonaco/Almanac
View the image library of a large number of the Olympic torches, find out what are counted as Olympic sports these days, and read the list of frequently asked questions to catch up on the trivia.

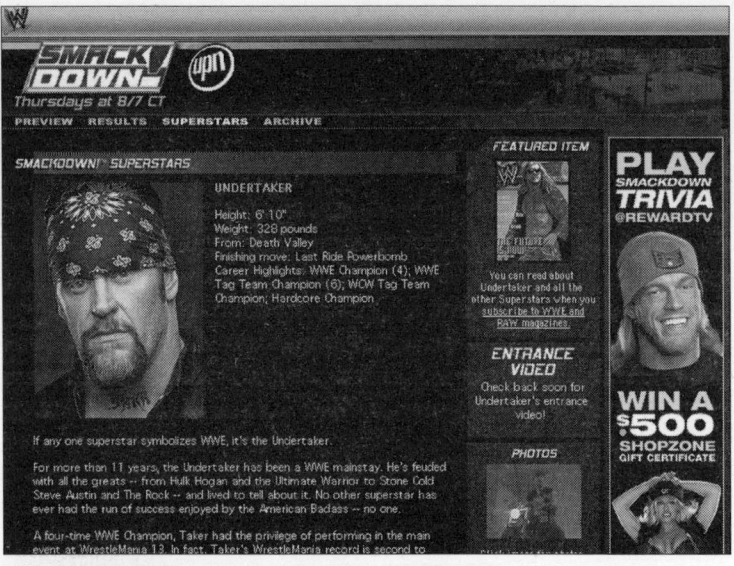

Catch American wrestling's finest (and funniest) at www.wwe.com

Contact sports

Boxing
www.skysports.com/skysports/boxing
Look up the boxing ratings, and see who's top of the pile. You can also find out when the next fight is due to be shown on Sky TV and remind yourself how to order Sky Box Office. There are boxing-related headlines, features on the day's important fights, and a round-up of the winners and the losers.

Powerlifting and bodybuilding
www.staff.washington.edu/griffin/weights.html
The author of this bodybuilding endeavour provides handy, scientific know-how to help build muscle and avoid damage. There is advice on what equipment to get, a sample workout for beginners, mental tricks to improve your lifting, and training spreadsheets for you to download.

World Wrestling Entertainment
www.wwe.com
After years of being confused with the World Wildlife Fund, those hairy wrestlers have finally admitted defeat and changed their name. Find out when your

favourite wrestler is pretending to give some damage – be it on television or at a live event – and view their particulars. Merchandise is, unsurprisingly, top of the bill, with the online shop featuring replica belts, clothes, and a Badd Ass Bear. There's news, gossip, videos, DVDs, chat, video gaming – and a whole lot more.

Equestrian sports

For all equestrians
www.equestriansonline.com
If you have ever suffered a horse balking at the ingate at one time or another, this well-constructed horsey site is the place for you. There are training tips, online chat forums, and articles on many different aspects of the horsing world, including breeding and grooming. For all your horsing goods, there is a classified section.

Horse racing tips
www.racetips365.com
Racing forecasts and racing cards are to be found here, along with the NAP of the day (the best selection of the day, that is, it's the horse which the site's systems have calculated as having the best chance of winning and is not odds-on). There's an interactive league to join in with, too.

Extreme sports

Aviation Aspirations
www.avasp.com
This impressive site features information on how to find a flight school and what you should expect from training courses. It also reveals those hidden expenses. If you want to get a private pilot's licence, then this is a good place to visit. UK- and US-specific sections are highlighted for ease of use.

Avidly extreme ironing
www.extremeironing.com
Welcome to extreme ironing – the latest danger sport that combines the thrills of an extreme outdoor activity with the satisfaction of a well-pressed shirt. For truly bizarre photos of precarious ironing, check the gallery. There's a webzine to download, and you can find out all about the stars of this relatively new sport. They are serious, you know.

Boarding: surf ... snow ... skate ...
www.extremesports.com

Find out all about the latest extreme news and details of events and competitions here. There are photos, movies, rankings, a calendar, industry details, and links to many other sporting sites. Surfing, kiteboarding, BMX, wakeboarding, snowboarding and more – it's all covered here, dude.

British Hang Gliding and Paragliding Association
www.bhpa.co.uk

If your idea of fun is to find yourself high in the sky with nothing keeping you there except more air, then visit this site and locate your nearest club. There are competitions to see who can fall most accurately and links to equipment shops. Flyability promotes opportunities for disabled people to get involved, too.

British Mountaineering Council
www.thebmc.co.uk

This is the place to seek out rock-climbing clubs, advice on fundamental safety techniques, and a directory of climbing walls in the United Kingdom. You can also find out how accessible the various places for climbing are at the moment. There's a subsite (Gripped) for young climbers, with information to calm concerned parents.

Bungee jumping
www.bungeezone.com

Locate a bungee jump near you, and take your life into your own hands. The database includes the United Kingdom, United States, Hong Kong, and seemingly everywhere else in the world, too. There is a full background on the history of risking life and limb on the end of an elastic band, a category describing the different types of jumps, and a photo gallery if you still need convincing that it's perfectly "safe". The unfunny cartoons are unlikely to take your mind off any reservations, and it's best to avoid the disasters section if you still need convincing.

Cross-country skiing
www.xcskiworld.com

For those who would rather eschew the safety of the regular runs, there is the gruelling cross-country skiing experience. You can learn about the different techniques, discover roller skiing, and read the hefty guide to the equipment you'll need to use. There are also suppliers close at hand ...

Extreme Knitting
www.sfbg.com/SFLife/36/10/stitch.html

Ahh, the beauty of the Net. If you can think of something, it's probably already been

Not for the fainthearted – skydivers should drop in at www.dropzone.com

done. Knitting is hip again and a favourite among San Francisco hipsters, college students, and cool kids nationwide. From sewing circle to stitch and bitch, today's knitters are rabid with the fervour for the fibres apparently. Find out more here.

Power kiting
www.kites.org/jo
Taking kites out of the realm of children in the park and turning it into an extreme sport, power kiting involves using very efficient kites that can end up dragging the kiter around. This works particularly well if the said kiter is sitting on a go-kart or buggy. Interested? The site also includes loads of links, some to UK kite shops.

Skydiving
www.dropzone.com
Read reviews of skydiving equipment, view information on safety and training, browse a database of global parachute centres, and find out where the most happening events will be going down. A chat forum for skydiving students, photo galleries, auctions, and, amazingly, skydiving software are all available.

Snowboarding
www.snowboarding-online.com
This site from Transworld Snowboarding offers everything from action photos and videos to chat and buyers guides and snowboarding features. Weather reports and

resort and travel information are covered, and there is an online calendar of events. The latest tricks and tips are also ably demonstrated.

Surfer resources
www.surfstation.co.uk
Up-to-date surf report information for the United Kingdom. Find out about surfcams, clubs, schools, shops, and boards of all kinds. Message boards mean that you can find out who is going where and locate where the best waves are.

Triathletes
www.triathletemag.com
This must be the most gruelling sport. The site has the latest information on the race calendar, invaluable guides to nutrition, and the gear that is needed to be a success in this sport of endurance. We were exhausted just navigating the site.

Martial arts

Aikido
www.aikiweb.com
Find out about the aikido martial art: its philosophy, techniques, weapons, and language. There's a comprehensive dojo search, so you can find your local centre of learning. And don't think it won't cover your area – the database seems to span the entire world. There are at least three dojos in one small part of Cornwall!

Black Belt magazine
www.blackbeltmag.com
Whether you want to consult the martial arts dictionary, search for a local dojo (in any martial art), or pick up a few tips, then this is a good starting place. You will also find advice on how to choose a suitable art and then a school – there are tips for beginners that are easy to follow, though don't try them while online. The dojo search is more suitable for US residents, as the European entries are really a little Spartan.

The Wing Chun Kuen Archives
www.wingchunkuen.com/archives
Read about the history and technical details of the martial art known as wing chun kuen. The lineage of this southern Chinese kung fu is tracked through different families, with detailed lists. The site includes a dictionary of martial arts terms in Cantonese (using the English alphabet) and further reading lists.

Motor sports

Autosport online
www.autosportmag.com
Everything you'll ever want to know about fast cars, who's driving them, and which team has been accused of cheating this month. Competitions including Formula One, Nascar, and World Rally are all covered with regular news stories, while the driver profiles should keep the statisticians happy.

Ford Rallye Sport
www.fordrallyesport.net
If you are interested in rally driving, including national and world championships, you should check out Ford's dedicated site. It includes the lowdown on events, drivers, and cars, as well as photos, video footage, and race diaries. The latest results and standings are all here as well.

Formula One
www.formula1.com
Due to relaunch in Spring 2003 as the official Formula One site. It offers a strong news section, analysis of popular stories, and graphical walkthroughs of the circuits – complete with statistics. Read the personal profiles of the drivers for a little excitement – especially as it's a no-holds-barred, speak-as-you-find affair. Live commentary is broadcast in season, with testing summaries out of season.

Formula One from ITV
www.itv-f1.com
The juicy gossip from the pits is flowing from this Formula One news site, and you can have the daily news from the F1 scene delivered direct to you by e-mail. Alternatively, you can download pictures and movies complete with sound for free (apart from your phone bill). Just to set the tone, be aware that there is a "Pit Babes" section, too ...

Sports news and information

British Wheelchair Sports
www.britishwheelchairsports.org
Promoting the British Wheelchair Sports Foundation, this site highlights the many sporting competitions that are available to people with physical disabilities –

which includes those with visual impairments right through to people in a wheelchair. Contacts are included with each of the numerous entries so that you can learn where local events are and how to attend.

The science behind sport
www.exploratorium.edu/sports
Taking a scientific approach to sport, "Sport! Science @ the Exploratorium" analyses a number of sports, discussing the chemical makeup of "fast ice" in ice hockey, the physics behind hitting the perfect baseball home run, and why climbing up a mountain can be more tiring than you'd think.

Sport globally
www.sports.com
A truly global sporting site with mirror sites based all over the world, but sharing all the sports in the world. You can therefore read the site in most European languages. The emphasis is mostly on football here, but other sports are also covered in depth.

Sporting Life
www.sporting-life.com
This exceptional sports news resource covers most of the popular sports, including soccer, racing, ruby, golf, cricket, and tennis. There is a radio for all your sports news and coverage. "Betting Headlines" will give you the odds on sporting events to come. If you have a strong opinion, then you can have it published in the "Fanzine" section.

Sport on Air
www.sportonair.com
This news site contains stories spanning the most popular sports, many of which feature audio interviews. An hourly audio bulletin allows you to "hear all about it". You can also read a round-up of what the papers have said that day and take part in the polls, normally for who is the best footballer.

Sportszine UK
www.sportszine.co.uk
The news on this site is handily divided into sporting categories, so that you can easily view all the stories relating to your favourite type of competition or pastime. The rest of the site acts as a useful directory to other websites on a huge range of subjects on just about every sort of event going – including kayaking, skydiving, and snooker. You can also locate online sports gear stores to help get you fully equipped for your sport.

Target sports

British Association for Shooting & Conservation
www.basc.org.uk
If you are interested in taking part in shooting in the United Kingdom, then you'll need to know about the recent changes of the law. It's all spelled out here, along with a set of links to other gun and conservation-type sites.

Darts
www.shootersedge.com
Buy darts, flights, boards, and other accessories from this online shop, which also features an online darts game that you can play from your web browsing program. Orders from outside the United States are acceptable, so get that nylon athletic jacket that you've had your eye on …

News for archers and bowhunters
www.archeryinfonet.com
You can pick up some interesting introductory hints on shooting a bow and also follow the large number of outdoors and hunting-based links at this site. The chat forum is surprisingly (if somewhat disturbingly) busy, with much talk about guns and hunting with your bare teeth (nearly). Hearing about the "ones that got away" can be pretty cheering for the non-hunting type, though.

Water sports

British Canoe Union
www.bcu.org.uk
Find out where you can learn to canoe, the different sorts of boats available, and what other equipment you'll need. There are lists of general outdoor events and details of the benefits of joining the union. If you want to know where to paddle, for relaxation or competition, the information is here.

Sailing
www.rya.org.uk
The site of the Royal Yachting Association contains details of affiliated UK sailing clubs, classes, events, and sections on racing, powerboats, windsurfing, and motor boats. It should prove to be a useful starting place for those sailors who are not yet familiar with navigating the web.

Swimming
www.swiminfo.com
Maybe you just want to swim to get fit, or perhaps you're a serious triathlete needing some help on tweaking your performance. Either way, the workout and techniques sections of this site should help. There is also an online shop and a new service that will keep you fully equipped with goggles and gossip.

— see also... —

For general sports information, you can head to Sports Info Central (**www.sportsinfocentral.com**) and Sport Quest (**www.sportquest.com**) for information and links to the best sites. Sports on Line (**www.sportsonline.co.uk**) provides a search engine for British sports sites, while a more general sports-related index is available at SportSearch (**www.sportsearch.com**). If you like playing fantasy sports games, see page 126 in Games, or give Fantasy League Net (**www.fantasyleague.com**) a shot, as it provides info to help you pick winning teams. For football news, player, and team information, there are dozens of sites (well, it is the global game); Sportal (**www.sportal.com**) and TEAMtalk Football (**www.teamtalk.com**) are among the most popular, the latter for its very speculative transfer gossip.

Visit the Ezbets (**www.ezbets.com**) online casino and sports betting emporium in all the sports you could dream of. Armchair athletes will discover decent coverage of future international sporting events at Sportcal International (**www.sportcal.co.uk**). Real nerds will find the results and statistics at Soccer STATS (**www.soccerstats.com**) irresistible. Darts fans should try Planet Darts (**www.planetdarts.com**), which has playing hints, tips, and a tournament calendar.

Tennis fans simply won't be able to tear themselves away from 1st Serve (**www.1stserve.com**), with its scores lists, date a tennis player, and player profiles, and The Tennis Directory (**www.tennisnetwork.com/directory**) lists courts (both public and private), rules, fitness routines, and many other tennis-related articles. If you need someone to actually play with, try the Fitness Jumpsite at **primusweb.com/fitnesspartner**. Badminton players can check out the latest on rules, technique, and equipment, as well as the world's best players, at **www.badmintoncentral.com**. Otherwise, simply look up your local club in the directory, then go out there and play a game!

World T.E.A.M. Sports (**www.worldteamsports.org**) encourages sportspeople of all ages and abilities, publishing details of events it has organized on its site. Lone sportspeople may find the articles on Runner's Web (**www.runnersweb.com**) handy. They include a marathon calendar, editorial columns, news, and sports medicine links. Swim News (**www.swimnews.com**) publishes swimming news, rankings, and an online magazine. For white-knuckle stories and books, try *Climbing* magazine (**www.climbing.com**).

Feel the wind in your hair at the Adventure Cycling Association (**www.advcycling.org**), which has touring resources including maps and details of cycling clubs. Cyber Cyclery (**www.cyclery.com**) has forums, links, happenings, and opportunities for jobs in bike shops. If you'd rather be behind a windscreen, then you may find the performance motoring sites Auto 1000 (**www.auto1000.com**) much more appealing.

Karate Net (**karatenet.com**) provides an "ask the experts" section, seminar ratings, and downloadable video files. Boxing lovers will be knocked against the ropes by visiting **www.boxing.com**. Baseball fans will find thousands of sites to encourage their interest. To begin with, try the All American Amateur Baseball Association (**www.johnstownpa.com/aaaba**) and the United States Amateur Baseball Association (**www.usaba.com**) for results, tournament information, and directions to playing grounds.

TRAVEL

You can use the Internet to plan and book a holiday, read about other people's experiences, or just check that your daily morning train ride to work won't be delayed. The quantity of travel-based sites available worldwide is astounding, and you'll save a fortune on travel guides by trying the web first. Even if you want a paper companion to take with you, there are sites that review them and can recommend an appropriate title. Of course, an online bookshop is usually just one click away. Medical advice and information on safe places to travel are always instantly available.

Cruises and flights

Airline Network
www.airline-network.co.uk
You can make sure that you don't overspend on your airfares by searching this database of discounts on flights from the United Kingdom to international destinations. There are also travel insurance and limited car hire services. The hotel price guide seems wide-reaching, although travellers to more exotic places may experience a little trouble.

British Airways
www.britishairways.com
Find out where and when BA is flying, and tell the site your future plans – it will respond with appropriate special offers when they become available. Occasionally there are auctions for flight seats announced here, too. Frequent flyers can take advantage of the benefits of Executive Club.

Cunard cruises
www.cunard.co.uk
Not a place to visit for those who are low on funds, the company that owns the *QE2* has its own site for the well-at-heeled to find a cruise that suits them. Find

Bob Geldof has created the simple yet useful www.deckchair.com for picking up cheap flights

out all about the history of their ships and details of the various destinations that those still on the water visit. There is even a section for memorabilia.

Deckchair
www.deckchair.com
This site is mostly famous for its knighted benefactor, Sir Bob Geldof, but it is a deceptively simple search engine for cheap flights. Register your details then search for the cheapest flight that money can buy. You can also now get deals for car hire, accommodation, holiday packages, cruises and insurance.

Expedia Travel
www.expedia.com
This site deals in all aspects of travel – flights, hotels, cars, holidays. Just enter the dates that you need in the search engine, and the database will do the rest. Its prices are extremely competitive, and there are many other bargains to be had here – check out the best deals at the bottom of the home page. It also includes useful tools such as a currency converter, flight status, and an airport guide.

P&O Cruises
www.pocruises.com
Have a look at the ships, itineraries, and what to expect if you book a cruise with this well-known company. You can sort of book online, by sending in a reservation by e-mail, but it's probably wise to request a brochure first (by e-mail, too). The online database lets you search for the best option to suit your vacation time.

Thomson Holidays
www.thomson-holidays.com
Find out all about Thomson's holiday cruises and resorts. You can now book online. There aren't any online brochures available, but you can get an idea of the holidays that are on offer and see which are available for (cheaper) late booking.

Travel Master
www.travelmaster.com
Plan your trip to the second with this set of online tools. You can book flights, car pickups, and hotel reservations in a huge number of countries, with any dangerous options thoughtfully flagged with warning notices. Specify your preferred airline and how you want your ticket options sorted (by price, departure time, or vendor, for example). You can also say when you want to pick up and drop off your car once you have chosen your car rental company. Focussed business travellers will probably gain the most from this service.

Virgin Atlantic
www.virgin-atlantic.com
Providing more than just trans-Atlantic flights, this airline has a website containing a full route list and map, a searchable schedule timetable, and useful information for passengers – including baggage allowances. Frequent flyers can also read about the perks that they may be able to claim.

For the adventurous

Adventure Network
www.adventurenetwork.com
Offering the core activities of rock climbing and kayaking, Adventure Network also emphasizes the need to be fit, follow safety procedures, and use appropriate equipment. There are articles on camping, layering your clothing, choosing different technical items such as harnesses, and the best ways to walk yourself fit.

Backpacker magazine
www.backpacker.com
Pick up essential tips on how to pack and carry a heavy rucksack safely without crippling yourself, choose the best gear for you and the requirements of your trip, find out what to do if it rains, and learn how to make tasty, easy meals while you are away. Features are provided to tempt you into leaving the house, and the gear finder takes note of your specific needs and suggests something suitable.

If you fancy Antarctica rather than the Algarve then we suggest that you visit www.gorp.com

Berghaus
www.berghaus.com
Browse through this specialist clothing and equipment site, complete with price guides. You can also find out what features you should be looking for when shopping, and there are articles on how the gear is tested. The site also explains which skills you might need in the outdoors – some of this information has been written by celebrity explorers Chris Bonington and Alan Hinkes.

The Great Outdoors
www.gorp.com
A big site providing help and information on just about any outdoor activity that you can imagine. As well as helping you to plan trips and providing tips on know-how, there are debates on dealing with high altitudes and staying healthy in the wilderness, as well as more mundane but lethal subjects as boredom and loneliness, and forecasting weather.

Outdoor equipment
www.cotswold-outdoor.com
Buy your mountaineering, cycling, walking, and camping gear from the online shop, and order a catalogue if you want to browse in bed. There is a seriously comprehensive set of links for travellers, including in-house technical information on choosing a sleeping bag, as well as contact details and websites of travel companies and map suppliers.

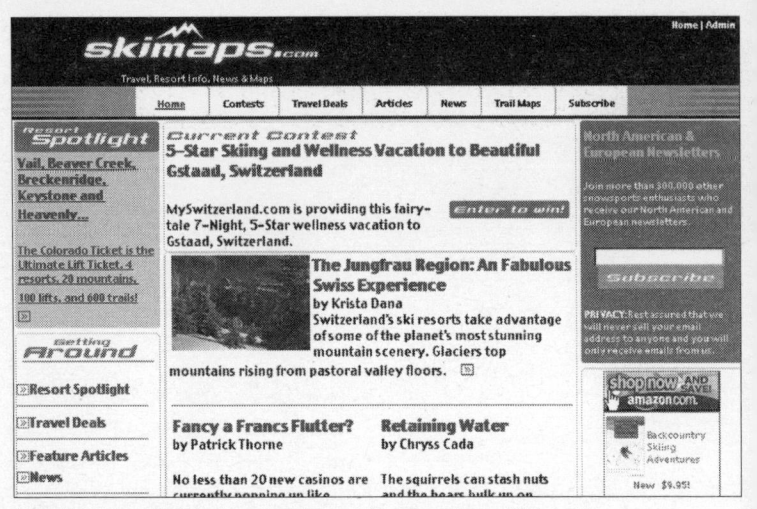

www.skimaps.com has the largest database of ski maps that you will find online

Outdoor gear for women
www.mountainwoman.com
Buying outdoor gear if you're a woman has traditionally been tricky, but things have improved, and now there is even a website devoted to supplying women with clothes, safety equipment, and packs – right down to a selection of specialized mountaineering underwear. Articles on not getting into the wrong sleeping bag and untangling ropes are not as patronizing as they sound.

Ski Resorts
www.skiresorts.com
Find a ski resort to suit your needs (and your costs). There are online snow reports for when you're out there (just remember to pack a PC) and a section where you can gain a local perspective on what to do and when, which are the best runs, and where the action is. Webcams will reveal the current skiing conditions for you. A calendar will also tell you about the events both on and off the slopes in your chosen resort.

Skiing: piste maps, resort guides, and reviews
www.skimaps.com
Claiming to host the largest online collection of skiing trail maps, SkiMaps provides just that. Well, that, and a resort guide with contact details and reviews from the people who regularly visit. Articles on resort casinos and retaining water, among other things, could prove handy, and there are also links to online ski equipment shops and auctions.

Space Adventures
www.spaceadventures.com
Book yourself a trip around space mission launch sites, ancient places of astronomy, and high-tech labs. If you feel really adventurous, you can pay (lots) to take a zero-gravity flight or even pre-book a proper sub-orbital experience. The innerspace adventure lets you dive down to the *Titanic*, and the 'G' training will spin you in a centrifuge like astronauts do in their training. This is the starting point for the holiday you never dreamed would happen.

Trailfinders
www.trailfinder.com
Priding itself on providing tailor-made holidays, Trailfinders can put together flights, hotel reservations, local tours, and car connections to suit your special needs. You can also sort out travel insurance online, order a brochure, and find your nearest agent here.

Holiday bargains

Bargain flights and holidays
www.onetravel.com
Discover a pile of cheap flights, alternative airports, and other money-saving schemes. Go through the fast fare finder to get the best prices. There is the "rules of the air", which publishes various airlines' rules and regulations, as well as a page that will tell you how delayed your flight is.

Bargain holidays
www.bargainholidays.com
Use this site to choose your holiday location according to the style of break you want, whether it be "Ski Bargain" or "Holiday Sun". You can pick up discounted city breaks, flights, and last-minute deals on package holidays. A live weather link lets you check out the current conditions all over the world.

Budget Travel
www.budgettravel.com
Designed for people who don't want to spend a fortune to travel the world, Budget Travel's avoidance of design frills (or any element of friendly design) will put many people off this site. But if you are a true bargain hunter, and want advice on how and where to get the best deals, you should put up with the basic look as there is plenty here.

Cheap Flights
www.cheapflights.com
The simple design of this bargain-holiday finding site is quite brilliant. Choose your intended destination, and you'll find a list of flights from the United Kingdom complete with links to the company offering them, some of which can take your order directly online. Other links will take you to extremely useful facts about legroom reports and deep vein thrombosis.

EasyJet
www.easyjet.com
One of the cheapest airlines and a pioneer of online buying – the company cuts down on costs by eliminating the middle man (ie travel agencies) and running a ticketless, therefore less bureaucratic, business. There are often-ridiculous offers (flights from £4) regularly throughout the year, so it is worth subscribing to its newsletters to find out about these bargains first. You get an extra discount for booking your flights online.

Flights, hotels, and holiday offers
www.ebookers.com
Grab discounted flights and other offers, and find the appropriate flight, car hire, hotel, and insurance deals easily, using the customizable search engine. You can even tell the site to inform you when a flight to your destination becomes available at a palatable price.

Last-minute ideas
www.lastminute.com
You can buy airline tickets, reserve hotel rooms, hunt for presents and concert tickets, or just stay at home and order a takeaway from this online shop with a difference. Each item for sale is only available for a short length of time, and details change frequently. Lastminute.com gets special offers directly from the suppliers, claiming that in doing so it can give you the very lowest prices. A useful site. Add it to your favourites.

Thomas Cook
www.thomascook.co.uk
Late holiday deals, and the ability to search for your ideal holiday without leafing through thick brochures, make this otherwise sparse site ideal for when you are weighing up the holiday budget. There's a Thomas Cook TV satellite channel devoted to holiday programmes, and there are also a fair number of late deals at extra discount.

Get everything last minute at www.lastminute.com, but especially flights and weekend breaks

Travelcare
www.travelcare.co.uk
Choose from a selection of special deals from holiday and airline companies on this site. You can specify your budget, time of departure, and destination, and you will be provided with loads of options, making choosing a holiday much less painful than running between travel agents in the high street. Go on, try it.

Tripquote
www.tripquote.com
This site aims to find you the optimum price for flight tickets for North American travellers. The online shop should still be able to sell you luggage, though, wherever you are in the world – what a surprise! There is also a handy "Link Library", connecting you to other travel-related websites for whatever your destination, and these are all sorted by category such as cruises, maps, and business travel.

US bargain flights
www.priceline.com
This US company has an innovative system which lets you name your ideal price

for a flight, then offers your deal to the airline companies. If one of the airlines accepts your price, the tickets are yours. They also do the same deals for car rentals, hotel rooms, cruises, vacations, and even home finance. Another great site to bookmark.

Holidays in Europe

British Tourist Authority
www.visitbritain.com
Visit Britain is the official British Tourist Authority's website, and it is available to read in numerous languages with the express purpose of offering plenty of ideas and information for those wishing to spend their holidays in the United Kingdom. There are lists of activities, attractions, virtual tours, and plenty of pretty images of Great Britain.

Canal boat breaks in the United Kingdom
www.drifters.co.uk
If you prefer the idea of messing around in boats to hanging around in airports, then suss out what it takes to organize a canal boat holiday with the information on this site. There is a list of UK operators, plus a map of the country marking out the different water systems.

Ferry and Channel crossing guide
www.a2beurope.com
Search the timetables for UK ferry services, the Eurostar trains, and Le Shuttle. You can also choose breaks in Europe based on price and town, and select the nature of your holiday – with suggestions including luxury, activity, and touring. There is also a guide to shopping in Calais, with online calculators for metric/imperial conversions and live weather forecasts to tell you how choppy the water will be during your crossing.

France
www.tourisme.fr/us
The English may not be that good on this site, but the average Francophile will still get a great deal out of it nonetheless. There is a search engine that lets you search for the town in France that you want to visit, and it has links into the tourist board for that region for information. You can also search the whole site by activities or type of accommodation, and find what monuments can be found in the vicinity of where you want to go.

For those who want more than a package deal, visit the Spanish tourist site www.tourspain.es

French tourism
www.alltravelfrance.com
From a hotel in Paris to an ancient château in the Loire, gîtes in Provence to camping in Bordeaux. All Travel France will arrange your stay, rent you a car, map your route, point out attractions, and even tell you what the weather is doing. A handy currency converter is also available to get you on your way.

Spain
www.tourspain.es
Available in English, this is the official guide to many a tourist's favourite – Spain. There is general information on vacationing in the country, resources to find hotels, a breakdown on the climate (ie it's very hot), the cuisine, the many festivals, and much more.

Virtual London
www.virtual-london.com
This site aims to hold your hand, virtually of course, from the moment of your arrival in London, through each visit to the theatre, the shops, and the sights, and ending up with handy tips on transport, news stories, and weather reports. There are live webcams that allow you to spy on the bustling shoppers and motorists stuck in traffic jams. If this is your first trip to London and you want the real skinny, you can "Ask a Londoner", who'll e-mail you back with the lowdown.

Travelling to the United States? Then visit www.usatourist.com before embarking on your trip

Holidays in North America

American tourism
www.usatourist.com
Ignore the embarrassing name and revel in this site, which is full of great information, as well as having a "Hot Tips" section with advice on visas, driving, and shopping. It focusses mainly on the major tourist areas and attractions (such as New York, Las Vegas, and the Grand Canyon), with long descriptions of each location accompanied by excellent photographs and handy tips. You need never buy a travel book again if you use this site, although USA Tourist also sells these through its online shop — surprise, surprise …

California
www.gocalif.ca.gov
California, the sunshine state, where dreams come true etc. This is the site to come if you want to know about this place of extremes. There is a good search facility for hotels and motels, as well as many useful maps. The list of theme parks and fairytale castles alone will have the kids clamouring to go, even if you're still not quite convinced.

Interstate travel
www.freetrip.com
Sort out your US or Canada interstate trip, finding the best route and booking accommodation along the way, using this trip planner. You can choose to avoid or favour certain types of road and specify what kind of places you'd like to stay at and what kind of price you are willing to pay. An excellent resource.

Universal Studios
www.uescape.com
Home of Universal Studios in Florida and various other resorts, this is the place to come when you want details of that "holiday of a lifetime". You can view the offers and special package deals available at various resorts, some of which you can book and pay for online, and generally work the kids into a frenzy with the photos and descriptions of the attractions.

See also "Disney online" in Entertainment, page 101.

Information and advice

The Currency Site
www.oanda.com
Find out what your holiday change is worth, or when the best time to buy your travel currency is. The FX (foreign exchange) converter will show the worth of any amount of any currency in any other currency that you choose. Other features offer multiple conversions, currency trends, and forecasts.

European route planner
www.viamichelin.com
Want to know the best route from A to B when travelling through Europe? Then put your starting point and your destination into this site, and it will give you a map of how to get there. Maps, traffic information and weather forecasts are all included. Don't leave home without a look.

For a smooth holiday experience
www.ticked.com
The advice offered by this site aims to help you prevent annoyances ruining your trip. "Cheap Charlie's" column points you towards the bargains, and there are details on how to save money in other, sometimes possibly unscrupulous, ways. Health and safety concerns are also addressed.

Foreign and Commonwealth Office
www.fco.gov.uk
If you intend to travel anywhere off the beaten track, then check here first to find out the official government line. There are lists of countries that the Trade Advice Unit advises against visiting, as well as ones that should be avoided unless it is absolutely necessary. You can search here for the Foreign and Commonwealth Office's opinion on more than 150 countries.

Hotel finder service
www.hotelnet.co.uk
Locate hotels all over the world, and find directions on how to reach them when you finally arrive in your chosen country. The companies whose hotels appear on the site have little pages showing where their other branches are to be found.

Holidays with the under fives
www.babygoes2.com
This site offers lots of information on where, when, and how to have a perfect holiday with the little ones. It lists recommended resorts, childcare options, and many offers and discounts, and £35 gets you a tailor-made holiday suggestion to suit your family's needs. There are ideas for single parents, too.

International Student Travel Confederation
www.istc.org
Aimed at encouraging students to blow their loans seeing the world, the information here highlights the value of the various student and youth cards available, as well as giving details of which countries and cities support student discounts and benefits. Further information on what to do and see, and where to eat is also provided.

MASTA online
www.masta.org
For those travelling to exotic parts of the world, health advice is an absolute must. And the information you'll get from MASTA (Medical Advisory Services for Travellers Abroad) is the best you'll find online. A range of travel ailments is discussed, including antimalarial drugs, with treatment advice and precautionary measures suggested. If in doubt, though, see a doctor!

Online travel information and booking resource
www.a2btravel.com
Completely organize your holiday using the features on this website, which include mileage counters, accommodation locators, last-minute bookings, links to

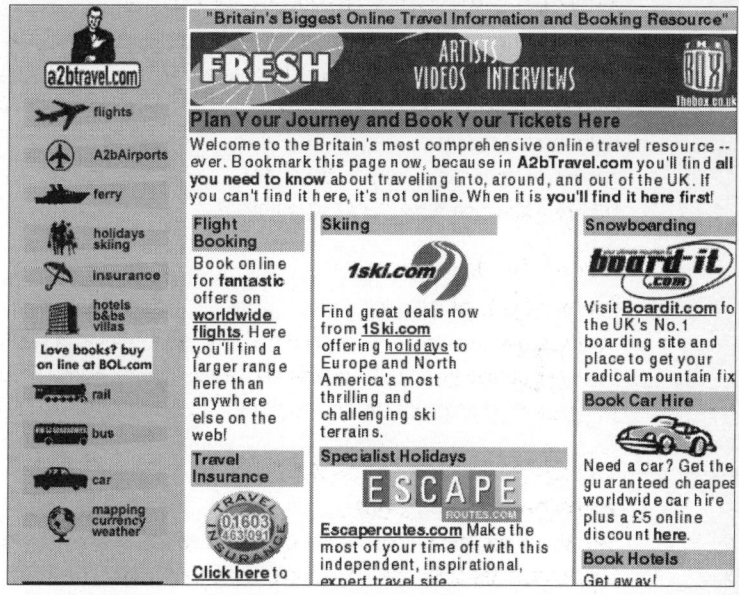

Visit www.a2btravel.com to organize every aspect of your holiday

specialized holiday sites, and live flight arrival information. There are also links to auction sites, shops that stock travel books, and travel insurance sites.

Holidaymakers' rights
www.holidaytravelwatch.org
If you like a moan, you'll love this. They assist, advise, and support any consumer or holidaymaker that has suffered an appalling holiday with a British tour operator. Holiday TravelWatch has an extensive database of holiday and travel complaints to peruse. There are tips and advice to allow you to get the most out of your holiday, and you can report it here if things don't come up to scratch.

Take the fuss out of business travel
www.biztraveler.org
Aimed at business travellers, the tips and advice found here should help to clarify your rights and ensure that your luggage stays in one piece. There is even a complaints procedure that lets you moan online; the site will forward your grievances to the people who need to hear them.

Tropical Medical Bureau
tmb.exodus.ie
Before you go anywhere too exotic, visit this top site to find out which jabs you

should have and how far in advance of travelling you need to get them done. There are some general health tips, too. However, don't bother wasting your time on the "news" and "chat forum" sections, as they are more or less dead now.

Virtual Tourist
www.vtourist.com
A place where travellers can exchange information – click on the world map on the home page and create your own travel pages, perhaps even about your own town, and have a look at others and rate them. There are lots of forums where you can find good, personal advice that you will never find in the travel guides.

Worldwide tourist information
www.travel-library.com
Find the tourist boards of other countries, read other travellers' travelogues, and locate tour companies. There is a guide to planning your round-the-world tour and useful info on which side of the road to drive on and bucket shops.

Transport and maps

Hertz: car rental
www.hertz.com
If you need to rent a car, Hertz's site will make sure that, when you do, it'll be from one of its fleet. You can specify all sorts of requirements, and get a price quoted online immediately. Cars are available in just about every country, whether it's safe to visit or not. There is a vehicle guide to help you decide on your car.

Maps and atlases
www.maps.com
View detailed maps, in various formats, and even check out satellite imagery at this commercial site. The hope is that you'll buy the digital images for use in research and other projects. There are also travel guides to buy, an online route planner, and map games to keep you amused.

Online atlas
www.multimap.com
Explore the world from your armchair with this online atlas. Type in anything from a road name (in the United Kingdom) to a country (worldwide), and adjust the scale to produce handy maps. You don't pay anything to use this service, but you're not supposed to copy maps to your own website.

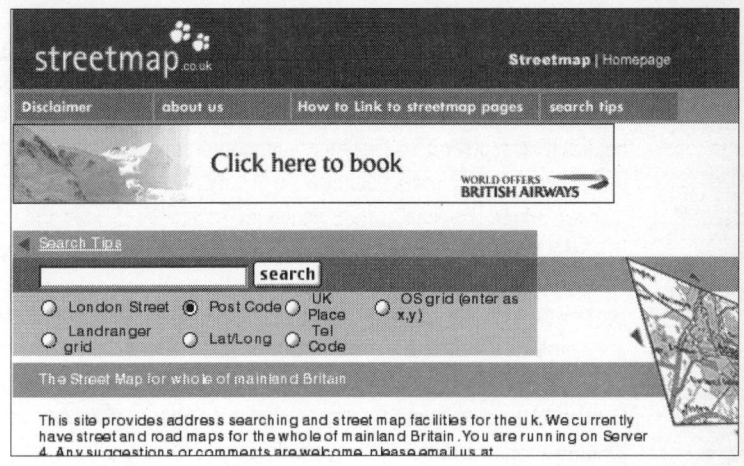

You will never need to ask for directions again once you've visited www.streetmap.co.uk

Street Map
www.streetmap.co.uk
This seemingly simple site will take a postcode or OS map reference and produce a map of the area, which can be enlarged, printed, or panned to find the places you are looking for. London street names are also recognized. The maps are ideal additions to party invitations, when no one knows where you live. US residents or visitors will find **www.streetmap.com** useful.

UK railway information
www.rail.co.uk
Access Railtrack's train timetables, find out why your transport is late in "real time", and get the contact details of the operating companies so that you can complain. Live departure boards, service alterations, and special offers are featured.

Travel guides

Guides to getting away
www.away.com
This site provides information and inspiration for would-be travellers, whether you are on your own or with others. There are articles written by guide book consultants and tips for making the most out of your visit. You can read international travelogues and a searchable database of 500 trips to plow through. A good selection of travel books, maps, and guides are also available.

Lonely Planet online
www.lonelyplanet.com
Pick up some essential, general travelling tips, as well as the lowdown on your destination. If you want a different opinion to that voiced in these great online guides, then you can also check out information supplied directly to the site from other travellers – this will doubtless be of varying quality.

Rough Guides to Travel
www.travel.roughguides.com
Browse through the spotlighted features, including insights into different cultures and religions, or just find out the history behind some of the world's most popular cities and the world's "cool places". Places to eat, seek entertainment, and rest are listed, and the site claims to carry the complete texts of the paper versions of the Rough Guides.

UK travel guide
www.uktravel.com
Do you tip hairdressers, hotel staff, and waiters in the United Kingdom? This site offers plenty of advice on where to go and how to get by in London and other places in Britain. Learn about the Royal Family, send a virtual postcard home, or discover the histories of Britain's castles.

US travel guides
www.ego.net
Planning a trip to the United States may be made easier with the services of this site. It offers travel guides, profiles of "favourite destinations", and a list of contact details for hotels. The map can produce a few national statistics for each state, as well as links to other, more informative, sites.

see also...

The beauty of the free travel guides you'll find on the Internet is that many have been created from the personal experiences of "real" people. The huge list of guides-based sites includes the UK Travel Guide (**www.ukguide.org**), which contains interactive guides to UK cities, with extra information on London, and the World Travel Guide.Net (**www.travel-guides.com**), providing a wider range of guides to countries all over the globe. Follow the author of Magical Places (**www.earthwisdom.com**) through her holidays at spiritually charged locations. If you decide you just can't make it out of the house, check out CAM Scape's (**www.onworld.com/CAM**) live, or nearly live, cameras at worldwide locations.

It's not hard to find a travel agent online. If you have no luck with the links listed above, try **www.access-ability.co.uk/tagencies.html**). Uniglobe Travel (**www.uniglobe.com**) will also help. Cape Tours (**www.capetours.co.uk**) can organize a holiday for you in South Africa, while Castaways Travel (**www.travelnude.com**) specializes in naturist holidays (you have to state your age before entering the site)! You can go to Orient-Express (**www.orient-expresstrains.com**) for a more sophisticated journey. Great Train Escapes (**www.greattrainescapes.com**) will also do you a deal on a rail-based break, and, if you like to shoot animals to relax, try the Hawkeye Sporting Agency (**www.hawkeye-sporting.co.uk**). More "normal" packages may be found at Lunn Poly (**www.lunn-poly.co.uk**) and the coach operator Wallace Arnold Holidays (**www.wallacearnold.com**). Some of the best cruise ship rates can be found at **www.cruise.com**. You can sometimes get flights direct from some of the major airlines such as American Airlines (**www.aa.com**), KLM (**www.klm.com**), and United Airlines (**www.ual.com**), or cheap flights at Ryanair (**www.ryanair.com**).

Travellers on a budget will find advice at Frommer's (**www.frommers.com**), which also provides discussion noticeboards. There are more hints at Backpack Europe on a Budget (**www.backpackeurope.com**), and, for real bargains, try buying a holiday from an online auction house, such as Internet Holiday Auctions (**www.holidayauctions.net**). Some of the most beautiful scenery in the world can be found Down Under, so visit the Australia Tourism Net site at **www.atn.com.au** to find out more about accommodation and the tours available. Holiday Wizard (**www.holidaywizard.co.uk**) will allow you to browse and order brochures online. Air tickets, hotels, and holidays can be bought, booked, and reserved at **www.travelocity.com**.

For those with a special interest in train travel, including commuters who have to use them every day, there is plenty on offer. The Trainline (**www.thetrainline.com**) has timetables and an online service where you can buy and reserve tickets and seats. Enthusiasts will love Rail Serve (**www.railserve.com**), with its directory of all things to do with trains – from models to the real thing. Trains Community (**communities.prodigy.net/trains**) is a truly awesome directory of train links.

You can also find your way around the United States via the Internet – with **maps.lycos.com**. Mapquest (**www.mapquest.com**) will provide you with map, directions, and local city information for just about anywhere in the world, as will MapBlast! (**www.mapblast.com**). Try the Ordnance Survey (**www.ordsvy.gov.uk**) for free online maps of the United Kingdom.

t

NETIQUETTE AND SECURITY

The Internet can be a very impersonal place, where people communicate with each other using hastily typed notes. Web chat forums, e-mail mailing lists, and newsgroups are all places where people can get together and share their ideas and opinions. But in an environment like this, where you can't hear voice tones or see faces, and are often dealing with complete strangers, this collective goodwill can sometimes turn more than a little sour. "So what?" you may ask. Well, believe me, the vitriol some people are capable of putting into an e-mail message would ruin anyone's day. However, if you follow a few simple rules, then you'll find that most people are very nice. And when a nasty message inevitably pops up, you'll be likely to find support from more reasonable "cyber-citizens". Many of the following suggestions apply when using e-mail with your own friends and family, too.

— Do's and don'ts on the Net —

Know your environment
This is crucial. If you want to participate in a particular discussion group, then you should spend some time reading other people's messages there first. You will then get a flavour of what is and isn't acceptable. You might even find that the group is not for you. Don't jump straight in and start firing off questions. If you've misjudged what a group is about, you may be politely told to ask somewhere else. Unlucky souls will be harshly abused, which is totally unnecessary, but an unfortunate fact of life. The Internet is used by people from all walks of life and, as ever, there are plenty of mean ones around, especially when they can hide behind their PCs.

Avoid humour
This might sound a bit harsh, but unless you are completely convinced that your correspondent will "get you", you run the risk of causing offence. Irony rarely comes across well, which is a shame. Some people try to spell things out by using a device called a smiley. For example, on a rainy day you could type:
What a great day we're having :-)

There are other such devices, which are called emoticons. If you can't "see" any of them, try leaning your head to your left shoulder and look again:

:-(Sad
;-)   Winking (this is one of the best if you do decide to use humour)
:-p   Cheeky – sticking your tongue out
:-o   Surprised
:*)   Drunk

For a comprehensive list of "amusing" emoticons, visit The Unofficial Smiley Dictionary (**paul.merton.ox.ac.uk/ascii/smileys.html**).

Type with care
Using poor punctuation, spelling, and grammar doesn't help when asking questions. The cardinal sin is to type every word using capital letters. This is hard for some people to read, and in Internet circles is counted as shouting. Silly, but these are the people that you will be relying on for help, so humour them.

Be careful who you reply to
Sometimes you'll receive an e-mail that has been sent to lots of other people, too. If you want to reply to the sender, make sure that you do just this and use the standard Reply option. Some e-mail programs have a Reply to All (or similar) feature, which sends your reply to everyone as well as the original sender. Do this and you risk an annoyed e-mail from at least a few of those e-mail addresses. If you do make a mistake, don't compound it by sending apologies to everyone!

Reply quickly
E-mail is fast to write and faster to send. This means that some people will expect to receive a reply within a day. If someone is offering you help and needs more information, then don't keep them waiting. They're doing you a favour, after all.

Some e-mail programs have a feature that will send automatic replies when you are on holiday. Don't use this if you are a member of a mailing list. Every time someone sends a message to the list, each member (and we could be talking hundreds of people here) receives a copy. So will you. And your e-mail program will reply. Everyone will be informed that you are on vacation right now, and will reply to their message as soon as possible. This will go on until you return or, more likely, until the person in charge of the list removes you from the group.

A few terms and their explanations

A "troll" is someone who causes mischief by posting a contentious view on a newsgroup or chat forum, with the express purpose of stirring up a fuss. For example, Christian forums might expect regular contributions from Satanists, while PC-based chat rooms are frequently invited to debate whether a Mac is better than a PC. The troll doesn't really care about God, Satan, or Macintosh computers, so there is no point in responding.

A few members of the group won't be able to resist replying, though, and may post reprimanding messages. If they send angry messages directly to the perpetrator, they are said to be "flaming" them. If you ask inappropriate questions on a chat forum, you run the risk of being flamed yourself. Again, the best defence is to ignore it, although you should maybe think about why you've received such a harsh response.

"Spam" is a term used for unsolicited e-mail. If you receive e-mail messages promising quick and easy money, or access to pornography, then you have been "spammed". Spamming also occurs when messages advertising goods or services appear on chat forums or mailing lists. Don't respond, even if the message invites you to unsubscribe from a mailing list you've never joined and you are itching to sort the "mix-up" out. All you'll achieve is to confirm to the advertiser that there is a real person using your e-mail account, and then you'll receive even more spam. Sometimes, you may receive e-mails from companies selling you their wares – most likely you accidentally allowed a site that you have registered to in good faith to pass on your information to other companies. The best advice that can be offered in this situation is to always read the small print before you submit your details to an online company.

Security on the Internet

There are three things related to the Internet that are guaranteed to make headlines: viruses, hackers, and child pornography. Movies, books, and news reports would have you believe that not only are we all vulnerable to these threats, but also it is almost inevitable that we will be attacked at some point. Let's clear up a few of these myths first.

Computer viruses

You cannot get a computer virus without downloading and running a program. Just using the Internet to access the web will not put you at risk. There are a few ways that bad web authors could, theoretically, attack your computer. However, software updates for all the main web browsers become available whenever a loophole is discovered. These updates can be downloaded from the web or are often found on CDs mounted on the front of computer magazines. A relatively new type of virus has been found circulating via e-mail. It abuses a feature in Microsoft's Outlook Express e-mail program to automatically distribute itself.

There is a straightforward way to avoid such viruses. If you receive an e-mail from someone you don't know, don't open any attached files – whatever they are. Even if a friend sends a program, try to avoid running it unless you are expecting something important. Joke animations, computerized birthday cards, and other "entertainments" are usually very uninspiring at the best of times. Add the fact that they have the potential to carry computer viruses and you can see that they are just not worth the time it takes to download them. It goes without saying that you ought to consider not forwarding these things on to other friends. And always use a virus checker, such as Norton AntiVirus, to check any attachments that you might receive with your e-mails.

To keep up to date with the latest virus software, get your browser patches from the download areas at Microsoft (**www.microsoft.com/downloads**) and Netscape (**www.netscape.com/computing/download**). You can also find the latest virus announcements at Symantec's AntiVirus Research Center (**www.symantec.com/avcenter**). Is the virus warning you've received through the e-mail system a hoax? Find out at the Computer Incident Advisory Capability website (**www.ciac.org**).

Hackers

The term "hacker" is usually used to refer to a computer-literate criminal who has misused a network to commit fraud or damage files. There is a community of computer experts who consider themselves to be hackers, but become upset when tarred with the same brush as vandals and fraudsters. They label the irresponsible people as crackers, among other things. Whatever you call them, the sort of people who infiltrate computer systems to blackmail companies, steal software, or create general havoc are not interested in touching your computer. They may try to steal your credit card number from an online store's system, but your PC is quite safe! A hacker would need a certain type of software, called server applications, to be running on your computer before he or she could even think about gaining control of your system. Ordinary home PCs do not have any of this server software.

Even if your details are stolen from a third party, such as a shop, credit card companies will indemnify you against misuse of your card, with the proviso that you've looked after it properly and taken reasonable steps to secure its use. Most consider Internet shopping to be safe, while Visa even goes as far as to claim that Internet shopping is more secure than giving your number over the phone. Check with your bank, if you're unsure of its Internet policy.

When you buy something from the Internet using a secure server, your details are encoded using quite strong encryption. However, what can you do to protect your e-mail from prying eyes? There are a number of free encryption programs available on the Internet that will do the job nicely, the most famous being Pretty Good Privacy (PGP). Considering the millions of messages that are flying around the Internet at once, you can see that the probability of yours being compromised is low. But although a stereotypical hacker would find it hard to access your e-mail, it's not so hard for the various people who work at your ISP, the ISP of your correspondent, and even co-workers in your office to do so. E-mail stays on your computer, and copies are made on others as the message progresses on its journey. Encryption protects your right to privacy, even if you have nothing to hide. Get PGP from The International PGP Home Page (**www.pgpi.org**).

Filtering out the filth

One criticism of the Internet, which is unfortunately true, is the proliferation of pornography. You can find it purely by accident, although most of the time you'll need a credit card handy before you can even gain any access to the bulk of the material. But often a few introductory pictures of the most explicit nature are flashed up first. There are programs and special web browsers that aim to filter out this kind of content, to avoid the corruption of minors. The latest versions of the main web browsers now feature built-in filters that aim to avoid sexual pictures, as well as articles containing swearing and violence. Many of these programs are quite effective, but nothing will work as well as a parental presence when children are online. More details on NetNanny, a content filtering and blocking program, can be found at **www.netnanny.com**.

Finally, a word about child pornography. It is true that the Internet can and is used to distribute this illegal material. However, it is very rare that someone can gain access to it, accidentally or otherwise. This is because the Internet is not completely open, and there are secret areas that are available only to those in the know. And the paedophiles who use these areas have a vested interest in keeping them secret. They want to avoid you, and the police, so you'd be very unlucky to uncover pornographic images of this nature. That said, some live chat forums have been used by men to contact and mislead children. This is a strong reason to provide parental guidance when using the Internet. You wouldn't let your child talk to strangers or use telephone chat services on their own – the Internet falls into the same category. The Internet is the perfect place for people to hide their identities and/or create new ones, so beware. Having said that, follow the simple advice above and soon you will be having hours of fun browsing with your family!

GLOSSARY

Adobe Acrobat
A file format (PDF) that keeps large documents together in a single file, including pictures. The advantage to this is that the content looks the same on every computer. The disadvantage is that it is usually a very large file to download.

ADSL
Asymmetric digital subscriber line. This is a very fast type of Internet connection using ordinary phone lines. Requires special hardware and a costly service subscription.

ASCII
American Standard Code for Information Interchange. The predominant way of encoding characters for computers. It includes upper and lower case letters, but no accented letters or those not used in English, such as the German sharp-S, "ß".

Cable
Very fast Internet access can be offered using cable networks. Often cheaper than ADSL, cable is certainly also more widely available. There are potential speed problems when lots of local people use the service simultaneously, however.

Chat
Live chat lets you "talk" to other people using your web browser in real time. You type your reply, then read the answers as soon as they are written. Chat forums are web-based bulletin boards. You leave questions and answers on a web page, and visit the site later to see the replies.

Cookie
Some retail sites store your personal information on your hard drive to "personalize" the page when you log back in. Don't worry, it is completely safe!

Directory
A massive list of websites, organized into handy categories to aid searching.

Domain
An essential part of a web address, the domain name of a site offers substantial clues about its nature. Yahoo.com and Apple.com are both domain names.

Download
When you open a web page in your computer's web browser program, you are actually downloading information onto your hard disk. This information will be automatically deleted from your computer after a certain period of time. You can also download files from the Internet, such as software drivers for your printer, or shareware programs.

Emoticon
A picture made out of text characters used to denote an emotion. They are handy to use to depict the mood you are trying to express, which can otherwise be difficult in an e-mail (see page 303 for examples).

Encryption
Used to encode information to prevent unauthorized access. All good online shops will use encryption to protect their customers' details from criminals.

Flame
An angry, aggressive e-mail message that is likely to be of a very personal nature.

Flash
Software used by web authors to make their sites look more attractive and interactive. If you don't have a Macromedia Flash plug-in installed, you will often be given the chance to download it, and some considerate sites will offer a non-Flash version for older browsers.

Frames
A technique used on websites that creates separate areas on a screen.

FTP
File transfer protocol. A way of providing files that can be downloaded using either a web browser or a dedicated FTP program. You would also use FTP to upload your files when creating a website.

Gif
A type of graphics file often used to create small pictures, logos, and buttons.

Hacker
Someone who can access computers using advanced networking techniques. They are far more likely to infiltrate the networks of large companies than your home computer.

HTML
Hypertext markup language. This is the computer language that is used to create web pages.

HTTP
Stands for hypertext transport protocol. This is the software that is used to send web page information from the server directly to your browser.

Hyperlink
A selected word or phrase, picture, or button that provides access to another part of the website when clicked with a mouse.

Internet
A global network of computers, providing many services, including the world wide web.

Intranet
A network of computers that provides services similar to those found on the Internet. However, this network is located within a company or building, and will have been tailored to suit its own specific needs.

ISDN
Integrated services digital network. A reasonably fast but rather overpriced service that brings you quicker Internet access.

ISP
Internet service provider. This is the company that you use to gain access to the Internet. Home computers use modems to dial into the ISP, which then forwards information from the Internet onto your screen. When you send an e-mail message, it leaves your computer and passes through the ISP on to the Internet, towards its final destination.

Java
A programming language that allows programs to run in your web browser, regardless of the operating system or type of computer that you have.

Jpeg
A type of graphic file that uses compression to allow the production of photo-quality pictures that download quickly.

Lurker
Someone who reads messages posted in chat forums and on newsgroups, without ever contributing. Lurk for a while before joining a discussion group to

Glossary

check whether it is suitable for you, but don't spend too long doing it!

Mac
A type of personal computer made by Apple.

Mirror
A copy of a website. Mirrors of very popular websites are made all over the world, so that Internet users can use the closest one and therefore get the fastest possible performance.

Modem
A device used by computers to establish Internet connections over a phone line. Most can also be used to send and receive faxes.

MP3
Mpeg 1 layer 3. This is a type of sound file that offers near-CD quality. MP3 files are around one-tenth of the size of a normal sound file, making them ideal for distributing music over the Internet. MP4s also exist, although they are not widespread as yet.

Network
A network is formed when at least two computers are wired together and are able to communicate with each other. The Internet is the largest network in the world. You can connect two PCs together, forming the most basic kind of network. This is useful for sharing files and printers, and when playing games.

Newsgroups
An area of the Internet consisting of thousands of very specific bulletin boards within which people can share their ideas and opinions with others.

Offline
It is possible to download pages from the Internet onto your hard disk, and then view them after disconnecting. Doing this is called working offline.

Online
When a computer is connected to the Internet, it is online.

Operating system
The software that allows a computer to run programs such as word processors, web browsers, and games.

PC
The most popular type of home computer, PCs are made by a large number of different companies.

PGP
Pretty Good Privacy. An encryption program available free via the Internet to help protect your e-mail from prying eyes.

Plug-in
A piece of software that increases the abilities of a web browser program.

Search engine
A website that attempts to index the websites on the Internet, providing visitors with the opportunity to search through its records.

Secure site
If a site is secure, then it is encrypted, meaning that any details that you submit should be safe. The URL often begins with https://

Server
A computer program that provides a service. Websites exist on web servers, e-mail is dealt with by e-mail servers, and files by FTP servers.

Shareware
Software, available on the Internet, for which the author requests payment, usually in the accompanying documentation files or in an announcement made by the software itself.

Shockwave
As with Flash, a website that uses Shockwave requires you to install a plug-in to reap the benefit of its features. It is used to improve a website's design.

Site
A collection of web pages held under the same domain name.

Spam
Unsolicited, junk e-mail that usually bears unlikely promises of wealth, health, and sexual fulfilment.

SSL
Secure socket layer. This security feature, which is found in all good web browsers, uses encryption to exchange information between computers. It is used by conscientious online shops to protect customers' details from the potential threat of criminals.

TLD
Top tevel domain. The ".com", ".org", and ".co.uk" part of a web address.

Troll
Someone who agitates the inhabitants of Internet chat forums and other "virtual communities". Also a verb, as in to utter a posting on Usenet designed to attract predictable responses.

URL
Uniform resource locator. The technical name for a web address, for example, **http://www.apple.com/press.htm**, which is made up of the following components:
http:// – The network software used to distribute web page data.
www. – The first part of the web server's name.
apple – The name of the computer that holds all of the pages.
.com – The top level domain name (TLD).
/press.htm – A web page.

Virus
This is a malignant computer program, more likely to be found hyped up in newspaper reports and Hollywood films than actually on your hard disk. Viruses are usually transferred when programs are downloaded, and they are often received as an attachment to an e-mail.

WAP
Wireless application protocol. Specially created Internet pages can be accessed through mobile phones. Originally just text, more development has meant that pictures can now be included in the latest models of phone.

Web browser
A program that displays web pages. There are different types and versions, although they all perform basically the same function. Later versions tend to work better with some websites. Microsoft's Internet Explorer and Netscape's Navigator are among the most popular browsers around.

Webmaster
The person responsible at a site providing world wide web information for maintaining the public pages and keeping the web server running.

www
The world wide web. Arguably the easiest part of the Internet to use, the web contains more than a billion pages of information.

Zip
A file format that creates a compressed archive, thus reducing the size of large files and making them faster to download.

INDEX

A

A Levels 69
abortion 146
accountants 193
actors 93, 99
acupuncture 132–3, 148
Adobe Acrobat 307
ADSL (asymmetric digital subscriber line) 307
adult material 14
Advanced Micro Devices 55
advanced searching 16
adventure holidays 286–9
advertising 102, 167, 174
aerobics 138–9
aesthetics 35
AIDS 83, 144, 148
aikido 278
aliens 161
allergies 148
alligators 219
Altavista 57
alternative teaching 67–8
alternative technology 220
alternative therapies 132–4, 148
Amazon 19–22, 43–4
American football 269
amphibians 219
animal rescuers 152
animals 150–2, 162, 221
   conservation groups 212, 213, 224–5
animation 31, 86, 106
Antarctica 225
anthropology 82
antiquarian bookshops 39, 44

antiques 31, 162, 169–70
Apple Computer 55, 309
aquaria 150, 162, 224
arcade games 128
archery 281
architecture 26–7, 31
art 28–31
art galleries 28, 29, 34, 253
   virtual 31, 34, 35
art museums 29, 30, 34, 252
artificial life 219
artists 28–31
ASCII (American Standard Code for Information Interchange) 307
Ask Jeeves 57
astronomy 161, 215
athletics 268–9, 273, 282
atlases 298
auctions 29
   on Internet 24, 153, 167, 301
Australia 301
Australian football 271
authors 36–8, 48
automatons 30

B

babies 137, 148
backpackers 286–7, 301
badminton 282
ball sports 269–72
ballroom dancing 162
bankruptcy 196, 250
banks 195
   Internet 180–3
banned books 49

banned music 209
barbecues 112
bargains 166
   holiday 289–92, 295
baseball 269, 283
basketball 270, 272
basses 199
beauty 134–5, 148, 179
beauty contests 90
beef issues 225
beer 108, 110
bellringing 210
betting 282
Bible 40
billiards 272
bingo 124
binoculars 89
biodiversity 212, 222, 225
biorhythms 132
birds 150, 162, 212, 221, 225
birth control 146
blind, reading codes for 40
board games 123–4, 128, 131
bodybuilding 274
bonds 191
book clubs 44
bookbinding 49
Bookmark (Netscape Navigator) list 8
books 36–49
   antiquarian 39, 44
   authors 36–8
   banned 49
   browsers 38–9
   computer 54
   conservation 39
   news 42–3

Index

online shops 43–5, 49
online texts 45
publishers 46–7
reviews 42–3
Boolean operators 16
bowling 270
boxing 274, 283
browsers 7, 9, 16, 306, 310
  books 38–9
Buddhism 262–3
building 178
buildings 27
bungee jumping 276
business
  courses 68, 74
  news 226–8, 237
  technology in 52–3
  travel 297
butterflies 220
buying tips 22–3

C

cable 307
California 294
cameras 33, 89
camping 286, 287
canal holidays 292
cancer 136–7, 143
candles 155–6
canoeing 281
car loans 187
car rental 298
card games 123, 127, 131
carpets 176
cars 158, 160, 279
cartoons 31, 35, 76, 86–9, 106, 235
castles 26
Catholicism 263
cats 220–1

CDs 97, 197, 200, 201, 204–5, 206, 232, 305
cemetery records 157
censorship 49, 209
ceramics 152, 162
charities 256–7
chat 307
chat forums 60, 302, 306, 307, 308, 310
cheese 110, 112
chemistry 80
chess 122
child pornography 306
children
  chat services 306
  child pornography 306
  computer games 121
  entertaining 90–1
  health 148
  holidays 296
  news 241
  on stage 102
  wildlife preservation 222
chimneys 176
chocolate 111
Church of England 263
Church of Scientology 263
CIA 265
Citizens Advice Bureau 265
classical music 203–4
climbing 280, 283, 286
clothes 164–6, 176–7
clubs 90, 91, 198
cocktails 108–9
coins 152–3
collections 152–4, 162
  toys 128–30
comics 38, 54, 86–9, 106
Commonwealth Games 273
composing 200

computers 50–66
  books 54
  dictionaries 51, 53
  downloads 60–2
  games 54, 66, 89, 98, 119–21, 130, 235
  hardware 53, 61
  literature 54–5
  magazines 65
  manufacturers 55–7, 65–6
  music 199, 209
  news 54
  personal (see PC (personal computer))
  programming 61
  search engines (see search engines)
  software 60–2
  stores 62–3, 65, 89
  support 51, 66
  technology 54–5
concerts 197–8
conservation
  books 39
  groups 211–13, 224–5
  historic buildings 27
  natural world 211–13
  volunteers 211
console systems, games 119–20, 121, 122, 130, 131
conspiracy theories 253–4, 258
Consumers' Association 23, 175
contact sports 274–5
contraception 146
cookies 22, 307
copyright 198
cosmetic surgery 148
cosmetics 134–5
costume 31

counselling 137
country music 205, 209
countryside magazine 211
courts (UK) 249
crafts 35, 154–6, 162
credit cards 18, 20, 22, 24, 25, 181, 183, 305
cricket 270, 280
crime fiction 38
criminology 82
crocodiles 219
cross-country skiing 276
cruises 284–6, 301
cults 263, 266
currencies 295
current affairs 258–9
curry 116, 117
customer service, Internet 23
customs 23
Cyberpatrol 14
cycling 283, 287

D

dance 31, 101–2, 162
darts 281, 282
debit cards 22, 25
debt 250
decorating 171–3, 178
defence news 233
deforestation 215, 216
delicatessens 111
Dell Computer 56
dental health 135
design 29, 35, 81, 154
dictionaries 245–9
   computing 51, 53
   gaming 127–8
   medical 143
   music 209
   rap 248
   rhyming 36, 48, 199
diet 118, 139, 140, 145, 148
digital photographs 33–4, 35
digital video tape format 107
dinosaurs 221, 224
direct marketing 174
directories 10–11, 307
disability
   dating agency 267
   information 266
   services 70
   sports 272, 279–80
disasters 255
discounts 166–8
   computers 62–3
   courses 69
   home goods 167–8
disorders, health 135–7, 148
distance learning 84
divorce 249–50, 267
DIY 171, 178
Dogpile 57
dogs 220–1
domains 13, 307
downloading 60–2, 307
drink 108–10, 118
drivers 60, 61
drug abuse 141, 148
drugs 143, 145
Druids 266
DVDs 89, 90, 92, 93, 96–7

E

e-books 38, 41–2, 45, 49
e-texts 38–9, 45, 49
earth 214, 225
ecology 212, 214
eczema 148
education 67–85
   alternative teaching 67–8
   exhibitions 76
   graduates 68
   intelligence 74
   language 75–6, 84
   learning 76–8
   mathematics 78–9
   parents 71–4
   revision 79–80
   science 80–1
   social sciences 82–3
   students 69–71
   teachers 71–4, 84
electrical equipment 179
electronic books see e-books
electronic equipment 89–90
electronic parts 156–7
elements, periodic table 255
elephants 224
email 303
emoticon 307
encryption 62, 306, 307
encyclopedias 245–9
   art 29
   education 78
   philosophy 82
endangered species 212, 224
entertainers 162
entertainment 86–107
   cartoons 86–9, 106
   comics 86–9, 106
   electronic equipment 89–90
   events 90–2
   films 92–3, 95–6, 105
   jokes 94

magic 94–5
music 96–9
radio 103
sci-fi 99
television 95, 102–7
theatre 100–1
theme parks 101
videos 96–9
environment 82, 214–18
equestrian sports 275
Europe 292–3, 295
restaurants 117
Eurostar trains 292
evening courses, London 85
events 197–8
entertainment 90–2
sporting 273
evolution 82, 219, 223
Excite 58
exercise 138–40
exhibitions, educational 76
expatriates 228–30
experts 242
extinct species 212
extinction 222
extreme knitting 276–7
extreme sports 275–8

F

family games 124, 131
family health 137–8
family life 138
fantasy games 126
fantasy sports 282
FAQ (frequently asked questions) 243–4
farming 215, 225
fashion 31–3, 35, 179, 235
fast food 117–18

Favourites (Internet Explorer) list 8
feng shui 172
ferries 292
fertility 148
festivals 90, 232
film music 209
films 92–3, 95–6, 105
news 93
financial advice 185, 186, 194, 195, 285
financial journals 190–1
financial news 185–6, 192, 226–8, 241
first aid 141
fish 150, 162, 213, 225
fishing 213
fitness 138–40
flame 304, 307
Flash 7, 308
flights 284–6, 289, 290, 291, 292, 301
flying 275
folk art 35
food 83, 110–18, 145
fast 117–18
GM 118, 212, 214, 216, 225
luxury 110–11
recipes 112–13, 117
reviews 114–15
safety 115
supermarkets 116
world 116–17
football 123, 271, 272, 280, 282
American 269
Australian 271
Foreign and Commonwealth Office 296
foreign websites, buying from 23

Formula One 279
fossils 223
frames 308
France 292–3
fraud 250
protection 174
free access 9
free stuff 107
Freeserve 58
frogs 221
FTP (file transfer protocol) 202, 308
fungi 211
furniture 154, 168–70

G

gadgets 89, 156
gambling 127
games 98, 119–31
card 123, 127, 131
collectibles 128–30
computers 54, 66, 89, 98, 119–21, 130
dictionary 127–8
educational 77
family 124, 131
favourites 122–3
news 121–2
online 123–6
PC 130–1
role-playing 126–7
rules 127–8
toy histories 128–30
war 128
word 124, 126, 248
gardening 171, 172, 173, 178, 179
gargoyles 35
GCSE 79, 81
genealogy 157
genetically modified foods see GM foods

geographical names 247
geography 214–18
ghost websites 58
gif 308
glossary 307–10
GM foods 118, 212, 214, 216, 225
golf 280
Google 14, 15, 17, 59
gorillas 225
gossip 241
government 71–2, 186
graduates 68, 85
grammar 247, 249, 303
grandparents 138
graphics, computer 50–1
guides, travel 299–300
guitarists 209
guitars 199

H

hackers 25, 305–6, 308
hair loss 148
hamsters 151
hang gliding 276
hardware, computers 53, 61
hayfever 148
health 132–49
   alternative therapies 132–4
   beauty 134–5
   dental 135
   disorders 135–7, 148
   family 137–8
   fitness 138–40
   illnesses 135–7, 148
   interactive sites 144
   nutrition 145
   pharmaceuticals 145
   psychology 146

   sexual matters 146–7
   travel 296, 297
healthcare 142, 143, 144, 149
heart 135–6, 139, 144
hi-fi 170
historic buildings, conservation 27
history 82, 84
   computers 51
   Internet 63
   web 8–9
HM Customs and Excise 23, 194
hobbies 150–63
   animals 150–2
   collections 152–4
   crafts 154–6
   electronic parts 156–7
   genealogy 157
   motoring 157–60
holiday bargains 289–92
   America 294–5
   Europe 292–3
home entertainment 89–90
home tutoring 67–8
homeopathy 133
homes 164–79
   furnishings 168–70
   improvement 171–3
   upkeep 176–7, 178
   utilities 177
   see also property
horse racing 275, 280
horses 225
HotBot 59
hotels 296
HTML (hypertext markup language) 54, 64, 308
HTTP (hypertext transport protocol) 308, 310
hummingbirds 221

hunting 213, 281
hurricanes 216
hyperlinks 8, 308

I

IBM 56
ice hockey 271, 280
illnesses 135–7, 148
industrial placements 71
Infospace 59
Inland Revenue 194
insurance 157, 158, 185, 186, 188, 194
Intel 56
intelligence, education 74
intelligence (security) 241
interactive sites, health 144
international news 240
Internet 308
   customer service 23
   etiquette 52, 302–4
   free access 9
   history 63
Internet service providers (ISPs) 9, 308
Internet trading 191
intranet 308
investments 184–7, 189–93, 226–7
ISDN (integrated services digital network) 308
Islam 266
ISP (Internet service provider) 9, 308

J

Java 308
jazz 204, 206
jewellery 165, 166, 179

job hunting 68, 72, 73, 85, 183–4, 195
jokes 94
journalists 241
jpeg 308
Judaism 264, 266
juggling 160

K

karaoke 209
karate 283
kayaking 280, 286
kites 160, 277
knitting 155
  extreme 276–7

L

lace 155
language 75–6, 84
Le Shuttle 292
learning, education 76–8
legal issues 249–50, 255
libraries 47–8, 209, 252, 255
life systems, computer synthesis 219
Linux 54
literary terms 247
literature 36–8, 42, 45
  computers 54–5
  see also books
local information 11–12
London 293, 301
  evening courses 85
lorryspotting 159
love life 143
loyalty schemes 193
lurkers 308–9
Lycos 59, 202
lyrics 199

M

Mac 309
magazines
  books 42, 43
  business 227
  computers 54, 65
  consumers 175
  entertainment 90–1, 101–2
  fashion 32, 35
  gambling 127
  health 132
  home entertainment 90
  music 200–1, 203
  natural history 223
  news 231–6
  for students 70
magic 94–5, 162
mammals 224, 225
manufacturers, computer 55–7, 65–6
maps 84, 216, 298–9, 301
maritime museum 252–3
martial arts 278
masks 35
mathematics 78–9, 84
mechanical sculpture 30
media 174, 214
  awareness of 78
  news 237, 241
  reviews 229
medical dictionary 143
mental health 137, 148
metasearch engines 16, 57, 66
meteors 161
Metropolitan Police 266
Microsoft 12, 56
  games 131
  Windows 51
migraine 137
mirror sites 12, 309
model airplanes 162
modem 309
money 180–96
  Internet banks 180–3
  job hunting 183–4
  money management 184–7
  property 187–9, 196
  stocks and shares 189–93, 196
mortgages 184, 185, 186, 188
Mosaic 8–9
motor sports 279, 283
motorbikes 158, 163
mountaineering 276, 287
MP3 59, 197, 201–3, 210, 309
MP4 309
museums 91, 250–3, 255
  art 29, 30, 34
  computer history 51
  costume 31
  maritime 252–3
  natural world 222–4
  science 251–2
  technology 253
  transport 251
  war 251
music 31, 54, 96–9, 197–210
  banned 209
  classical 203–4
  concerts 197–8
  magazines 200–1, 203
  MP3 59, 197, 201–3, 210, 309
  MP4 309
  musicals 203–4
  musicians 198–200
  popular 204–7, 210
  radio 207–8
music industry 199

music therapy 209
music venues 91
musicals 203–4
musicians 198–200
mysteries 225
mystery fiction 38
mythology 247, 253
myths 253–4

N

Napster 203
national culture (UK) 257–8
National Curriculum 72, 84
National Trust 27–8, 212
natural health 133–4
natural world 211–25
   conservation 211–13
   environment 214–18
   geography 214–18
   museums 222–4
   nature 218–22
   parks 222–4
   zoos 222–4
nature 218–22
   sounds of 225
nature conservation 211
naturist holidays 301
netball 271
netiquette 52, 302–4
NetNanny 14, 306
networks 62, 63, 309
news 226–41
   art 29
   books 42–3
   business 226–8, 237
   children 241
   computers 54, 61
   defence 233
   environment 215, 217

expatriates 228–30
films 93
financial 185–6, 192, 226–8, 241
games 121–2
gossip 241
international 240
magazines 231–6
popular music 205–6
positive 241
radio 236–7
satire 229
search engine 230
spoof 229
sports 280
summaries 241
technology 237–8, 240–1
transport 233
TV 238–40
weather 240
newsgroups 17, 243, 302, 309
newspapers 7, 231–6, 241
Nobel awards 255
North America 294–5
nuclear issues 82, 216
nursing 149
nutrition 132, 139, 140, 143, 145

O

oceanography 216
offensive websites 14
offline 309
old houses 176
older web users 59
Olympics 273
online 309
online discussions 17
online high street 18–19
opera 31

operating system 309
orchids 218
outdoor equipment 287
ozone depletion 214

P

paganism 263
palaeontology 223, 224
Palm 56
paragliding 276
parenting 73, 137, 138, 148, 178
parks
   natural world 222–4
   US 225
passenger rights 297
patents 160
patient support groups 138
PC (personal computer) 53, 60, 61, 62, 309
   games 66, 89, 98, 119–21, 121, 130–1
penguins 225
pensions 185, 187, 196
people finders 85, 162–3, 243, 244
periodic table of elements 255
Perl 54
pets 151, 162
PGP (Pretty Good Privacy) 62, 306, 309
pharmaceuticals 145
philosophy, encyclopedia 82
photography 33–4, 35, 163, 277
pictures 244
planets 218
plumbing 178
poetry 31, 40, 41, 45, 48

Pokémon cards 153
police 266, 267
political parties 258–62
politics 258–62, 266–7
pollution 83, 212, 218
ponies 225
pool 272
popular music 204–7, 210
population 214, 215
pornography 306
positive news 241
power kiting 277
power suppliers 177
powerlifting 274
pregnancy 138
price comparison 22
print 49
privacy 62, 309
private healthcare 144, 149
programming 61
pronunciation 167, 249
property 187–9, 196
Psion 57
psychology 146
publishers 42, 43, 46–7
pubs 108, 272
puppetry 161, 162
puzzles 123–6

Q

quizzes 106, 124, 125
quotations 255

R

rabbits 162
racing 280
racism 264–5
radio 207–8, 210, 236–7, 240
rail travel 163, 292, 299, 301
rainforests 217–18
rally driving 279
rap dictionary 248
reading 84
recipes 112–13, 117
reference 242–55
 conspiracies 253–4
 dictionaries 245–9
 encyclopedias 245–9
 legal issues 249–50, 255
 museums 250–3
 myths 253–4
 questions 242–4
relationships 267
religion 262–4
restaurants 91, 114, 115, 116–17
retirement 250
reviews
 books 42–3
 computers 55, 61
 films 93
 food 114–15
 media 229
 music 207
revision 79–80
rhyming dictionaries 36, 48, 199
rocketry 157
role-playing games 126–7
roofs 178
royal families 258
rugby 272, 280
running 268–9

S

safety, personal and domestic 174
sailing 281–2
salsa 102
SAT 79–80
schizophrenia 137
schools 68, 71–4, 84
sci-fi 99, 105
 collectibles 129
 comics 88
science 80–1
 museums 251–2
Scoot 12, 58, 142, 243
scrapbooks 153
sculpture 35
search engines 14–16, 57–60, 66, 309
 news 230
 sports 282
searching 15–16
 advanced 16
secure connections 25
secure site 309
security 62, 304–6
 shopping on the Internet 24–5, 174–5, 305
security services
 UK 265
 USA 265
security systems 14
SeniorSearch UK 59
servers 309
sewing 154
sexual matters 146–7
shamanism 266
shareware 61–2, 199–200, 309
sheet music 199
Shockwave 310
shooting 281, 301
shopping on the Internet 18–25, 179
 auctions 24
 books 43–5, 49
 buying tips 22–3
 computers 62–3, 65

Index

delivery 23
entertainment 106
foreign websites 23
online high street 18–19
security 24–5, 174–5, 305
Sikhism 264
sites
  defined 310
  see also websites
skateboarding 276
skiing 276, 288
  cross-country 276
skydiving 277, 280
smoking 140
snooker 280
snowboarding 276, 277–8
soccer see football
social issues 264–6, 267
social sciences, education 82–3
Society for Promoting Christian Knowledge 264
sociology 82–3
software 60–2
  games 121
  Windows 51
South Africa 301
space 161, 216, 218, 221, 240, 289
space exploration 81
Spain 293
spam 304, 310
spiritual healing 133
sport 268–83
  athletics 268–9, 282
  ball sports 269–72
  big events 273
  contact 274–5
  equestrian 275
  extreme 275–8
  martial arts 278

motor 279
news 279–80
search engine 282
target sports 281
water sports 281–2
SSL (secure socket layer) 25, 310
stamps 153–4
statistics 83, 267
  religions 264
stock brokers 190, 193
stocks and shares 189–93, 196
students 67, 69–71, 72, 84, 85, 255
  travel 296
supermarkets 116
surfing 276, 278
surfing the Internet 10–17
  guessing web addresses 12–14
  local information 11–12
  search engines 14–16, 57–60
  Usenet 17
  web directories 10–11
surgery, cosmetic 148
sustainable development 83
swimming 283
symbols 255
synthesizers 199, 209

T

table football 123
target sports 281
tax 194
tea 108
teachers 71–4, 78, 84
technical terms 6
technology 52, 81, 107, 240–1

alternative 220
computers 54–5
museums 253
news 237–8, 240–1
teenage health 147
telephone services 177
television see TV
tennis 280, 282
texts online 38–9, 45
theatre 100–1
theme parks 101
thesauri 247, 248, 255
threads 17
tiddlywinks 123
time, global 255
TLD (top level domain) 13–14, 310
toilet repairs 177
toxic waste 216
toy soldiers 154
toys 128–30
transport museum 251
transport news 233
travel 284–301
  adventure holidays 286–9
  cruises 284–6
  Europe 292–3
  flights 284–6, 289, 290, 291, 292
  guides 299–300
  health 296, 297
  holiday bargains 289–92
  information 295–8, 301
  maps 298–9
  North America 294–5
  transport 298–9
travel agents 301
triathletes 278
trolls 304, 310
tropical fish 150
tsunami 218

TV 92, 93, 95, 102–7
  listings 232, 241
  music 209
  news 238–40

U

underground writing 38
universities 70–1, 84–5
unknown species 225
urbanization 83
URLs (uniform resource locators) 6, 9, 12–14, 310
  common suffixes 13–14
US Customs 23, 194–5
Usenet 17, 243
utilities 177

V

Vatican 266
vegans 115
vegetarians 115, 118
Viagra 147
video games 129
videos 96–9
virtual animals 162
virtual expeditions 221–2
virtual game reserve 222
virtual Jerusalem 264
virtual newsroom 229–30
virtual tourist 298
viruses 66, 304–5, 310
volcanoes 218

W

walking 287
WAP (wireless application protocol) 9, 310
war games 128
war museums 251
water sports 281–2
weather 217, 221, 240
web 6
  history 8–9
  learning 77
web addresses see URLs (uniform resource locators)
web browsers see browsers
web directories 10–11, 307
web pages see websites
webmaster 310
Webring 60
websites 6
  construction 63–5
  foreign, buying from 23
  ghost 58
  links 8
  navigating 8
whaling 216
wheelchair sports 272, 279–80
whisky 110
wild plants 212
wills 181, 196, 249, 250
Windows software 51
wine 109–10, 114, 118
wing chun kuen 278
wolves 224
women 144, 175, 288
wood, fuel 178
woodwork 154
word games 124, 126, 248
world 83
  entertainment guides 91–2
  food 116–17
  music charts 205
  reference 249
  royal families 258
  sport 280
  time 255
  travel 298
wrestling 274
writers 41
  prizes 47–8
www 310
  see also web

Y

Yahoo! 10–11, 60
Yellow Pages 59, 167
yoga 139, 140
youth orchestras 209

Z

zip 310
zoos 222–4